A NOVEL
COMING
BACK
BY
NWANGANGA SHIELDS

Expl**O**ra
BOOKS

EXPLORA BOOKS

700 – 838 West Hastings St. Vancouver, BC V6C 0A6
www.explorabooks.com
Phone: (604) 330 6795

ISBN: 978-1-998394-37-1

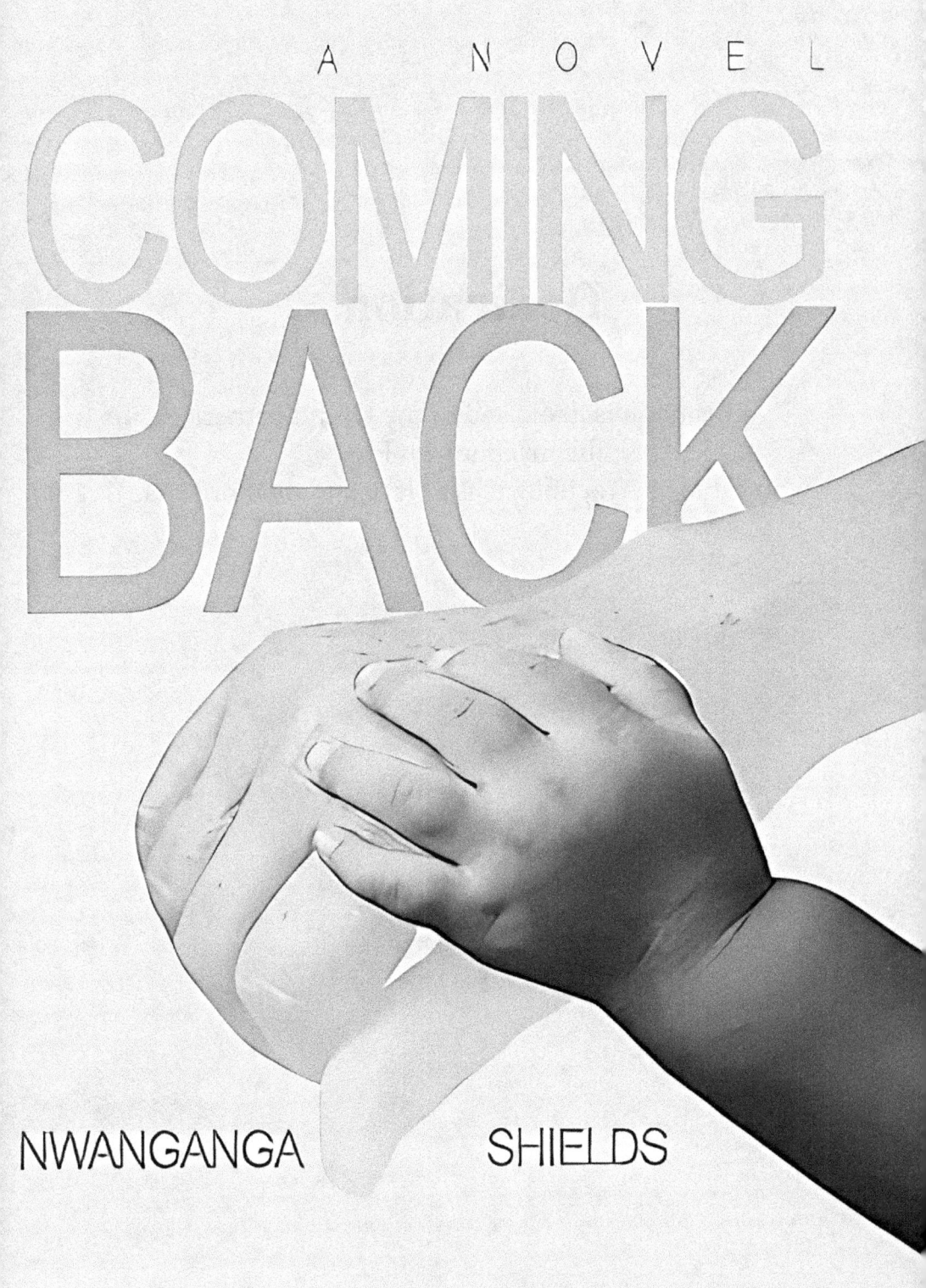

A NOVEL

COMING BACK

NWANGANGA   SHIELDS

Dedication

This book is dedicated to my Grand Father,
Iheonyebuokwu Eni,
who came to Arochukwu as a slave and died in 1958.

Table of Contents

A NOVEL

COMING
BACK

CHAPTER ONE

At twenty-two, Clint had the rest of his life before him. He spent a lazy day at home in early June, while Peace and Peter, his Nigerian parents, were at work. He graduated from college only three weeks earlier and looked forward to law school at American University, following in his father's footsteps. He agreed with his parents it would be more economical for him to live at home during law school, since it was on Massachusetts Avenue NW, very close to his parents' home in Tenley Park.

To all appearances, he was quite happy. His parents, relatively well-off, were able to pay for his schooling, but he rejected their offer to pay his tuition, preferring to finance his further education with student loans. He was grateful for what his parents already gave him, a student loan to cover his tuition and incidentals. Living at home meant he didn't have to worry too much about money, and he could let them satisfy their desire to provide for him. He felt it was the least he could do.

They were reticent about their lives in Nigeria. He knew they emigrated from there, but beyond that, he knew very little. What he heard were humorous, disparaging anecdotes about incidents that occurred during his parents' visits to Nigeria or what they read in the papers.

One such incident apparently occurred the only time he was taken to Nigeria with them during the summer of their move to Tenley Park when he was five. That visit became part of their family lore. Whatever happened was something that made his parents decide Clint didn't need to accompany them to visit Nigeria again.

He smiled at their amusement when discussing the visit. They arrived in Port Harcourt in the second week of December. Clint had just turned five, while his sister, Sarah, was a baby.

One night at dinner, Peter mentioned the visit, and Peace laughed. "Don't remind me of that dank, dilapidated airport hotel where we stayed," she said.

"What did you expect?" Peter asked. "I was told the hotel was quite pleasant before the war."

"I didn't expect a palace. What I minded was the women crowding the bar and the expatriates thinking all Nigerian women were available to be picked up." Her expression showed disgust.

"That's the reason you gave when you asked for room service, as I recall."

"What I remember most are the cracked plates and lukewarm coffee. Let's talk about other things. I want to forget that experience." She stood to clear the table.

At another time, Peace recalled a different incident from that visit. "I wonder what happened to the driver my parents, or maybe it was yours, sent to meet us at Port Harcourt. I remember the car ride. The air-conditioning wasn't functioning, and the children cried and complained about the heat."

"I must say I was taken aback by the pandemonium on the road leading out of Port Harcourt," Peter said, scratching his nose and pursing his mouth like someone remembering a difficult moment. "Somehow, I didn't expect so much traffic. The roads were congested, and the noxious smell of gasoline permeated the air. Cars competed with pushcarts, bicycles, motorcycles, and pedestrians."

Laughing, Peace added, "The car horns and shouts from the pedestrians were deafening."

"After living in the U.S. for so long, we forgot how things were in Nigeria. There was no visible order, as drivers tried to outmaneuver each other."

"Can you imagine how I felt sitting in back with these two rascals?" She smiled at Clint and Sarah, who listened to the conversation with wide eyes.

"Don't stop," they begged. "Tell us what happened, Mummy."

"It was inevitable, I suppose," Peace continued. "As our car approached the junction to the turnoff to Aba Road, the driver swerved to avoid hitting another car. Unfortunately, he hit a young boy trying to cross the road." She clasped her hands. "A crowd gathered. Even though the boy suffered only minor scrapes, his guardian saw it as an opportunity to make money."

"I got out of the car, hoping to deescalate the situation," Peter said, "and went to the young man to see where he'd been hit, but my presence made matters worse. Before the boy could respond, someone shouted, 'Make them take him to the hospital. These big shots think they can get away with anything." There was a chorus of agreement from the crowd. It was the worst thing that could have happened on our first day in Nigeria."

"Remember the man who said he was the boy's father?" Peace asked.

"How can I forget? I was afraid the situation would get out of hand, and the crowd might take it upon themselves to administer justice to the driver, so I tried to keep calm."

Peter continued the story. "As I approached the young man, his so-called father rushed out from his shed when he heard of the accident and said, 'Don't touch him! You must take him to the hospital for the doctor to look at him, or you can pay me to charter a taxi to take him there. You must also pay for his treatment.'"

Peter raised his hands to demonstrate. "I didn't know what to do. There was no policeman around, and if one were present,

I knew it would cost even more time and money before we could leave the area. The crowd immediately took sides and gesticulated wildly."

Peace, fidgeting on the dining room chair, explained, "The argument was between those who agreed with the guardian's position and those who thought the child wasn't seriously hurt, and the guardian just wanted money."

"That was the case. With five people in the car, there wasn't enough room for a sixth, plus the self-appointed guardian. The hot air was stifling. I was in a quandary. All of you were hot and uncomfortable in the car, and Peace was ready to jump into the fray and make matters worse. Rather than give in to the avaricious man, I opted to take the boy to the hospital. We all squeezed into a car meant for only five passengers."

"Did I sit with you in front?" Clint asked.

"Poor Peace had both of you in her lap. It was very uncomfortable for everyone. Even now, I can visualize her holding her children tightly, not able to hide her irritation. Halfway to the hospital, the guardian said, 'Oga. Just pay us so we can go on our way. You know how it is in this country. We'll waste a lot of time at the hospital, and I won't be able to sell anything today. Settle with me, and let us out of the car.' By then, I was so angry, I couldn't hide it anymore."

Peace laughed. "I knew he was a fraud when he asked for 100 naira."

Smiling, Peter nodded. "In my frustration, I lashed out, saying, 'I don't have it. Besides, it wasn't our fault. Your boy should've been watching where he was going. He ran in front of the car. If the driver hadn't stopped, the boy would've been seriously hurt. You've already wasted our time. By now, we would've been at Aba.' I tossed sixty naira at him and ordered him out of the car. I intended to give him only fifty, but I added ten for taxi fare back to the junction."

The visit hardened his parents' resolve not to risk their children's lives taking them to Nigeria again. They showed a strong disinclination to visit the country despite requests by their parents to bring the children again. Instead, they were prepared to pay their parents' tickets to bring them to the U.S. to visit.

Recalling the conversation, Clint felt sympathy for his parents for distancing themselves from Nigeria. Unlike his fellow college students, he felt his background was incomplete, and he needed to learn more about his heritage.

He lay on the bed, glancing at his childhood trophies from swimming and track, as well as his diplomas from elementary, middle school, and high school. Soon, he would add college diplomas to those.

On that warm June day, though, he felt a sense of unease.

Something was missing in his life. Did he really want to go to law school? Was that his true wish? He applied at his father's urging. Until then, he always followed the script given by his parents, who, like most Nigerian middle-class parents, tried to control all aspects of their children's lives. They wanted him to have a successful professional career and were determined that he would either be a doctor or a lawyer. His father, in particular, wanted him to follow in his footsteps and join the legal profession.

They lived in a predominantly White neighborhood, because they wanted their son to have the best education, and so far, they've succeeded. He strove to meet their expectations. In high school, any grade other than an A was the subject of much discussion and a warning of impending failure and a slide into poverty. He excelled in school, earning a 4+ grade-point average. He was accepted at several liberal-arts colleges, and his final decision of a school in Massachusetts was based on criteria his father provided, even though his personal choice would have been Howard University, a predominantly Black college in Washington, DC.

During his first year of college, he began to feel dissatisfied with his life. Deep in his gut, he felt something was missing, and he needed to know more about himself and what he wanted from life. He wanted to make his own decisions.

In his first semester, he met and befriended several foreign students from different parts of the globe through his membership in the International Students Club. Unlike him, they were unrestrained in their thoughts and actions, unafraid to say what they meant and befriend whomever they wanted. He was fascinated by their tales of African customs and traditions, about which he, though Nigerian, had no inkling.

Three of his closest friends were from Nigeria and Malawi. Tunde, a Yoruba from a royal family in Abeokuta in southwestern Nigeria, who talked incessantly about his father, the ruler of Abeokuta, and Nigerian politics. Tunde majored in economics. Given his father's position, he was certain he would one day become Governor of his state. He appeared to have unlimited funds and was often in Washington, DC, to meet visiting relatives or attend important functions at the Nigerian embassy. He often pressed Clint to accompany him to Nigeria whenever he went. Clint assured him that he wanted to accept the offer in the summer, but he felt his parents would be affronted. During summer vacations, Clint was expected to earn pocket money.

His other friend, Justin Banda, was from Malawi, and Clint at first assumed he was related to the late strong man Kamuzu Banda. Justin assured him that Banda was a common surname, and he wasn't related. Justin talked often about the changes in his country after the death of Kamuzu. He was very dismissive of the democratic ideals Clint had been raised with as the ideal form of government. Justin firmly believed that most African countries were better off ruled by dictators, saying, "Banda knew what was good for Malawi." During his rule, Malawi avoided most of the problems of corruption and the diversion of government funds that plagued many African governments, including Nigeria.

"Look at what happened since his death and the arrival of democracy," Justin said when other students teased him. "It's chaos and corruption."

During those discussions, Tunde often argued it would be difficult for a dictatorship to work in Nigeria. "Nigerians are too individualistic and would rise up against anyone who tries to curb their natural instincts."

His third friend was Uche, who, like Clint, was born in the U.S. Unlike Clint, he always visited Nigeria each summer. His father, a professor in the Engineering Department of New York State University, made sure Uche knew his roots and let him and his siblings spend school holidays with relatives in Nigeria.

Seeing how grounded Uche was in his identity made Clint question his parents' choice to turn their backs on their homeland. While discussing that aspect of his life, Uche vehemently understood why it would appear that way, but, since Peter and Peace never gave up their Nigerian citizenship, it appeared they regarded themselves as Nigerians.

"We Nigerians have a love-hate relationship with our country," Uche said. "That your parents haven't visited Nigeria since you were five shouldn't be interpreted as turning their backs on the country."

Justin attended the elite Kamuzu Academy and worried that, given the changes taking place in his country, the academy might lose its elite position.

During those countless discussions of social issues in the dorm or in associations with other African students, Clint's thinking began to change. He wondered if the American press' emphasis on fraud, corruption, poverty, famine, and other miseries, coupled with his parents' lack of empathy for their homeland, were wrong.

He considered expanding his knowledge by taking a course on African literature. During a Christmas break, when Clint mentioned this idea to his father, Peter said such esoteric studies would only distract him from the goal of being admitted to a good law school. Peter convinced him that he could always read African literature for enjoyment, so there was no point taking it as a class subject.

During his holidays, all his attempts to get his parents to share their knowledge of their homeland by mentioning information he garnered from his friends were dismissed offhand. It was as if they wanted to wipe away their past and treasure only the experiences they acquired in the U.S. In some regard, he found that strange, but he felt he should give them the benefit of the doubt. In time, they might eventually open up.

Looking out his bedroom window, he gazed at the spring flowers blooming in the neighbors' yards, but his mind was elsewhere, wondering what his college friends were doing. Tunde went home for the holidays and invited him to visit during the summer before the commencement of graduate school. Justin, who also majored in economics, had a job offer from the Bank of Malawi. Both appeared sure of their plans and aspirations and of their roles in the future of their countries. Interacting with them and other students from Iran and the Middle East in social situations, Clint realized all the decisions for his future had been made for him, and he always acquiesced without dissent. Furthermore, he knew very little about his heritage or family.

He glanced at his watch. He'd been sitting in his room all morning, and it was already midday. He knew what he had to do. The more he thought about it, the stronger he felt he needed to break the mold and act. Not wanting to dwell on his feelings too long and talk himself out of doing something, he picked up the filed labeled Law School, went to the family room where the house phone was, and called the admissions office.

He explained he wanted to defer his admission, because he had been offered the chance to travel to Nigeria to gather information on its legal systems. He intended to specialize in human rights in law school, and it was an opportunity he didn't want to forego.

After some discussion, the dean told him to put his request into writing. If it was denied, he could re-apply the following year. The dean kindly advised him how to couch the letter.

Clint began writing to request a deferment. To avoid a full-scale family meeting, during which both parents would band together to persuade him to change his mind and point out the reasons for continuing his education, he affixed a stamp onto the envelope and ran to the mailbox at the end of the street.

Uncharacteristically, he felt at peace. The deed was done, and he had to bear the consequences. Next, he called the manager at the Bethesda Barnes and Noble, who agreed to see him at 4:00 that afternoon. Having worked several summers at the store, he didn't have any trouble being rehired, although that summer his job would be in the café, because there were no other openings. He could start as early as the following day.

CHAPTER TWO

Peace, a doctor at a nearby medical clinic, was the first family member to arrive home. "Hi, Clint," she said, depositing her bag on the hall table. "How was your day? Do anything interesting? Did any of your friends stop by or call?"

She continued talking, as she walked into her bedroom to change out of her work clothes.

Clint waited to answer until she returned to the family room, where he lay on the sofa, listening to jazz on the radio. Peace tousled his hair and pulled a chair up close, gazing at him expectantly.

"Well, I'm listening. What did you do today?"

His attention went from the music to her face. "Nothing much, except I went to Barnes and Noble. I have a summer job starting tomorrow."

"But, Clint," she said, raising her voice, "I thought we agreed you would use the summer to prepare for law school and perhaps volunteer in Dad's firm. Why the sudden change of mind?'

You agreed, not me, he thought, hearing the irritation in her voice.

He hesitated, thinking the timing was a bit off, and he should defer discussing his plans.

Peace didn't press him. "We'll talk about it when Dad comes home. Right now, I have to get your sister from the YMCA." Standing, she left the room.

Very typical of this family, he thought. Dad has the final word.

We'll see about that, he added resentfully.

Clint bided his time until after the family dinner. He listened to his parents discuss their day, and his sister talked about summer school.

In a determined voice, he finally said, "Mom, Dad, I have something to tell you."

Looking up, he saw them staring at him and plunged ahead. "I've decided to defer law school for at least a year." "Defer law school?" his parents shouted.

"What do you mean?" his father demanded. "What nonsense am I hearing?" He slammed his hands on the table. Peter, a stocky, darkbrown man with gold-rimmed glasses, always made it clear to his children that he knew what was best for them and tolerated no argument. In his wildest dreams, he never imagined any of his children stepping off the path he carefully carved for them. His colleagues at work often complained about their children's decision to skip or drop out of college to pursue alternative lifestyles, but Peter was certain it wouldn't happen in his household. Visibly annoyed, he glared at Clint, challenging him to take back his words.

"Listen to me!" Clint shouted back.

His parents stared angrily at him, as if they never expected him to use such a tone.

"All right, Clint," Peace said, breaking the silence, "we're listening."

"I've given this a lot of thought. I'm not sure I want to go to law school. I want a year off to think about it. I already called the university and spoke to the dean." He nervously wrung his hands.

"You did what?" Peter shouted. "Are you out of your mind?"

"I don't see why you're so annoyed. It's my life, not yours," he said vehemently.

"Rubbish! It might be your life, but we have the responsibility of bailing you out if things go wrong. Don't you think we, as your parents, deserve the right to discuss such an important decision that will affect your whole life?"

"Isn't that what we're discussing right now?"

"Don't be facetious. There's a difference, and you know it. We're discussing this as a fait accompli." He used the tone of voice reserved for someone he considered stupid.

"Oh, boy." Clint's long pent-up anger erupted. "Did you ask me when you decided to move to Tenley Park? Do you remember what happened? You made the arrangements without any hint to me. I only learned about it when you came to day care on the last day of school, picked me up, and brought me here."

"Talk about a decision that changes someone's life! That was it? Do you know how unhappy I was in middle and high school? Did you ever try to find out my feelings? It was always, 'Clint, do your homework. Clint, you must study. We don't want anything below an A from school.'

"Do you remember how many times you pointed at the garbage men and beggars near the Tenley metro station and told me that's what I would become if I didn't study? When I was in high school, if I looked tired, you ransacked my room for illegal drugs, as if I had any urge to take them.

"Do you remember the argument over my wish to apply to Howard University? You didn't want to hear of it. Rather than fight you, I bent to your wishes."

Everyone stared at him aghast, their mouths open.

Confronted with the steady deterioration of public services, schools, and the increasing level of drug use, Clint's parents, like most middle-class families, decided to move from their inner-city apartment on Fourteenth Street NW across town in search of a safe haven and environment for their children. Distraught, Peace didn't know how to explain to Clint the trauma of being pregnant and having to avoid hordes of unemployed youths loitering in the apartment building entrance, having to walk down streets with garbage bins full of discarded drug paraphernalia, condoms, and half- eaten hamburgers.

"Enough, Clint!" she snapped. "You can't talk to your father like that. Every decision we made, since we had you, was for your benefit. Stop this at once!"

Emboldened, he said, "For my own benefit? Ha! While we're at it, did you ever try to find out if I was interested in going to Nigeria? The only thing I know about it is hearing you two talk of your experiences from your honeymoon and the one time we visited just before I began kindergarten. Whether you like it or not, I'm deferring law school and will try to save enough money to go to

Africa for a year."

Peace, unable to restrain herself, stood up and folded her arms tightly around herself. She didn't know how to tell Clint about the problems he'd face in Africa and her fear she'd lose him either in the upheavals and constant violence or from lack of timely medical care if he fell ill. "Africa? What's this?"

Her words were immediately echoed by Peter, who seemed too upset to look at Clint. He stood and began pacing.

"I have homework to do," Sarah said, who finished clearing the table. She dashed from the room, not wanting to get involved in the row.

After what seemed like a lifetime, Peter finally spoke in a calmer voice. "Clint, you must be joking. I hope you haven't written the letter."

"I have."

"You did what?" Peter, losing control, pounded the table with his fist again. "Why didn't you wait to consult us before doing such a thing? This decision will affect your entire life, and you felt you had to make it by yourself? What's wrong with you? Are you out of your mind? What will you do in Africa, travel around, get a job? Where? You have no skills, and even graduates from African universities have difficulty finding jobs. Clint, use your brain. We won't subsidize any such harebrained activity." He sat down heavily, covering his face with his hands.

"Let's calm down," Peace said, trying to reason with him. "As long as you haven't posted the letter, no harm has been done."

"I posted it this afternoon, because I didn't want to change my mind," Clint said.

"Then write another letter saying you made a mistake," she said, unperturbed.

"I can't do that, Mom," he said firmly. "I don't care if my request for deferment is turned down. I don't want to go to law school this fall. I'm not sure what I want to do in the long run. I know I want to take a year off and decide whether to become a lawyer. I've been thinking about this for some time."

"Are you out of your mind, Clint?" Peter asked, grasping at any straw. "Did we force you to apply for law school? You had ample time to tell us what was on your mind."

"If I told you what I wanted, would you have listened?" he asked softly. "You wanted me to go to law school, so you could boast about my achievement to your family and friends." He took a deep breath. "I applied, because I wanted to please you, if you really want to know, and because I thought that was what I wanted. I plan to save money and travel to Grandpa's village. Perhaps I might find something to do there. It'll give me time to think of my future."

"What future? You won't have any without professional qualifications!" Peter pounded the table again.

"You aren't listening to me. I might as well talk to a stone." He stood, too angry to continue the discussion, and went to his room, where he slammed the door.

He stared at a painting of an Africa village scene that hung in the room he shared with his parents when he was born, a tableau of men and women carrying pots, firewood, and other goods on their heads, returning from or going somewhere, and clumps of men under a tree, talking and drinking from gourd cups. A woman carried a load, her right hand stretched out behind as if to catch a little boy running after her.

He remembered when his father brought him to Tenley Park the first time. It was one of this childhood memories that always came to him when he studied the painting. His father picked him up at the day care and drove past their old apartment without a word of explanation. On arrival at the house, Clint hesitated before leaving the car, because he was in a strange part of the city filled with houses, not apartments. It didn't resemble anywhere he lived before with his parents.

They entered the house, and he heard his mother, who was pregnant with Sarah, call that she was in the kitchen. He saw unopened cartons everywhere and was very confused.

"Clint, you have a room of your own instead of sleeping with us in the same room," Peace said. "Peter, why don't you show him his new room? It isn't organized yet, but the bed is made. This is your surprise, Clint."

"Come with me, Young Man." Peter led him to his room.

The first thing Clint saw was the painting. His mother bought it at a flea market in Washington before his birth, and it hung in his new room.

Just as they entered the room, the phone rang. It was his grandfather in Africa. Clint overheard snatches of the discussion, something about land given to the family when someone bought his freedom, and the ownership was being challenged. Still feeling confused and slightly ill, he was hustled to dinner.

At dinner, his parents ignored him except for occasionally asking him to pass the salt or a plate. The conversation was about the phone call. His father was visibly annoyed.

"I don't know why he wanted to involve me in that fight," Peter said. "He knows I'm not interested in anything to do with that."

"It's a shame that the Aros like to dwell in the past," Peace replied. "Slavery was abolished a long time ago, but will they let it go? Who cares whether your antecedents were slaves? What matters is what you are today."

"My father's a bit self-conscious about it," Peter said. "I don't know why, though. I thought having achieved much in his life and living as he does in a big estate would make him feel different. When it comes to quarreling with Igwe's family, he inevitably feels inferior.

Clint felt confused and forgotten until his mother turned to him and asked him to get ready for bed. He remembered walking into his room filled with anger, because he'd been wrenched from the apartment where he'd been happy and the day care where he had friends to a place where he knew nobody. That night began the mysterious dreams that plagued him all his life.

He remembered sitting on that spot on the bed and staring at the painting. He thought of himself as the little boy, hurrying after his mother. Suddenly, he was no longer in Tenley Park but in the village square in Africa as the little boy. He saw himself at a stream in Africa, playing with friends, a happy day of Hide-and-Seek and splashing in the water. Startled by a loud noise from the village above, the children hid behind a tree.

As the noise abated, they ran toward the village, only to find people calling to their loved ones, telling them to run to the safety of the forest, because unknown, warlike strangers had been sighted.

His mother beckoned to him, but, when he reached for her hand, she was distraught and told him to hurry, because the village was under attack. Commotion and confusion surrounded him. As if propelled by an inner force, people fled the village. Women dragged their children, some carrying meager possessions, while others wore nothing but loincloths.

"Hurry up, My Son," Peace shouted. "We have to get my sister. She's preparing the evening sacrifice to our deity. Where's your

younger brother? You're supposed to look after him."

"I don't have a brother." Panting, he asked, "Mummy, wait. What's wrong? Why aren't we going home?"

"Hurry. The village is under attack. Come on. There's no time to waste. I don't want to lose you, too. We have to go. Put down that bowl of mushrooms you're carrying. Where'd you get them?"

Without waiting for a response, she prattled on. "I heard they're bad people from far away who have a powerful oracle that protects them at all times. Hurry up! Their warriors have been sighted. Our men, who made the journey to consult the powerful oracle of these people, said their coming this far prophesizes something evil. The chiefs have ordered us to run away."

Running along the narrow path to the shrine, his mother dragged him with her. She needed to persuade her sister to accompany them.

As they approached the shrine where the god worshipped by the villagers resided, Clint's body shook with fright. The shrine was a forbidden place. No one but the chief priestess and village heads were allowed inside. The hut sat within a grove of massive iroko trees, its external walls covered with human skulls and paintings of leopards and other wild animals in various poses.

It was a frightening place, especially to a young boy who often wondered what was inside the forbidden building. As the pair approached, they saw smoke coming from the hole in the roof, evidence of the latest sacrifice to the god.

They stopped a few yards from the entrance.

"Sister!" Peace shouted, hoping her voice would be heard inside. "Come out! The village is deserted. We have to leave. Something bad is about to happen. We have very little time to hide. Come with us immediately."

Her voice must've carried. The woman who walked out was like an apparition Clint saw in photographs in National Geographic that his father occasionally brought home. She wore a leopard-skin vest, grass skirt, and several strings of cowries. Ivory bands covered her legs from the ankle to the knee. Her body was covered in clay and charcoal markings, giving her the look of a leopard on the prowl. She had a leopard-skin cap adorned with feathers and cowry shells, multicolored feathered fans in both hands, and a carved cane shaped like a snake.

Seeing his aunt in her garb as high priestess terrified Clint, and he clung to his mother. By then, she was crying, and he couldn't bear to see her tearstained face. His heart raced.

"Come with us, My Sister. I beg you!" Peace, looking around, saw most of the other wives running wildly toward the forest.

"Get away from here," the woman called back. "Nothing will happen to me. The gods will protect me."

Turning to him, Peace said, "We must hurry. This isn't a raid like the others. These people don't act like crop raiders who make for the yam barns. Instead, they prefer to hide under thick bushes and bide their time. That's what's so frightening about their sudden appearance. They're said to be people who lived next to the Cross River and who had the protection of a powerful oracle.

"Let's hurry. I wish I hadn't wasted time looking for Nwada. All the women are far away, and we must catch up."

Everywhere Clint looked, he saw families running into the forest.

Groups of them coalesced and disintegrated, depending on how fast the younger members could run. The first night, he and a group of children slept near the river. The air was filled with the sound of crying from the children and the hushing sounds of mothers trying to still them by invoking the danger from the marauders. The children weren't easily quieted. In the dark, he felt the presence of other children, many too tired to stay awake. In their flight, some mothers abandoned their children. That was when he realized he'd been separated from his own mother.

Huddled under a tree, praying for daylight, the little boy he became finally fell asleep.

At dawn, the children left behind were in the river, splashing around, crying and not knowing where they were. Confused, Clint followed the older children, who were bent on returning to the village.

All along the narrow bush track, unseen eyes watched them, as they walked single file. Without warning, some of the children were captured by the marauders.

"Let me go! Let me go! Mummy, where are you?" Clint shouted, as a man bound him with a rope and tethered him to the other children.

—⚉—

"Wake up, Clint. Why are you crying? You're all tangled in the bedspread. Did you have a bad dream?"

He woke to find his mother shaking him. "That was quite a dream, Clint. When I came to your room, you said in your sleep that you were bound, and the ropes dug into your side. I kept telling you no one was attacking you, but you kept struggling."

"I dreamed I was separated from you, as we ran away. We ran into a big forest to hide from bad people. That was where I was separated from you."

"No wonder you were thrashing about. Poor Clint. You were just worried because of the move. I'm here now, aren't I?"

"But, Mama, even now I'm frightened of the dream."

"Clint, stop your nonsense. I don't want to hear this again. I'm your mother, and I'm not running from anything. You're imagining things. What book are you reading now? Is there a forest in it? It must be all the talk about land in Africa that put the forest in your head. It's only a dream. We could visit the Air and Space Museum today. Would you like that?"

—⚉—

Lying in bed the morning after the fight with his parents, alone in the house, Clint remembered how lonely and sad he felt the summer of the move. He changed from a sunny, carefree child into an introverted, moody one who preferred his own company.

Peace and Peter, noticing the change in him, tried to distract him with various excursions they thought might appeal to him. They assumed that by the end of the summer, he would revert to his usual self. They constantly emphasized how the move would give him the best opportunities life could offer, which became their mantra while Clint grew up.

One Saturday, his parents took him to the zoo. Knowing his fascination with animals, they thought the visit would draw him out.

At the big cat area, Peter said, "Clint, look at the leopard. When I was a young man in the village, I was initiated into the Ekpe (leopard) Society. My parents were flabbergasted, because they labeled such societies pagan." "How young?" Clint asked.

"It was a long time ago. It was in the time between high school and university. Leopards are part of the burial ceremony for important chiefs in our area."

Clint's interest was piqued. He wanted to hear more about the leopard society, but Peter didn't elaborate.

"Let's not visit the reptile section," Peace said. "I can't abide snakes. I usually have nightmares after I see them."

"But Mama, these can't come out to bite you," Clint said.

"How do you know?" she asked belligerently. "When I was growing up, a snake bit me. It wasn't uncommon to hear of someone being bitten by a snake lurking in a corner of the house or the undergrowth on the farmland. I remembered a time when a snake swallowed a baby left under a tree, while her mother was weeding her farm plot."

She strode down the opposite path as if pursued by a demon. Trying to keep pace, Clint tugged her hand to slow down. Anxious to know more about the horrifying incident, he said without thinking, "I saw a snake killed once."

"Rubbish!" She was taken aback. "What are you saying? You've never seen a snake except at the zoo. Is this one of your fibs?"

Instead of answering, Clint clutched his father's hand protectively, as Peace pushed the pram and put more distance between herself and the reptile enclosure.

Suddenly, the zoo and the people faded away. It was as if Clint was once again in the big forest. He felt the presence of other captives, as he tried to keep pace with the group. Sweat glistened on their bodies, and their feet were covered with chalk-colored dust from the forest floor. He heard the calls of unseen animals and birds, as the party marched through the thick forest. Occasionally, a hare or porcupine scampered across their path. Each time, the men made a halfheartedly attempt to catch it before it disappeared. When they caught one, they roasted it for their evening meal.

At first, Clint refused to eat, but when hunger overcame him, he had no option but to eat whatever was offered.

The trees became denser, until the marchers could barely see the sun. The air was dank with the smell of rotting leaves on the ground, and they saw snake skins shed not long ago. They had to be vigilant to avoid stepping on dangerous snakes that sometimes hid under the rotting leaves beneath the canopy. Afraid of snakes, Clint watched his step constantly.

One of the three men who captured with him stepped on a snake and was bitten. The lead man cauterized the wound and bound it with leaves, so he could keep pace. Clint knew the man was in pain, but their captors were determined to complete the journey at all costs. Occasionally, the men pushed aside tree branches and, finding a stream, stopped to drink water and wash off some of the sweat and dirt.

The next thing Clint knew, his father shouted to watch where he was going. Suddenly, the zoo returned, and he heard birds, noise, and the chatter of children and adults all around.

Sitting in his room that afternoon, staring at the picture, he relived the experience. He wanted to know what happened to the little boy he temporarily became. Lost in thought, he recalled another time when his parents took him to the Smithsonian for his birthday.

Remembering the first time he saw the space capsules, and the idea of space travel made him smile. The visit to the Air and Space Museum went well. The family enjoyed seeing I Can Fly at the IMAX theater. It was a relaxing day, and Peace noticed Clint seemed captivated by the capsules and astronauts, and he enjoyed the film.

During lunch at the cafeteria, she suggested going to the African Museum near the Castle. She wanted to see the photographic exhibition of Women in the Harem by a Moroccan named Lalla Essaydi.

"This won't take long," she said. "I know you two are tired."

As they entered the museum, Peace said, "Listen. I think there's an event in the auditorium. Do you hear the drums?"

Clint heard them, and he was reluctant to take the elevator that carried them to the auditorium where the sound emanated from, but he did. When the elevator stopped on the floor leading to the auditorium, though, he hesitated.

"Let's see what it is," Peace said. "Look, Clint. There are children your age here." She pointed at them. "Why don't you sit here and listen to the drums while we wander around and look at the other photographic exhibits?"

Some of the photographs had been described as "erotic" by the guard and thus not suitable for children.

"We won't be long," she added.

She found a spot for him in the auditorium. Tired and shaken, he was glad to sit down He must've fallen asleep, lulled by the drums, because he was again transported to the forest floor, where he heard someone say, "I hear drums. They're faint. Can you hear them?"

"It means we're close to a farm village," replied the head of the warriors. "It's probably two days' journey before we're home."

Fearing for their lives, the men chatted among themselves at the sound of the drums, while the captives looked at each other and whimpered.

"Stop that noise immediately," one man ordered, "or your fate will be decided here! We can leave you for the animals to eat, if that's what you want. Give them some palm wine if there's any left. That should silence them. I can't think with them making all that noise."

Thirsty and dehydrated, Clint was glad to drink anything. He sniffled.

"Wouldn't it be nice if, in addition to them, we brought back a leopard?" one captor asked, amid general laughter, coughing, and slapping of thighs.

"That reminds me. I wonder whether the group looking for leopard caught any," said the head man. "Perhaps we should look for one."

It was two days since they'd been taken from their homes. During that time, the party avoided places of human habitation. They ate guinea fowl eggs, wild cocoyam, and, occasionally, bananas or plantains picked up at an abandoned compound and prepared on a makeshift hearth in the forest.

By midafternoon on the third day of their march, the sound of drums grew louder, and the men's attitude changed. They followed a narrow path that led them to a small village near a stream. Relaxing, they joked and congratulated each other on the success of their mission.

"I hope we get home before it's too late," one man said. "When we left, the illustrious one was still breathing."

"The priest said it wouldn't be immediate, and we had time," the head man said. "We've still got a day's journey ahead. Let's start at dawn. We can get something for the next leg of the journey in the village. I just hope he's still alive. We've been gone nearly four days. No one will blame us, though. We couldn't find what we wanted nearby. We had to go too far for them."

As they approached the village, one man took out a small drum and tapped out a message, then they listened for a reply

The farm village was a cluster of several compounds, each totally enclosed by farmland, where yam and other root crops were planted. Cassava was planted around the perimeter.

They walked past an area thick with cassava plants until they reached a large compound with several huts. Cocoyam and several vegetable plants competed for space in and around each hut, with plantain and pawpaw occupying the back spaces. The smell of food from pots on the charcoal hearth outside each hut permeated the air.

In the middle of the compound was a substantial house, from which the drumming emanated. The group went toward that house, which had a veranda, and they saw a group of ten men surrounding the drum, waiting in anticipation for their arrival. The drumming intensified, as they neared, and a man came out to welcome them, indicating a corner where the captives could be kept, so the men could confer.

Clint saw women holding onto their children and peeping out of the doors of smaller huts, watching as if waiting for something to happen. Occasionally, someone stepped outside to coax the embers of the fire on the hearth or to stir food in a pot.

"I see you've been very successful," the village headman said, surveying the captives huddled on one side of the hut.

"Yes, but it took a while," the warrior leader said. "We'll stay only until tomorrow morning, because we're pressed for time. Have you heard anything?"

The village headman lifted his hands as if asking for a blessing. "No. We sent someone to the nearest farming village for news, but, can you believe that since you left, we've seen no one? It's as if we've been forgotten. Usually at this time, farmers till the soil and prepare the farmland in the settlement nearest us, and we exchange visitors. It's as if all are staying indoors, fearing to venture out." He looked at the warriors, seeking confirmation.

"I can understand," the warrior headman said in a tight voice. "These are trying days. One needs to be careful to avoid falling into a trap."

Later that night, the men of the hunting party discussed their next move. The captives, chained together, were taken outside to be fed.

The headman sat at the far end of the room, lost in thought.

"You heard what the man said," one man said. "He advised us to take the western route into Aro Chukwu."

In the confusion following the party's unexpected arrival, the little boy separated from the group and hid in a corner to listen to the men argue.

The headman was silent for a long time, as if lost in his own world. Finally, he said, "Ay! But we have to be careful. I don't believe the headman has heard nothing. You know this village belongs to us. Surely our people will want to protect it from harm, so he must know what's happening at home. I don't believe him when he says he has no news."

"I can't see one of the captives," another man said. "It's a child. I thought we chained them together."

The boy trembled, hoping he wouldn't be discovered.

"My God, you're right," said a man the boy had been shackled to during the journey. "He must've slipped out. I don't see him eating. He couldn't have gone far. I thought he went outside with the other children before we came in."

The men scrambled to their feet to search.

"That one is something else," the headman muttered. "He's always watching and listening. If I catch him, I'll beat him to prepare him for a journey to the next world."

Hiding in a dark corner, the child listened. He was still trembling when a man approached his hiding place.

"Come out of there, you little plotter," the man said. "Let's teach you a lesson." Slapping the boy, he shoved him outside, where he hit him again with a stick. "No food for you tonight."

Tears rolled down his cheeks, and mucous came from his nose. He wiped his nose with his hands and plucked a cocoyam leaf to clean them, while his fellow prisoners, who were eating, watched. He cried silently, calling for his mother.

—ᴔ—

The next thing Clint knew, Peace was shaking him.

"Clint, it's time to go," she whispered. "You seem so far away. You're crying and calling out, 'Nne, moo.' You love to say those words when you're tired. Why are you crying and wiping your hands? We've been gone for only thirty minutes."

"Mama!" he said, rubbing sleep from his eyes, but he didn't answer the question.

"Did you have a snooze? The drumming was quite loud, so I don't know how you could sleep through that."

She helped him stand. "Did you enjoy the drumming? Would you like to learn how to drum? We can buy you a small drum from the museum shop. Look. Here's a photograph your father took of you listening to the drums. You seem quite enthralled, and you didn't know he took it."

In a daze, Clint said, "We still had a day's travel ahead after we arrived at the place where the sound of drums beckoned us. That was what the man said."

She looked at him. "What man? What place?"

Still fuzzy with sleep, Clint said, "The drums directed us to that place." Waking more fully, he said, "My body aches. I feel like I've been beaten up." He lifted his shirt. "Mama, do I have welts on me?"

"What are you talking about?" Peace became agitated. "You must've been dreaming. You've been here all the time. I don't see any welts on you, but you certainly feel hot and sweaty. Are you ill? Do you have a fever? Let's take you home, so you can sleep properly."

She and Peter hurried Clint to the car and drove home.

Recalling the experience on the last day of May, sitting in his room, Clint felt his parents' unease and worry about the changes he went through. Their efforts to cheer him were intended to bring back his good mood before the move. Instead, he became more introverted and less spontaneous about expressing his inner thoughts. Always protective of himself, willing to please, and never giving offense, he spoke only when necessary.

Those attributes persisted throughout his life.

CHAPTER THREE

For days, his parents wouldn't talk to him. He went to work at the bookstore, came home, and stayed in his room most nights, reading or listening to music. He wondered how long the silent treatment would last, but he was determined not to change his decision, and changing was the only thing his father would accept.

At the beginning of the following week, he was home alone with his mother. Sarah was sleeping over at a friend's house, and Peter wasn't around. Sarah was the only family member who sought out Clint's company during those day. She came to his room after dinner and tried to make him give in to their parents.

"Why do you want to throw away everything you've worked for?" she asked. "Go to Dad and tell him you've changed your mind." Despite her pleading, Clint was adamant.

That particular evening, surprised by his father's absence at dinner, instead of moodily staring at his plate, Clint turned to his mother and asked, "Where's Dad?"

"He's out of town at a conference." She stared at him sadly. "Clint, we need to talk. We can't go on like this, with you so angry with us. Come sit with me."

"What's there to talk about?" He sat near her.

"We knew you were unhappy with the move. We saw changes in you that worried us. You went from a sunny, carefree child to an introvert who preferred his own company. You refused to socialize with the neighborhood children, preferring to watch TV and play with your toys."

Clint raised his hand to stop her, but she shook her head.

"No, Clint. You have to let me have my say." She sighed. "I was on maternity leave during the first part of that summer, so I tried to spend as much time as possible with you. I tried to distract you by taking you to the parks, so you could play with the other children, but you refused to have anything to do with them. You clung to me as if you feared to lose me and didn't show any interest in the swings and slides. I don't know if you remember. We took you to the zoo many times and even the Smithsonian, though, like most Nigerians, we would rather visit friends or stay home to watch TV."

Looking into her face, seeing her sadness, Clint said, "I remember the zoo visit. You're afraid of snakes, and Dad has something to do with leopards."

"I'm glad you remember. Our move from the inner city was inevitable. We were expecting Sarah, and we wanted both of you to have a good education. We came from a culture where parents make the decisions without consulting their children, and children acquiesce without argument. It would be unthinkable of me to argue with my father over the decisions he made for me. Even now, Peter has trouble arguing with his father, though he's a successful lawyer."

Holding Clint's hands so he would face her, she said, "Peter and I attended boarding schools from an early age. That was our fathers' decision. We considered sending you to a boarding school in Nigeria for your secondary education, so you could be spared the trauma of the Washington school system. We decided we wanted you with us, and we wanted to see you grow up here. Our visit to Nigeria that summer was part of our attempt to distract you. You already know the story."

"Yes." Clint chuckled. "I've told it many times."

"I can still see you climbing the orange trees at Peter's father's estate. You appeared happy and carefree there."

"I vaguely remember Grandpa worrying that I would fall."

"Do you remember us telling you during your primary school years that you should be more assertive and friendly, because your teachers often remarked you seemed aloof and unable to make friends?"

"Seriously, Mama, I was unhappy in elementary school. I didn't feel like I belonged. In one of the classes, I was the only Black kid."

"Your teachers liked you and thought you were very smart. They paid more attention to you than the other kids."

"But being liked inevitably lands you in trouble. It happened in middle and high school, when we had a sizable number of Black students bused in from different parts of the city. I became a pariah, because I didn't side with them all the time when they felt they were being singled out by teachers for punishment for minor infractions. I was upset by the general attitude of Black students to blame all their problems on racism."

"I remember those letters from the principals to the parents on issues of insubordination. It always puzzled Peter and me that, despite all the opportunities available to Black students here, many failed to take advantage of them. We felt many Africans would welcome such opportunities and thrive on them. There are many deserving African children who aren't in school, because their parents can't afford the fees and associated expenditures. It seemed to us then that your fellow students didn't understand the importance of education in opening doors to good jobs and the realization of the American dream."

"Mom, you often said Dad wouldn't feel so negative about Black students if he had been subjected to institutional racism from birth."

"Indeed, I did, but also added it wasn't our fight. We didn't want you participating in it."

"Mom, you said that being Black doesn't mean they always have to be our friends. You told me that after I had a fight with a Black student, who called me African and asked what I was doing here. He said I should go back to the bush where I came from. I was so affronted, I was ready to hit him, but Frank stopped me in time."

"I remember that." She smiled. "Poor Frank and the many battles he fought for you. Clint, we moved here to give you the bestpossible education, and we wanted you to take advantage of the opportunities you had. We didn't ever want you suspended from school. That was our objective. I'm sorry if you feel differently," she said, sighing.

"I don't fault you for that."

"Incidentally, I saw Jumon, your high school basketball friend, the other day, waiting tables at Clyde's in Friendship Heights. He asked about you. Remember how he was going to college on a basketball scholarship? It appears he didn't make the cut, and his parents couldn't afford to pay for college. He said college is presently out of his reach, since he now has to provide for a wife and child," she said sadly.

Clint shook his head. "That's a shame. He showed promise in high school. Talking of high school, you should've warned me about dating."

"I thought of it, but I knew you wouldn't listen. You wanted to copy Frank, and I wanted you to learn from the experience."

"Why are you and Dad so upset about my decision? I know you'd rather see me complete my education, but that doesn't seem a good reason. I actually thought you two would be happy that I wanted to spend time in Nigeria, learning about our family and culture. I'm puzzled."

Peace thought the conversation was over and was ready to get on with her many Saturday chores, but she settled back down and gathered her thoughts. She knew of the daily indignities meted out to the ordinary people of Nigeria. There was the daily police and army harassment of motorists and ordinary people going about their business, the sycophantic worship of wealth no matter how it was earned, the lack of basic services from the government, the bribes everyone had to pay to get something that was due them, the stifling opposition of viewpoint in all levels of government, and the government's general insensitivity to the citizens' needs. What should she tell him?

"For my part, I was worried about you," she said. "Nigeria isn't like the U.S. It's a difficult place, and I feared for you. You're American and think like one. You want to take sides if you see injustice, but that might not be the right thing to do. You might be hurt or contract a disease, and your life could easily be threatened. The hospitals aren't always nearby in an emergency.

"Even if you're taken to a hospital, don't expect, even if your situation is dire, that you'll be immediately cared for. You're an African, even though you don't act like one. Your color won't spare you from any indignities. What Nigerians tolerate from expatriates in their midst won't be tolerated from you. Don't expect any favors from them.

"Rather, they'll take advantage of you, because they know you take things at face value. I don't expect you to understand."

She was silent for a while, then she looked endearingly at him and touched his hands. "Clint, Dear, I'm glad we had this discussion. I have some errands to run. I'll tell your dad you're a grown man, and even though we don't like your decision, we should respect it and help you find what you're looking for."

Clint wasn't convinced by her answer. Disease and violence were everywhere. Even in America, he could be shot while standing innocently on the pavement or hit by a car when he crossed the road. What did she mean? Was she trying to frighten him? He just hoped his father would come around.

Back in his room, Clint went over the discussion with his mother. In high school, he had his first experience of racism. Prom was an important ritual at his school, and, as the senior prom approached, the main conversation in the cafeteria, during breaks, and on the bus, centered on who was taking whom. Not having been socially interactive with any of the girls, particularly the Black girls, Clint had no intention of going.

One day during lunch hour, Frank, his buddy, announced he asked a girl to the prom. Clint was taken aback, because he didn't think Frank was interested in such things.

"I'm glad for you," Clint said. "Did she accept the invitation?" "Yes. She's the daughter of my mom's friend. Who are you thinking of asking?"

Clint frowned. "I never gave it any thought. I'd be uncomfortable asking any girl to go with me, since I've had no contact with any of them."

"Clint, that isn't true. You know many girls from the neighborhood, and I know some would like to go to the prom with you."

Clint pondered that for a moment. "I've spoken to only one girl in school, but she's bused in, and it would be a drag asking her to the prom. She would probably regard it as a joke."

"Clint, Man, I'd really like you to come. We've always done things together. You should think about it."

Clint knew Frank since kindergarten. Their houses abutted each other, and their parents tried to enroll them in the same after-school activities, so they could carpool, with Frank's mother picking them up at home, and Clint's parents bringing them back. Frank was the nearest thing to a friend Clint had.

As the date of prom approached, Frank raised the issue again.

"I have a date for you," Frank said. "It's someone who's anxious to go to the prom and really longs for you to ask."

"Who's this?" Clint made a face. "I'd be uncomfortable asking anyone to go with me."

"She's a friend of Mary's and is in all your classes. Her name is Imogene."

"Her? She's a very serious girl. I'm surprised she's even interested in the prom."

"Why don't you ask Imogene? The four of us could have a nice time together."

"I can't. I hardly know her. We've spoken a total of four times this year. I'm afraid of rejection."

"Nonsense. I know for sure she likes you. I heard her say

so many times. In fact, she asked me if you were going with anyone in particular."

"OK. I'll think about it." Clint knew he couldn't avoid thinking about it, because it dominated all conversations during the week.

The next time Clint saw Frank, he asked, "Would you do me a favor?" "What is it?"

"Ask Imogene if she'll go to the prom with me."

"I already did. She said if you asked her, she'd go."

Clint wrote a note to Imogene, asking if she'd like to go to the prom.

When Clint stood in line at the cafeteria the following day, she came up and said excitedly, "Yes!"

At dinner that week, Sarah asked Clint if he was going to the senior prom. Some of her friends' sisters in his grade were talking about it.

Embarrassed, he said, "Yes." "Who are you taking?" "Imogene."

"Who's she?" Peace asked. "A girl I know in school."

His parents sensed his reluctance to discuss it. Instead of pursuing the topic, his mother asked, "When is it?"

He told her the date. He saved enough money from his weekend job at the bookstore in Friendship Heights to buy an outfit for the prom. He started looking forward to it.

The day before the prom, as he left school to catch the bus, Imogene called to him.

"Clint, I want to talk to you."

He walked over to her, thinking it had to be about the arrangements for the prom.

"I'm sorry, Clint, but I can't go to the prom. My parents think it's a bad idea."

Speechless, he didn't know what to say. He didn't want to argue with her, because he knew how hard it was to disobey his own parents.

"OK. I understand."

She wanted to talk further, but he was so hurt, he walked away. When he told Frank the news, Clint learned there were intense discussions between Frank and Imogene's parents about the date. The only reason Imogene's parents gave for their disapproval was that Clint was Black, and they didn't want Imogene emotionally involved with him. Frank added that Imogene was under intense pressure from the other White students to break off the date.

Clint couldn't believe it. His parents raised him to believe in the equality of all. The knowledge that students at his school regarded him as inferior was unthinkable.

At home, when the discussion veered to the prom, Clint simply said, "I'm not going."

His parents heard why the date had been broken off and didn't ask questions. Sensing they knew more than they let on, Clint left the room in tears.

That night, overcome with grief, he tossed and turned in his sleep, feeling that even though he'd been reluctant to go to the prom, he never expected such an outcome. Somehow, he felt that the situation would turn out differently. He couldn't recall why.

When he woke the following morning, he was sick to his stomach and was glad he didn't have to go to school, knowing he would be a major topic of discussion among his acquaintances.

Clint came home from his Saturday job at the bookstore that afternoon.

"Clint," Peace said, "Dad and I want to talk to you." "About what?" he asked truculently.

"The prom."

"What's to discuss? I'm not going."

"We're sorry you had to learn the hard way that there are people who judge others by the color of their skin," Peter said. "We want you to understand one thing—you're as good, if not better, than they are. Don't let this diminish you in any way. Learn from it and strive to rise about it.

"We chose to live in a predominantly white neighborhood, because we wanted you and your sister to have the best education and go to university. If you have a good education, no one can take that from you. You can get any job you want. If you're qualified, the sky's the limit, and nobody can take that away. What differentiates us from many White people is that they don't have to work hard to succeed, but we do. You should always remember that."

"Clint, try not to think about what happened," Peace added. "You're too young to get involved with a girl right now. You still have college. You might meet someone there. Since today is prom, why don't we as a family go out to dinner and see a movie?"

When he next saw his father, everything was back to normal. Peter was in a good mood, chatting about the conference and asking Clint about the bookstore. A female associate recommended a book titled On Black Sisters' Street by Chika Unigwe, a Nigerian woman living in Brussels.

"I understand the book is about four disparate African women who left their homelands for the riches of Europe and are thrown together by bad luck and big dreams into a sisterhood that changed their lives. I'm thinking of getting it for Peace. Will the bookstore carry it?'

"I can find out for you. If they do, do you want me to buy a copy?"

"That would be nice. Your mom will probably want to read it. I think she said she knew the writer from her high-school days."

It was a happy evening at home, and they ended up watching and discussing a PBS documentary by David Attenborough. Going to his room, Clint's thoughts returned to the fight with his father. He remembered the final episode during his last week at the university, which was partly what precipitated his decision to go to Africa.

It had been a pleasant spring day, and, like his fellow graduates, Clint was outside at the quadrangle, lying under a tree, glad to have completed the final courses and papers for graduation. The smell of rows of hyacinth along the edge of the flowerbeds was intoxicating.

He must've fallen asleep. The next thing he knew, he stood at the doorway of a substantial mud house, holding a keg of palm wine and asking to see the chief, someone he called "the master."

He was accompanied by a boy carrying a basket of dried goat or lamb legs and some tubers, which Clint assumed were yams. His parents often brought home goat meat from the Latin store in Silver Spring, Maryland. He and his companions were admitted to the presence of a man in a loincloth sitting on a mud bench, who welcomed them.

Kneeling, Clint spoke like a supplicant. "My father, I have served you faithfully all these years. I'm here to ask you to make me a free man. I have brought these gifts to ask you to consider my request. I want to own my own home and work for myself."

The man replied. "Stand up, my son. You have served me faithfully all these years. I have grown to rely on you for everything. I intended to free you. Times are changing, and our oracle is under attack. Not only will I grant you your freedom, but I will show you where you can build your house directly opposite mine. Although you are free, I hope you will continue serving me when the opportunity arises."

He stood and accompanied the man outside, where he saw a plot marked out. In the dream, he saw his mud house being constructed.

Clint was awakened by a fellow student who came to remind him of the events taking place that evening.

Since Clint returned home, he often recalled that dream and others before it, wondering what they meant. Who was the man who haunted him since he was a boy? It seemed as if all his dreams and visions pointed him toward Africa, where all would be revealed. He was determined to go there.

Clint had no identity problem. He was a human being and an American. He grew up believing he could achieve any goal he set for himself. Until recently, he never expressed any interest in visiting Nigeria. It was merely the place where his parents were born and where some of his relatives still lived. Occasionally, someone from there visited and brought food, tie-dyed fabrics, and batik clothes. He knew his parents didn't understand the urge to seemingly throw away everything he'd been raised to value for a year in Nigeria. On reflection, he could appreciate their viewpoint, but he felt he had to do this for himself.

CHAPTER FOUR

Clint took a United Airlines flight from Reagan to Atlanta, where he could connect with an international flight to Lagos. After working at the bookstore for a month, Clint was glad that his father finally began making arrangements for him to stay with his grandparents at Aro Chukwu, their hometown in eastern Nigeria. He wanted to fly to Lagos and take public transport to his final destination, but his parents pointed out that Nigeria, unlike East African countries and even Ghana, wasn't set up for tourism. Having been raised in the United States, Clint was in danger of being taken advantage of by unscrupulous individuals. Arrangements were made for him to be met at the airports and driven to wherever he was going. Luckily, they had relatives in Lagos and Port Harcourt, who were willing to meet his plane and ensure he was out of danger.

His parents debated where he should stay at Aro Chukwu. Both had their parents living there. His mother wanted him to stay with Peter's father, but Peter was adamant that he preferred Esther, his mother-in-law, since she lived near the village.

"Clint wants to experience life in Africa," Peter said. "At Esther's, it will be easy for him to visit the villages without a car. Besides, living at my father's, he will be too pampered, as if he were still in the U.S."

"Although my parents' house isn't a palace," Peace said angrily, "it has electricity, at least, and it's spacious. It's not an example of village life."

"That's not what I implied. I was thinking of your uncle's house in the village. If we send him there, he'll have a really good African experience, fetching water from the stream for his bath and going to the bush to take care of business. Need I say more?"

"Then my uncle will demand we send him money for a borehole or an outhouse, so Clint won't be inconvenienced."

"Peace, my dear, what do you expect? Nigerian families are like that."

"You don't think much of them, do you, Dad?" Clint asked.

Before Peter could reply, Peace reluctantly agreed. "Perhaps you're right. My mom will welcome the company, given that she's alone. I doubt my brother and his wife, who live with her, are anything but grief for her."

In the end, arrangements were made for Clint to stay at Esther's.

Peter had to calm his father's unhappiness.

Once the arrangements were in place, Peter helped Clint buy his ticket and obtain a visa, since he was traveling with his U.S. passport.

At Reagan Airport, there was the usual chaos of Nigerians trying to check in huge amounts of freight as luggage. One family of four had twelve pieces of overweight suitcases. The head of the family, unable to convince the clerk that as an international passenger, he was entitled to check all the bags he was carrying, subjected other passengers in line to the spectacle of the family's suitcases being opened and reloaded to distribute the items into eight bags and four hand luggage.

In the end, much to Clint's amusement, the father asked Peace, "As a fellow Nigerian, can Clint take one of these items, since he carries so little?"

"I'm sorry, but no," Peace said. "The airlines require passengers to attest to the ownership of their checked baggage. I can't put him at risk if it turns out there are contraband items in the luggage. I hope you understand."

There were other passengers who chose to carry most of their excess luggage as hand luggage only to be told at the gate that the bags wouldn't fit into the overhead bins and had to be checked. Clint was shocked by how much luggage people had. Peace explained that most of the items were gifts for family members at home or things they expected to resell in Nigeria to recoup the cost of the airfare. Clint watched with interest, wondering what would happen when he reached Lagos.

———————

At the gate in Atlanta, there were some of the Nigerian passengers he recognized from the airport in Washington, and he was surprised at how few of them were white—only twelve. Some women clutched their children, and he surmised they might be wives returning to their husbands after a short trip to the U.S. or during their children's vacation.

Among them was a nun in a blue robe, who Clint assumed was a missionary. The White men, probably mid-level oil workers, returned to the rigs in Port Harcourt, stood stiffly apart from the other passengers, conversing quietly.

He wondered what they were thinking. Most of the passengers, he assumed, were Nigerian. They seemed primarily middle class, with the ladies in braids or corn-rowed hair, tight jeans that rode down when they bent over, and high-heeled shoes. The men, dressed casually, sported football team caps. A few elderly women looked harassed, as they tried to corral fidgety, active grandchildren.

In business class, Clint saw a few Nigerians looking smug, as they watched the embarking economy-class travelers, who must be businessmen returning home or embassy staff from the Atlanta office. He saw one greeted reverently, as he was embarking.

The plane was completely full. The energy in the cabin was high, with passengers jostling each other and trying to cram big bags into the small overhead bins. The hostesses had difficulty trying to control the Nigerian passengers, who, on meeting a friend at the airport, insisted on changing assigned seats to sit with that person. It was difficult to hear what was being said over the intercom, because the passengers all chattered loudly.

Clint sat beside a man who, to his surprise, said he was from Uganda and was a professor at Emory University.

"Are you going to Nigeria on business?" Clint asked. "No. I'm in transit to Kampala."

"Is there no direct flight to East Africa?"

"No. The routes through Europe and Brazil are very expensive, and this one through Nigeria is the cheapest and most direct I could get. I still have to change planes at Nairobi."

During the flight, passengers moved about often to talk to friends in other aisles. When the lights went out at night, the cabin finally calmed down with an occasional loud murmur from the seat behind him.

Clint, wedged between the Ugandan and a woman who spilled over into his seat, couldn't sleep.

Just after eleven o'clock the following morning, the plane landed at Lagos. The flight attendants had difficulty enforcing order, as the passengers, once freed from their seat belts, competed to be first off the plane. His Ugandan seatmate seemed bemused by all the raucous goings-on.

Clint went through customs in Lagos and found a crush of people waiting for loved ones to clear customs. That was followed by hugging, sobbing, and theatrical wailing, as the loved ones finally appeared. He stood there, hot, sweaty, confused, and was very glad to see his name on a placard held by a short, elderly man with cropped white hair. It was the driver sent by his uncle, a high official at the Nigerian airport authority, to meet him and take him to the domestic airport, where his uncle was waiting. Unfortunately, Clint missed his flight to Port Harcourt due to delays and the chaos at customs.

His mother's brother, who met him at the local terminal, rebooked his flight to Owerri. He insisted on taking Clint to a busy noisy restaurant at the airport to eat. Clint mentioned his parents bought an unlocked phone for him, and he needed to buy a sim card and acquire a number.

Despite Clint's vehement protests, the uncle told the driver to take care of getting the sim card and number. He handed Clint 100 naira for his immediate needs once he arrived at Aro Chukwu.

"It's the least I can do. You're family. Your mom would do the same for me. However, I doubt you'll need to spend any money. My mother will take care of your needs. Incidentally, I arranged for your cousin, Chima, to meet you at the Owerri airport and to cancel the Port Harcourt arrangements accordingly."

Clint made a mental note to tell his mother to thank his uncle for his generosity. Soon, it was time to board his flight to Owerri.

The Owerri flight was overfull. He was lucky to get a seat beside a civil servant going to Owerri on business.

On being introduced, the man said, "You missed your Port Harcourt flight."

"How'd you know?"

"Your name was called many times over the loudspeaker at the airport. Some lucky person was happy you never turned up."

They chatted briefly through the flight about the dangers of travel. At Owerri, the man not only helped Clint identify his luggage but insisted on staying with him to make sure he was met.

As they emerged from the airport, Clint anxiously scanned the faces of the assembled relatives of arriving passengers until he saw a placard bearing his name.

Turning to his companion, he said, "I see my name there. Someone called Chima was supposed to meet me."

They walked toward the placard. His traveling companion introduced himself to the man with the placard.

"Hey, Nna. I didn't know this young man was your relative. He said he's going to Aro Chukwu."

"We are, though I'd like to keep him for the night and show him Owerri tomorrow. My instructions, unfortunately, are to take him directly to my aunt."

"A pity. I'd better leave you. When will you be back in Owerri?" "Hopefully tomorrow, God willing," Chima replied.

The two chatted for a few minutes. Knowing that the young visitor was safe, the man said good-bye and walked away.

Turning to Clint, he said, "Hello. I'm Chima Oji. Your uncle asked me to meet you and deliver you to Aunty Esther. I hear you missed your Port Harcourt flight. I hope you didn't have to wait long for this one. Aro Chukwu is about two or three hours away depending on the state of the road. I know you're tired. You can sleep in the car." Without waiting for an answer, he added, "Let's go."

Chima was Esther's half-brother's son. He graduated in engineering from Nsukka University four years earlier and worked at the Imo State Ministry of Works and rose to a supervisory position. Rather than entrust Clint to his driver, he took compassionate leave to meet him at the airport.

The family was generous to Chima. He lived with Esther throughout his secondary school years. Esther's husband paid the fees, and Chima regarded their children as brothers and sisters, because he was raised with them. He was glad to be of service to them and looked forward to seeing Esther again.

As they drove down the road from the airport, Clint was fascinated by the scene unfolding before him. He saw palm and coconut trees laden with fruit. Clumps of palm fruit sat by the roadside, waiting to be loaded onto trucks.

Once the car entered the main road, traffic became thick. Heavily loaded trucks carried freight and people. He saw cyclists dwarfed by heavy loads. Some had two or three passengers. Men and women carried large bags and various household goods on their heads.

At one of the main junctions they passed, Clint saw a man attempting to direct traffic, only to make it worse.

Clint had many questions for Chima, who laughed and said, "You're now in Nigeria," as if that sufficed.

They came to a major town crowded with trucks, taxis, and crowds buying and selling. Men, women, and children, in T-shirts from Yale or Harvard, or with the faces of U.S. basketball heroes printed on them, peddled their wares of peanuts, handkerchiefs, and assorted manufactured goods. They bombarded the window on the passenger side with requests to buy.

Clint kept the window closed at Chima's instruction, as they passed through crowded areas. When a one-legged beggar approached and knocked on the window, Clint rummaged in his knapsack for a naira to give him.

"Don't do that," Chima said sharply, and berated the man for begging.

It was very confusing for Clint, who tried to take it all in.

———m———

As the car approached the first of the Ohafia villages, where yam barns stretched from the roadside and beyond, a chill went down Clint's spine. He became very quiet and didn't respond even when Chima tried to explain that yam seedlings were stored that way to preserve them for the next planting season.

By then, it was getting dark. Clint, lulled by the car's movements, started dozing.

"I never really liked this route," Chima said. "I always take the long route through Ikot Ekpene."

Instead of hearing Chima's voice, Clint was back in time at the farm village where captives were brought.

"Which route shall we take, then?" one man asked.

Instead of prevaricating as he did previously, the leader gave a forthright response. "This is what I think we should do." He stopped to put a pinch of snuff in his nose. "We'll let the people in this village think we've agreed with their suggestions to take the route cutting into Obinkita and proceed from there. Instead, we'll take the southern route through the mangrove swamps into our home village."

He paused to swat a circling mosquito. "On that route we can avoid inhabited places. Let's put the captives in a secure place for tonight. We can't afford to lose even one."

One man coughed loudly. "You're right. That'll do. That way, we can avoid inhabited places. We should start before the first cock's crow."

The other men nodded.

"Make sure we have fruit to stop hunger pangs," the leader added.

The party left the farm village of Bianko just as the first cock crowed, with their captives in tow. At first, the route took them through cassava farms, but, by sunrise, they were deep in a mangrove swamp. When rain began, the men persisted. Soon, they reached an area thick with palm trees of the sweet wine variety. Swarms of bees and wasps circled, attracted by the palm wine sap.

"The gourd containers are overflowing," one man said. "I doubt the tappers have been here for several days."

"I don't want any of you snatching a container and gulping down the liquid," the headman cautioned. "We need to retain our sanity. I mean it!"

Given his tone, no one dared to disobey. Swatting aside bees and wasps that were attracted by the sweet smell of the liquid in the containers, they continued their hot, damp journey. Without a clear path, they had to gauge their route by instinct. Many small streams originating from the Creek River flowed into Aro Chukwu. If they found the right one, it would eventually lead them to the Amanagwu freshwater stream.

By the time the sun was high in the sky, they finally reached a small stream that would bring them to the spot where it became the Amanagwu. They followed the stream for two miles until it became less brackish, and they could quench their thirst and wash away some of the dirt and sweat.

By midafternoon, they reached the spot where the stream widened. That was the village water source.

The headman shook his head. "I think the news is not good. I expected to see men and women collecting water and children splashing around, but there's no one. It's eerie, as if the whole place has shut down."

He sat dejectedly on a downed coconut tree near the riverbank, considering his next move, while the men and boys stood nearby in anticipation and despair.

Eventually, the leader got up, cut down a branch of a palm tree, and fashioned the leaves into his personal mark. Turning to a man, he said, "Take this into the village and give it to the elder of my compound. Make sure you aren't intercepted. He'll tell you if it's safe for us to proceed into the village. Remember, other hunting parties might try to intercept us and claim our spoils, so be careful. The rest of you, hide the captives in the bush."

"Clint? Clint, wake up!" Chima called, shaking Clint with one hand.

"We're at Aro Chukwu. Soon, we'll be at your grandfather's place. You slept through Ohafia, Ihe, and Ututu. At one point, you waved your hand around like you were warding off mosquitoes. I tried to point out the oil palm plantation, as we entered the first of the Aro villages, but you were lost to the world."

Clint roused reluctantly, wanting to know more about the fate of the captives in his dream. A moment later, Esther rushed from the house to welcome him.

The next morning, lying in bed in Grandmother Esther's house, Clint felt disoriented. His body ached. When he checked his watch, he saw it was a few minutes after five. He tried to get up, but his body refused, so he looked around the room to get his bearings.

His suitcase sat on a table on the opposite side of the bed near a window. Two wooden hangers dangled from a rope strung between two walls, inviting him to unpack. He felt unpacking wasn't necessary, because he didn't bring much.

He was in his maternal grandmother's house in Aro Chukwu, a town on the Cross River in eastern Nigeria. He arrived late the previous night and went straight to bed, worn out by the long journey.

The room had dark wooden flooring and no carpet. The walls and ceiling were painted light yellow with black trim. A chamber pot stood in a corner, and a floor fan was at the corner nearest the bed. There was no other furniture.

The four open windows let in the morning breeze through mosquito-net curtains, and he heard goats bleating and snatches of conversation in an unknown language. Two geckos on the ceiling pursued some flies, which must have entered the room when the door was open. Fascinated, he watched, willing the flies to escape. Unfortunately, one of the geckos prevailed. After eating its breakfast, it turned and crawled to the opposite side of the ceiling. When he looked for the remaining fly, he found it circling the lone electric light bulb in the center of the ceiling.

Through the windows, he saw the branches of coconut and mango tress swaying gently. A few birds flitted from branch to branch. The sun's strong rays on the neighbor's zinc roof made him realize the day was more advanced than he thought. He hadn't reset his watch to Nigerian time, so it was actually five hours later than his watch read.

Reaching to a shirt to wipe the sweat trickling down his face, he realized he wore only his pajama bottoms. It was a hot night, and he must have discarded his top sometime before morning.

Lifting the mosquito net, he struggled out of bed. His feet found his slippers nearby. Clutching his toiletry bag, he walked into a small corridor leading to the living room.

He looked toward the front yard and saw Grandmother Esther climbing the stairs leading to the corridor. He recalled meeting her briefly when he arrived from the airport well past midnight, then he was hustled off to bed. She smelled faintly of Yardley Brilliantine, a smell he always associated with her when she came to the U.S. for a visit. He was six-years-old, and Sarah was just a baby during Esther's first visit abroad.

She married her American-educated husband immediately after his return to Nigeria from the U.S., where he studied medicine. Her husband had such a bad experience in America, he never wanted to set foot in the country again, preferring travel to Europe whenever the opportunity came. Clint often heard his parents discussing that visit when Esther called to ask for a ticket to see them.

Clint understood from his parents that the visit had been very fractious, marred by Esther's constant harping on their home situation. Having come from a social class where she was pampered from birth and had a coterie of servants catering to all her needs, she couldn't get over the fact that in America, her eldest daughter didn't even have one maid to help with housework or care for her child. In Nigeria, she would have had at least two servants and a driver. With a newborn, a nursemaid would have been necessary. In America, her daughter had to take care of the household and drive to the supermarket for food in addition to looking after a new baby.

On the first day of Esther's visit, she was shocked to see her daughter cooking a meal. "Don't you have a maid? I can understand not having a driver, but you should at least have someone help you cook while you're recuperating from childbirth."

"Mama, we can't afford to hire help. Do you know what we'd have to pay per hour? The mortgage and housekeeping expenses take a big chunk of our combined income."

"Then let us send Onyeka to help." That sentence was often repeated by Peter whenever Esther's name came up.

"No, Mama. Not now. We value our privacy. Besides, we don't have room for a maid. Onyeka would want to attend school, and she wouldn't be much use from us."

"Mmechie onugi. Don't be silly. Onyeka would be happy to come help you. You don't have to put silly ideas about going to university in her head. I don't understand you. You're a doctor married to a lawyer, and you can't afford help? Nobody at home will believe this." She shook her head.

Peace remained quiet, knowing there was nothing she could say that would change her mother's mind.

Esther apparently decided she would shame Peter into doing her bidding. As soon as he came home from work on the first day of her visit, she confronted him.

"Peter, my son-in-law, are you going to get a nursemaid to help look after the baby? You aren't being fair to Peace. If we were in Nigeria, she would have three months' maternity leave, and, with help, she'd be well rested when she returned to work."

"Mama, did she tell you she needed a nursemaid? She knows we can't afford help." In an effort to calm her, he added, "We're hoping at the end of maternity leave, we can arrange for day care for Clint and the new baby."

"Ogom. Don't you think you should return to Nigeria, where, as you know, we have people who help in the house? It isn't that expensive, especially since both of you will hold responsible, wellpaid positions."

Peter expected that. During numerous calls while his wife was pregnant, Esther harangued him about returning to Nigeria to practice law. "No, Mama. We aren't thinking of going back to Nigeria —ever," he said firmly.

Throughout her stay, Esther harped on the need for Peter to pay for help or return to Nigeria. "What's wrong with Nigeria? It isn't as if you both can't get good jobs with a house better than this apartment." She wouldn't accept Peter's reply that they could neither afford full-time help, nor did they want to return to Nigeria.

Clint smiled at the memory of how often his father laughed and told Peace, "Whoever heard of a doctor and a lawyer not having enough money to hire help?"

Peace and Peter were relieved when Esther finally flew back to Nigeria. Determined not to repeat the experience, they deflected all future requests to visit the U.S. from both sets of parents. They argued that, since their parents were very old, it wasn't wise to undertake such a journey. Besides, with the cost of health care in the U.S., such visits couldn't be entertained.

To placate the grandparents', wish to see their grandchildren, Peter often responded, "Later."

Commenting on his height the previous night reminded Clint of that visit.

He watched her come up the stairs one at a time and saw a youthful sixty-five-year-old brown-skinned woman fashionably dressed in a rayon caftan with matching head tie. Her eyebrows were outlined with kohl, but there was no trace of lipstick on her lips. She wore silver earrings that were among the presents from his mother.

He handed her the parcel before going to bed. Several gold-toned bangles jingled on her right wrist, as she gestured while speaking.

He'd met her only twice before—the first time when he was five, and the only time she came to the U.S. for a visit.

She stopped at the top of the stairs to catch her breath. Her voice filled with concern, she asked, "Nnam, did you have a nice sleep? I told the servants not to wake up and to let you rest." "Good morning, Grandma." He rubbed his eyes.

"I went to the compound for an important errand this morning and hoped I'd be back before you woke." The speed of her words betrayed her anxiety, as she marched into the parlor and dropped the handbag she carried.

"No, problem, Grandma." He stifled a yawn. "I had a restful sleep. I'm just waking up and trying to find the bathroom."

"Come, then. Let me show you." She led him to an open door leading to the back stairs. "It's at the back of the house. This is an old house, and the facilities are in the backyard. I'll have servants bring you a bucket of warm water for your bath and get you a towel."

Bewildered, he followed, murmuring, "Thank you, Grandma, but if you tell me where things are, I can get them."

Esther ignored him and called to an unseen servant in the kitchen to set out a bucket of warm water for Clint.

Later, he sat in the alcove under the stairs that served as a breakfast room, sipping a sugary cup of tea and staring at a plate of fried plantain and fried eggs. He decided to forego the plantain, which had turned cold. As she nibbled the eggs, his gaze wandered to the courtyard, where Esther was conversing with Chima. As they came toward him, he stood up.

"Clint, have you rested?" Chima asked. "Is there anything you'd like to do today? I can show you around before I start off for Owerri later."

Clint shook the outstretched hand. Deciding he might as well take the opportunity to get a general view of his new home, he said, "I'm a bit tired, but perhaps I can come with you to get my bearings. I want to be able to walk around and get to know the place." He went into the house for his shoes.

In the car for his first sightseeing tour, Clint saw things that were familiar and unfamiliar. In was familiar, in that he felt as if he had once walked those same dusty roads filled with villagers going about their daily routines. As the car passed particular houses or village squares, he felt he knew those places, but they weren't quite as he remembered. Troubled, he tried to understand the conflicting emotions passing through his mind. He felt glad when they drove back to Esther's house, because he knew with certainty that the house wasn't a figment of his imagination.

CHAPTER FIVE

Clint spent his first two weeks in Nigeria in a daze. It rained intermittently, and, when it wasn't raining, the sun baked the red earth, sucking up all the moisture. At noon, the air was still, with no breeze. Goats and sheep lay under the shade of fruit trees, sleeping lazily. Cocks and hens strutted about, picking grubs from the dirt.

Clint sometimes sat on the verandah with a fan, trying to cool his burning skin. Occasionally, he saw small birds hopping from one branch to another or whistling to confirm each other's presence. Sometimes, he saw a single vulture in the sky, trying to find prey or a dead animal, so it could swoop down to feed.

Most of the time, he lay around the house, receiving visitors, who usually came in the morning or in late afternoon when the air was cooler. Unlike his parents' house in Tenley Park, where visitors were scarce, his grandmother's house was like a train station, where people came and went at all hours. A constant stream of visitors arrived from morning till night. After the initial greetings, the visitors sat and stared at him as if he came from outer space. When they left, others quickly took their place.

At first, he couldn't tell which ones were blood relatives, since his grandmother always said, "Clint, come and meet your sister," or "Come meet your brother." He eventually understood that the terms denoted anyone who was related, no matter how far removed.

During his first week, he often walked to the primary school grounds to watch the children play with an old, worn-out ball, which he learned was a gift from an Italian associate of an Aba-based businessman from one of the compounds. Clint fleetingly thought of offering his services as a soccer coach and mentioned the idea to his grandparents.

Esther and Igwe, his grandfather, adamantly opposed the idea. Esther argued that the house would be overrun by children looking for Clint, while Igwe said Clint would expose himself to all kinds of financial demands he couldn't meet. As an American, he was perceived as enormously wealthy.

Though Clint didn't share their concern, he felt the least he could do would be buy a soccer ball for the boys. He gave money to his Aba-bound uncle to buy one for him.

During the second week, Clint was bored and decided to disregard his grandparents' advice and meet the headmaster of the primary school. He wanted to organize an after-school soccer practice for the neighborhood kids. The headmaster, who lived in a compound adjacent to the school, was surprised by the offer, adding, "I don't see anything wrong with the current informal situation. You are free to join the game at any time. I can't approve of any activity that might place a financial burden on the parents, since they are already paying school fees and other mandated expenses."

"I want to be sure that by participating, I won't give offense," Clint said. "I need something to do. By acting as unpaid coach, I can help the children improve their skills."

After some deliberation, the headmaster said, "Young Man, it's kind of you to offer to organize a soccer practice, but don't expect regular attendance from the children. They have duties to their parents."

Once Clint bought a ball, he began spending late afternoons at the schoolyard, coaching soccer.

———⟋⟍———

One day, after the last of the morning's visitors left, and the maids were clearing the parlor of the used cups and bottles, Clint turned to Esther.

"Grandma, I'd like to visit the slave museum. I've heard there's one in the Ujari village. My parents visited one in Calabar during their honeymoon. Perhaps one of my cousins can go with me."

Esther arched her eyebrows and stared, running her tongue over her lips before saying emphatically, "There's no such place here."

She stood by the door leading to the courtyard, staring off into the distance. Almost as an afterthought, she added, "Those people in Ujari dug up some of their ancestors' skulls and bones. People pay them to look inside the graves. It's an abomination. Those are heathen practices, not to be condoned. You don't want to go there.

Your parents wouldn't like it."

Clint, deciding arguing would worsen the situation, let it go.

———⟋⟍———

The following week, Clint visited his grandfather at his palatial estate in the new extension. Igwe lived in the new area outside the villages, with big houses and immaculately landscaped yards surrounded by barbed wire and imposing gates. Completely insulated from the villages, the residents had generators to ensure a constant flow of power and water from their wells.

Clint knew Igwe could afford such a lifestyle, because Peter and his siblings abroad sent him monthly stipends. When Clint arrived, his grandfather broke away from a meeting to greet him. He took him aside to explain that the ten members present were government retirees in the area, the majority of whom hadn't received their pension or gratuities for over six months.

They hoped to pressure the government to meet its financial obligations in a timely manner.

As Clint entered the parlor, he saw empty beer bottles and platters of leftover roasted goat meat and fried chicken, indicating the social aspect of the meeting was almost over. A young man, holding a pitcher of cold water in one hand and a towel in the other, poured water into a basin on a nearby stool, so one of the men could wash his hands.

Clint's arrival diverted the group from their financial problems, and they welcomed him and commented on how well he looked. As Clint shook hands before taking a seat, one man mentioned his Americanborn grandchildren were currently attending boarding schools in Nigeria and would visit during the next school holidays.

"I'll get them to visit you when they come, if you're still here." Puzzled, Clint asked, "Why aren't they in school in the U.S.?

"Na long story," the man said, blowing lustily into his handkerchief. "My daughter, their mother, wanted her children to have American citizenship. Every time she was pregnant, she visited the U.S. and had the baby there, then came back with an American child. This happened three times. She doesn't really live in the U.S.. She has a well-paid job here. I think the intention is to send the children to university in the U.S. when the time comes."

"What an ingenious way of bypassing all the palaver of getting a visa to study in the U.S.," Igwe commented.

The other men nodded.

"Perhaps you can give my grandchildren hints on how to prepare for the SAT," the man continued. "They tell me this exam is like the entrance examination we taken here to get into university." He stood to look for the bathroom.

Clint, who had been instilled from birth to respect the law, wondered whether the U.S. government knew that the citizenship loophole was being abused. Then he remembered an article in the Washington Post detailing how Chinese citizens were doing the same thing. The practice seemed universal."

Shaking his head, he turned to the speaker. "I'll be glad to speak to them."

Soon after the meeting, the men bade his grandfather good-bye and left.

"Grandpa, have you heard of the slave museum?" Clint asked, as servants cleared the plates.

"Yes, of course," Igwe replied. "It's in Ujari. I hear it's been recognized by the Department of Antiquities. Professors from an American university in Mississippi visited it. It was quite an occasion."

"Really?" Clint was surprised. He took peanuts from a bowl before it was removed. "I'd like to visit it, but I want to go with someone who can interpret for me. I understand a few words, but I have difficulty following conversations."

Igwe scratched his head and stared at Clint. "You needn't worry on that account. The people who look after the museum speak English. It might not be perfect, but it's understandable." He paused to ask a servant to bring Clint food, then he sipped from his beer. "Do you know that my grandfather, Achi, was brought here as a slave?"

Clint's hands shook, and his heart rate doubled. With difficulty, he mumbled, "I didn't know that." He controlled himself and turned to Igwe.

"When he was your age," Igwe said, forestalling whatever Clint meant to say, "his master freed him. Despite that, until his death, he was regarded as a slave. There were places he wasn't allowed to enter and social events he couldn't participate in. When there was the rumor of the death of an important person, he stayed indoors to avoid being caught and sacrificed. Apparently, as a little boy, he was captured and brought to Aro Chukwu.

"He worried incessantly about his fate should anything happen to his master. He knew the family would have no compunction about putting him in the master's grave to serve him in the afterlife. The only difference in his status as a free man was that he became a house owner and could keep his earnings. He was particularly conscious of his status during the festivals, when Chief Igwe called upon him to perform certain functions as his slave. As Chief Igwe's feet, he was often sent on errands to other minor chiefs in the area. He told us that during one such visit in preparation for a war, he almost lost his life at Ujari."

Still trying to absorb the information, Clint didn't reply.

Finally, Igwe broke the silence. "When do you want to go?" He abruptly changed the subject. "I'm really cross with your parents. I don't know why they insisted you stay with Esther."

Clint sensed his grandfather's latent inferiority complex emerging. He knew that Esther was the daughter of a minor wife of the paramount chief of the area who married the scion of the Ibinukpabi priestly family. She never said it, but she might have felt socially superior to Igwe, the grandson of a slave. That wasn't the first time Igwe mentioned that slight by Clint's parents.

Clint didn't want to become embroiled in a intra-family conflict. "It's probably because she's alone," he said diplomatically, "since her husband passed away. My being there is expected to help her heal."

"That may be so." Igwe clearly disagreed, but he would let it stand. "Regarding your intended visit, I'm sure it will confirm what I've been telling you about the stupid things our ancestors did in the past, which we would rather forget."

The visit was arranged for a day in the next week.

CHAPTER SIX

The slave museum in Ujari was a few miles from the outskirts of Clint's mother's village. Clint's current abode was a house on the outskirts of the village a few meters from one of the ten compounds that made up Peace's father's village. Her father moved there when he retired from the civil service.

Clint and his companion, a young man from Igwe's compound, walked along a road that was once paved but reverted to its original dirt surface. This main road connecting various villages was busy, and villagers going or returning from their errands competed for space with cyclists and cars.

Soon the pair reached the first compound and decided to cut across the backyards of the houses in Peace's ancestral compound until they reached a narrow footpath. Mangrove swamps bordered each side of the sandy path, which soon widened enough to allow four people to walk abreast. Suddenly, they encountered a stream cutting across the path. Villagers constructed a makeshift bridge of two tree trunks held in place by two large boulders on both sides of the stream. Clint's companion quickly walked across to the other side.

Clint gazed at the opposite embankment, gripped by fear. Despite the sizzling heat of the sun directly overhead, cold sweat trickled down his spine. It was as if time stood still. The path, which a minute ago had been filled with the sounds of villagers walking along the road, interacting with each other, and the raucous noise from children feeling aggrieved by perceived slights, was deserted. He was alone, surrounded by the strong smell of sulfur emanating from the mangrove swamps around him.

In his mind's eye, he went back in time and saw himself stepping off the bridge from the other side in another time period. He carried an empty basket on his head. He walked fast, and, as he stepped off the bridge, a band of thirty warriors from the adjacent village accosted him. Pumped up by the accompanying war drums, the short, wiry men's faces and bodies were covered with clay markings.

"Where do you think you're going?" they shouted in unison. "Shouldn't you be with the warriors of your village? Don't let him pass. He must be a traitor."

His crumpled expression showed how uncomfortable he was with the situation. His master sent him to deliver an important message to the chief of Ibom, the village contiguous to Ujari. He knew of the tense feelings between the villages. At every gathering of chiefs, the threat of war was discussed and debated.

He had the eerie feeling something was about to happen, and he was already frightened. Recognizing his life was in danger, he searched the warriors' faces, looking for someone familiar.

Thinking he recognized the son of the Ujari chief among the warriors, he walked toward him. "Our father, I'd normally not be here at this time, but my chief gave me a message for the chief of Ibom. I'm on my way home now. He's expecting me. Tell your men to let me pass."

"Tell me your master's name," the son of the Ujari chief said, flexing his muscles. "Do you have his marker?"

"I belong to Chief Igwe of Amanagwu. You should know me. I am his feet."

"Come here so I can look at you." He was clearly held in respect by the other warriors.

He examined the young man's face for the small mark that showed he was owned by Igwe. Satisfied, he turned to his men. "He is the slave of Igwe. He's telling the truth. Let him pass."

—⚏—

As he stepped onto the bridge, Clint heard his companion calling him, urging him to hurry up. Dazed, he recovered, greeting passersby, and crossed to the other side toward Ujari. He resolved to learn more about his family history, and, in particular, the man who haunted him since he was a child.

—⚏—

The statue of a man sitting on a stool with his feet on a mat showed Clint and his companion they'd finally reached the compound where the museum sat. The statue, grimy with age, was in the village square. Clint saw small open sheds occupied by blacksmiths, car repairers, and tailors, while enclosed sheds served as the village's drinking places. Goats and chickens competed with small children, running around and playing with discarded plastic bottles. Clint and his companion exchanged greetings with a group of old men sitting under a huge iroko tree surrounded by all types of trash.

Looking around, Clint was dismayed by the general air of neglect. Trash was everywhere. He saw the same situation in all the compounds he visited so far. It wasn't the first time he saw a place littered with trash, cigarette butts, papers, drug paraphernalia, and food packages dropped by people who were too lazy or didn't care enough to use the trash cans provided by the city.

His mother, in one of her teaching moments, took him to Washington's northeast section where she owned a rental, to teach him to be grateful for what he had, but the situation in Africa was different. He saw piles of trash of all types—rotting fruit, kitchen waste, rusty tins, parts of roofing sheets, torn bits of clothing, and plastic containers of many types and sizes. More disgusting were the clumps of animal waste all down the path leading to the museum. Such disregard for the environment always amazed him, because the villagers were very particular about their appearance. Most people wouldn't leave their homes without grooming themselves and making sure they showed off their finery, and Ujari villagers were no exception. When he looked for trash cans, he saw none.

Trying not to step on broken glass and clumps of animal waste while following the small path, he came to the museum, housed in the old, ancestral home of the Ujari chief. The caretaker, a descendant of the chief, collected a nominal fee from Clint, who handed over part of the money his grandfather gave him that morning.

A short, light-brown-skinned man with cropped hair, the caretaker, wore a joji wrapper and a long shirt with images of a leopard stamped on it. As was the custom, he also wore a string of coral beads that he inherited from his forebears. Rubber flip-flops protected his feet, and they flapped as he walked.

Welcoming them, he offered his hand to shake. "Welcome to the house of my ancestor who lived long ago. This house has been in my family since the Aro people inhabited this place. This is the grave of one of my ancestors."

Clint peered into an open grave containing various skeletons and shivered. "Is this the grave of the chief who owned this house?" he asked softly.

The caretaker coughed, preparing to begin a long opening speech. "Yes it is, but you can see he didn't go alone. He was accompanied by some of his wives and slaves. This grave was uncovered when we tried to make changes to the house. There was a small house here before, where our ancestor, the chief, was buried. As you're well aware, we don't have cemeteries. We bury our dead in their houses.

"You should understand that in those days, human sacrifice was prevalent, particularly at the death of an important man in the village. It was believed that he required servants, wives, and retainers to accompany and serve him in the next world. It is a custom we no longer practice."

"How are the wives and slaves selected?" Clint shuddered at the image of the poor wives and slaves waiting, wondering if they would be chosen.

"Usually, a hunting party went out to find someone, if it was decided the chief needed more slaves than the ones he already had. In those days, when a chief as important as our ancestor died, the whole town was gripped with fear, because no one was sure who might be caught and required to go with him. It was very secretive."

Clint stared at the grave and saw the young Achi and the other slaves being taken to the square, where their fate would be decided. He heard the roar of the crowd in the square, welcoming the hunting party. Fear showed on the prisoners, as they heard the leader of the hunting party tell the chief, "I suppose all four will have to accompany him."

"We're only expected to contribute one or two, but we're also required to give a gift of one to the successor, who may decide that the gift also be sacrificed," the chief said. "Let's look at them."

He examined the slaves carefully. "We're grateful to you for quickly carrying out this dangerous task. For a short time, we thought the Ebem warriors got you. We should decide now what to do. The funeral rites are tonight."

The chief pointed at Achi. "I will sell this one to Igwe. He was looking for a small boy to be his feet. He should accompany me home now. The rest should be taken to the funeral venue immediately."

"I should warn you, my chief," the leader said, shaking his head, "the one you're sparing is a difficult one. He's given us nothing but grief since we caught him."

"You know how Igwe is," the chief said nonchalantly. "He can control even the wildest cat. You'll see."

Lost in thought, Clint heard the guide cough loudly and ask, "Do you need something to drink?"

Clint shook his head. "Is there a designated number of people to accompany the dead chief?"

The caretaker's voice dropped lower. "The number of people buried with the chief depended on his status in the community. I can't tell you the selection process for the wife. I suspect it was usually the most difficult one who was sacrificed." He laughed uproariously. "I presume no one would want her alive. What better way to get rid of a thorn in the flesh?"

"In your lifetime, do you know of any chief buried with less socially well-known persons?" Clint was shaken by what he heard and the man's lack of empathy.

The man merely laughed again.

A man standing beside the caretaker, who'd been quiet so far, said, "I think the last such sacrifice was in the fifties, but it was kept quiet. The story went that the sacrificed man was out hunting and was eaten by wild animals, but we all know what happened." Clint shuddered.

Outside, a group of women and children from the compound gaped at the visitors. They wanted to know where Clint came from. Normally, museum visitors were Black Americans or White men from the UK doing historical research.

Clint's companion explained that though Clint was visiting from America and was technically American, he was a son of the soil. When he mentioned Clint's patrimony, the audience gave sighs of amazement and joy. All wanted to shake his hand in welcome and affection. The caretaker warmly welcomed Clint and offered to send one of the women to get him a beer, because it was a hot day.

Clint politely refused, saying he still needed to visit his father's compound in the next village.

As he stared at the grave, Clint saw himself as Achi, naked and waiting for his fate to be decided when he was brought to Aro Chukwu as a young slave. He saw Achi being scrutinized by the Amanagwu chief, who spared him and separated him from the others to be Igwe's slave. Was that the chief whose death precipitated the hunt for afterlife companions? Were some of the young slaves buried there?

He couldn't ask those questions. Instead, he accompanied the men into a room that smelled of damp and mildew, which housed various objects for the museum. He saw the iron chains used to bind slaves together, the clubs and bows and arrows used in battle, and the drums that signaled the arrival of an important person.

There were other objects relating to the slave trade—various ritual items, including pots, animal skulls, leopard skins, and human skulls; several displays of old jojis; and photos of the chief performing rituals. He was fascinated by the counters the chief used to keep track of his debtors, as well as by cowries and iron and manila rods, which were used as money at the time.

Before leaving, Clint accepted bottled water and cabin biscuits offered by their guide.

As he ate, he asked the question that burned in his mind. "Did your ancestors participate in the war with the British?"

"Of course. All the chief houses in Aro Chukwu were involved. It was a tense period, I was told. My great-grandfather led our warriors to the battlefield at Oror. Do you know we're the only people in all of Nigeria to be called the People of God?"

"I didn't know that." He was unable to forget the image of slaves and women being buried with the dead chief. Were they buried alive? He couldn't bring himself to ask.

Feeling faint, he listened as the caretaker said grandly, "We're the keepers of the God Ibinukpabi, even though the White men brought their own God and imposed Him on us."

Recovering, Clint returned the man's gaze.

"Have you been to the site of the oracle?" the man asked.

"Not yet. That's another place I have to visit." He looked away. "Thank you for the refreshments and all the things you told me about the past." He couldn't wait to leave.

Clint walked from the museum with a heavy heart. He couldn't imagine burying people alive so they could be of service to the dead in the afterlife, and the guide's laughter troubled him. What did the men and women he knew in Africa think of such a tradition? How could they justify it?

He knew if he mentioned his feelings to his grandfather, Igwe, he would rant and rave and say anyone practicing such an act in the modern world would be jailed. From the snippets of conversations he heard in his grandmother's parlor, he had the impression that witchcraft with body parts was widely practiced among politicians, even those who professed to be Christians.

Turning to his companion, Clint asked, "Why don't we go home via Amanagwu? I'd like to pay my respects to my uncle, who lives in Ndi Igwe compound." He also wanted to walk the route Achi took from Ujari to Amanagwu.

As they walked, Clint said, "Look! There's a market today. I thought there was only one market on the way to Grandpa's house. Perhaps I can buy paper. I need to write a long letter to my parents.

The aerogram from the post office doesn't allow me to write much."

"Today is market day," the young man said. "Traders from all over

Aro Chukwu come to sell and buy things."

"How many market days are there?"

"Traditionally, we have eight days in the week with two big market days, of which one is today. Nowadays, there are several markets that operate every day, so the traditional marketplaces are no longer patronized as much as before. One of the new modern markets is the one you mentioned along the road to the new extension. You should visit that sometime."

They walked past women selling vegetables and foodstuffs, displays of dried and fresh snails and fish, mounds of crayfish, different types of pepper, piles of yams and plantains, edible seeds in containers, and past the butchers' stalls with huge chunks of fresh cow meat being cut. Clint found the mixed smell different and strange, and he was troubled by the dirt around the food area. Men carelessly urinated only a yard from where food was sold, while women sellers handed change to customers with one hand and cleaned snot from their children's noses with the other. He was relieved when they entered the manufactured goods section, where he could buy what he wanted.

Soon, they reached the Presbyterian Church, where men were repairing the roof.

"Most people in town belong to this church," his companion explained, "though the Pentecostal churches have made inroads."

Finally, they came to the Ndi Igwe compound and the house of Clint's uncle, Okoro, who just returned from the market. Okoro was Igwe's maternal brother. Igwe's father remarried after the death of his first wife during childbirth. The grief-stricken father, unable to care for the child, at first entrusted her to a neighbor's wife who was still lactating. Knowing that the arrangement was temporary, he sought advice from his close friends and confidants, who found a suitable girl to care for his motherless child. He married her and brought her to his home.

The woman subsequently gave him two sons—Clint's grandfather and Okoro. Igwe told Clint about the relationship, and Clint had yet to meet his half-sister and wondered what happened to her. Should he ask Okoro about her?

Before he could make up his mind, he saw Okoro standing in front of the house. Okoro ushered them into the front room that served as the parlor. He was a tall, dark-brown man with a head of white hair and a stubby white beard. Though younger, he looked older than Clint's grandfather, indicating the years hadn't been good to him. Clint knew he had no visible means of support but was fortunate in having a fairly wealthy brother who helped educate his seven children. They, in turn, supported Okoro in his old age.

He married young, a forced marriage to a girl from a prominent family he got pregnant. She died young after giving birth to seven children. Igwe also told Clint that, unlike Okoro, his children did very well. The sons held important positions in government and business, while his daughters married successful husbands. One of the sons was in the diplomatic corps in Germany.

"That is as it should be," Igwe added smugly. "In many families, success could be a curse in that you're forever being taxed by your family. You end up supporting the next generation."

Clint recalled all that, as Okoro welcomed him. "I see you bought a few things. Did you go to the market?"

"I've been to the slave museum in Ujari. I thought I should visit you." Sweating profusely, he wiped his face.

"Very kind of you." Okoro paced the floor. "You almost missed me. I'm just back from the market." As an afterthought, he added, "I remember now. You're staying in your mother's home. By the way, how is your grandmother, Esther? I saw her at church, and she said she was having difficulty getting you to accompany her on Sundays." Not giving his uncle his full attention, Clint let his gaze roam the room, seeing a photograph of a man in a long shirt with leopard design and a traditional joji wrapper. He held a staff in his hand with an ivory handle.

"The man in this photograph looks a lot like you," Clint said. "You're very observant. That isn't your grandfather but his father.

The photograph was taken when he was my age. It must be confusing to you. Our father married a second wife when his first wife died, but your grandfather and I came from the same mother."

"Okoro, who na dis boy?" shouted a man sitting in the doorway of the opposite house, where he'd been watching Clint since his arrival. "I no see am before." He stood and walked toward them, stretching out his hands.

"Mazi Nwankwo, this is Clint, my brother's grandson from Peter."

As they shook hands, a shudder passed through Clint, and he felt certain the man was no friend. He recoiled from the handshake, barely listening to the introduction.

Nwankwo addressed Clint in a mellifluous voice. "How long you go be with us?"

"Perhaps until Christmas," Clint said in a voice tinged with sadness.

"Your granddaddy and me, we be in school together. Him very clever. Go secondary school here in Aro Chukwu."

"Look where it got him," Okoro added. Both men laughed uproariously.

Puzzled, Clint's eyes flitted from one face to the other, looking for a clue what the joke was about.

"I sabi your papa," the old man said, wiping away tears of laughter with the tail end of his wrapper. "I de see am during his holidays from secondary school. The last he don com na for marry your mama. You think he go come now you be here?"

When Clint looked at him, what he saw wasn't a man so crippled by arthritis that he could hardly walk the few paces to his own house, which, unlike others, was a small, one-room building with a thatched roof. Instead, he saw a small man grinning, though the grin didn't reach his eyes. Clint saw the man scowling at Achi for his success and looking for a way to belittle him.

Beside the small house was a larger house occupying a bigger lot that had since fallen down. The original contours showed its past glory.

Trying to remain calm despite the loud thumping of his heart, Clint said wearily, "I don't think so, Sir."

The man lingered for a while before returning to his house. Watching him leave, Clint felt he'd just seen a serpent with two forked tongues slink away and shuddered.

Okoro studied him hard. "Are you all right? You look as if you've seen a ghost."

Startled, Clint said, "I'm tired, because I've been in the sun a long time, and I need to hurry home to rest. Tell me, Uncle, who is that man? I didn't catch his name."

"He's the direct descendant of Chief Igwe of our compound, who lived a long time ago. That broken-down structure you see was the big man's house. Unfortunately, his descendants fell on hard times and couldn't maintain the house. Now it's a ruin."

"How are we related to that old man?"

"A long time ago, my grandfather, Achi, served Chief Igwe, the founder of this compound. That's how we share the same surname."

Clint nodded. "Grandpa told me recently that Achi, his grandfather, was captured and sold to a chief. He eventually got his freedom and was granted a piece of land for a house. I presume that's the house he built."

Okoro nodded. "That's true. He was lucky he wasn't sacrificed, or we wouldn't be here." Laughing, he added, "Igwe bought him, you know?"

Clint nodded. "Did his situation change as a free man?" He wondered whether vestiges of that relationship between his family and the old man still survived.

"Not much. He was nominally a free man, but he continued to serve Chief Igwe in many ways. Your grandfather used to help Nwankwo, whom you just met, with his homework when they were in primary school, but they fell out at some point. Nobody knows why." He frowned in thought.

Clint waited.

After five minutes, Okoro abruptly changed the subject. "You must be bored, because the colleges are in session now, and there are very few young men of your age to talk to."

"Oh, no, Uncle," Clint said emphatically. "I'm not bored. I have a lot of things happening. I'm coaching some kids in soccer at the primary school in late afternoons. It's not as regular as I expected, but that's OK. It gives me something to do. I have a list of things I still have to do. I want to visit all the villages of Aro Chukwu."

"Did they tell you at Ujari that the next village is Amasu, where the canoes leave on the journey to Itu and beyond? You should go there sometime. It's a trading port on the Cross River." He paused again to study Clint.

Clint waited expectantly.

"Surely you've heard of the Cross River?"

"Of course. Grandfather said his grandfather traveled on it to Itu." He was glad to shift the topic away from the Igwe business.

"We have many creeks emptying into the Cross River. In one of the villages farther up, maybe even at Amasu, but I don't know, Mary Slessor, the Scottish woman who brought Christianity to us, lived in a hut. Of course, the hut is long gone, but there's a marker indicating where it was."

Okoro walked Clint and his companion to the compound entrance.

"I realize now, Uncle, there are many things to see and do while I'm here. I need to plan my days, because I want to visit as many places as possible during this time."

As Clint and his companion walked down the dusty road toward Esther's house, Clint didn't see any of the modern houses or many small shops lining the road. Nor did he see the men and women in beautiful patterned jojis or other cotton materials, or the women with gorgeous head ties and umbrellas. He ignored the cars, cyclists, and motorcycles plying the busy road.

Instead, he saw small men with strips of cotton tied around their waists, carrying hoes and machetes in their hands or slung across their backs. There were dusty, tired women of all ages, some naked to the waist, many with babies slung on their backs, carrying heavy loads on their way back from the market. Young girls with Uri patterns on their bodies trotted side-by-side with their mothers, carrying pots or other containers of palm oil or vegetables they sold or bought at the market.

By the time Clint returned home, he was very tired. Reflecting on all that happened that day, he wanted very much to confide to his grandparents about his memories. On second thought, he felt their attitude would be the same as his parents', so he let the thought slide.

CHAPTER SEVEN

"Hi Clint. I miss you." "Sarah?" he asked into the phone. "How have you been? With me out of the way, are you driving our parents crazy?" "You can't imagine what it's been like without you. I can't stay out late without Dad immediately organizing a search party, but let's talk about you. Mom said you must be sick by now of the power outages and the outhouse."

He laughed. "I know they wouldn't be surprised if the doorbell rang, and I appeared."

She laughed with him. "Is that likely? I miss you, especially now, when I need help choosing the course I should take during my first semester, deciding on a roommate, and what I should take to college. I can't make up my mind. You're always good at those things."

"Sarah, I wish I could be there to help you, but I'm too far away. I'm enjoying myself so much I can't think of leaving yet. It's very interesting. When we meet, I'll tell you all about it."

She told him her preparations for moving into the dorm, her decision about what classes to take, and her insecurity about her prospective roommates.

He tried to allay her fears and promised to call more often. "Are our parents well? Is mom still going to the gym?"

"Dad's at a conference in Chicago, and Mom's brother from New Orleans came to visit."

Talking to her reminded him of the excitement he felt when he started college.

He'd been in Aro Chukwu for almost a month, during which he visited the slave museum only once. Each day was the same. He saw his grandfather, had soccer practice if it wasn't raining, went to the bars, or visited his uncle. At least with Igwe, he could discuss local history and his grandfather's life. With his bar friends, he listened amid loud music to their ramblings about their lives, Abia state politics, and things he didn't really understand or care about. He often lounged at Grandmother's house, welcoming the people who dropped in to visit but with whom he had nothing in common. His days became very monotonous, and he craved excitement.

He missed his sister and being in Washington. He missed his daily jog on the trails at Rock Creek Park and the changing seasons, when leaves turned color in the fall. What wouldn't he give to read the Washington Post and argue with Sarah about her choices in music. He could use a dose of rap or jazz or anything from modern America. He enjoyed the popular Nigerian High Life, but he was bored with the beat. He also wanted to walk into a bar and play some of the new computer games his friends said were all the rage.

In the village, he had no access to exciting music or games, and he didn't have Internet. He went to a computer center in the village once only to find it closed due to a power outage. To his surprise, he missed playing chess in the evenings with his father while listening to Sarah's silly stories of school.

Esther wasn't good company. She barely had anything to say to him except, "Clint, what do you want to eat? Are you hungry? Have something to drink. Are you going to Igwe's house today?"

Any attempt on his part to obtain information on family history was met with, "What do you want to know about those people?

There's nothing to tell. I told you my husband's father was a teacher. There's nothing else. The rest of them were heathens."

She would have liked him to accompany her on some of her visits, but what would he do except listen to her and her friends talk?

When there was electricity in the evenings, which wasn't often, his grandmother sometimes turned on the radio to a church music station, or she watched TV news from the Nigerian Television Authority. Sometimes, they watched her favorite Nollywood movies, which he found disconcerting. They inevitably involved a heroine who was a wronged wife persecuted with witchcraft by her in-laws. After ten minutes, Clint would become bored and would read a book he brought with him.

Often the outages lasted for days. Sometimes at his grandfather's house, Clint saw the current news from the Al Jazeera network or from South African TV during the day, giving a glimpse of events happening outside Nigeria.

Overcome by homesickness, he began to consider returning. He realized his parents had known that would happen. Once they agreed to the visit, they agonized over which family to house him. Peter wanted him to stay at his father's house, where he would be comfortable, but Peace pointed out that her mother lived a short distance from the village where she was born. It would be a comfort to her mother, who was recently widowed, if Clint stayed with her. Besides, he could easily get around without transportation and would be better able to interact with villagers than if he stayed at Igwe's house.

Clint imagined that both agreed that the inconvenience of living without comforts like a shower, an indoor toilet, or electricity at the flick of a button, as well as accessibility to transportation, might give him incentive to shorten his trip. If he lived with Igwe, in the house at the new extension, he would have a chauffeur available to drive him anywhere he wanted to go. If there was a power outage, the generator would take over. They had a constant water supply from the borehole, and he would never know how ordinary people lived in Nigeria.

At Esther's house, the presence of poverty would be evident the moment Clint stepped outside. Besides, he would be constantly reminded of the stark reality of village life by the steady flow of visitors.

He imagined his parents in the privacy of their bedroom, making fun of his imagined reaction to the outhouse, using a pail of water for his bath, or to the sudden power outages that could last weeks. They hoped he would hurry back to the comforts of home.

Thinking it over, Clint felt they realized he might become accustomed to the inconveniences, but what they probably feared most was the loneliness he would experience without his friends and the real possibility of contracting malaria, dysentery, or typhoid. He might be involved in an accident.

Having been in Nigeria over a month, he felt empathy for his parents' decision to stay away from the country. With some many demands on a person, it was difficult to become independent. Peace and Peter used distance to accomplish that.

For a whole day, he considered what he wanted to do. He could travel, but where? Most places were the same as Aro Chukwu. He could organize children to clean the compounds, but he'd been told there were designated clean-up days, although he never witnessed such activity. He needed to keep busy while in Aro Chukwu, so he went to the courtyard to find his grandmother.

Seated on a mud bench in the room outside the kitchen, she seemed taken aback at seeing him and prepared to get up and accompany him back to the main house.

"No, no, Grandma. Sit down. I don't want to disturb you. I just wanted to know where I could rent a bicycle. I want to explore the other villages I haven't seen. I've been to the ones on this side of town, but I haven't been outside Ibom."

"Rent a bicycle? There's no place in Aro Chukwu, or even in Nigeria, where you can rent bicycles. Can't you hire a taxi? Do you want Mazi Igwe to give you his driver to take you places? I'm sure he'd let you use his car anytime. We already talked about it."

"I know, Grandma, but I don't want him to be inconvenienced. I just need an old bike to ride."

"Let me see. I'll send a message to Mazi Igwe to ask if he has one

at his house. We used to have some when my sons were growing up, but I gave them away to young men in my village. Your uncle, the shoemaker, had one, but that was a long time ago. I wonder what he did with it. Perhaps he sold the parts to bicycle repairmen."

Esther was clearly distressed by the request. Her grandson hadn't been a problem so far, and he never asked for anything. When her husband was alive, they owned a car. After his death, it was more trouble than it was worth, and she didn't want to waste the small amount of money her children sent each month on maintaining a car. She once owned a bike a long time ago, but she gave it up as she grew older. Whoever heard of a woman her age and stature riding a bike? She chuckled at the thought.

She had no need for a car, because she could easily walk to anyplace she wished to visit. Unlike many of her contemporaries, she had no knee problems. They complained about pain even when stepping out of their front door.

She wrung her hands in despair, her thoughts scattering like a hen rooting for worms without finding any. Where would she locate a bike for this young man?

She wondered why he was so reticent about asking Mazi Igwe to have his driver take him around. Something must have happened between them. Perhaps it was his jealous wife's fault. She knew Igwe would do anything for Clint.

Turning back to Clint, she said, "Let me think about it. Perhaps I can get one from a friend. It'll take me a day or two, because I want to find a good one for you."

As they talked, a visitor arrived, one of the women who came regularly. Often as she left, Clint saw Esther hand her a few naira or ask the maids to give her food to take home. Intrigued, he wondered what their relationship was. He couldn't ask Esther about it, because she was reticent about her actions and would probably tell him it was a woman who needed food and leave it at that.

He decided to visit the compound. As the lady left, Clint asked if he could accompany her to the compound. Esther rolled her eyes but didn't speak. He quickly told her, "I need to stretch my legs."

They walked companionably together, with him occasionally asking her the Igbo names of shrubs and trees. Passersby often stopped them to compliment her on her companion. When that happened, the woman laughed and took Clint's hand in hers.

Finally, they entered the compound, and she led Clint to her small home at the far end. They entered through a very small veranda with half-walls on the sides. A pile of ashes in the corner under a tripod stand showed him the hearth where she cooked.

As she opened her room to bring out a stool for him to sit on, he saw a door leading to a small backyard. In halting Igbo, he asked, "What's out there?'

She led him through a room without windows where she slept. A raffia mat was spread beside one wall. A big covered clay pot with a mug sat in a corner. Strung across the room was a rope on which she hung her clothes. The mud floor was swept recently, and he saw a broom to one side. Pots of different sizes and cracked plates were heaped in a corner.

She had very few possessions, but she tried to keep things clean. He followed her into the backyard through the small doorway, a tiny space, separated from the house by a few boundary shrubs. In a corner was a chicken coop with a hen inside and some chicks running around, pecking at the dirt. A pawpaw tree barely survived in another corner, and a bitter leaf plant was opposite. Two poles had a rope strung between them, probably for drying clothes. A rusty pail stood against the house wall.

Pointing to the chicks, she said, "I hope to give one to mama when they get bigger."

They lingered for a few minutes outside before returning to the porch.

"Would you like something to drink? I can send one of the boys next door to buy a small bottle of a soft drink from the trader outside the compound."

Touched, he replied, "Thank you, but I'm not thirsty." As he bade her good-bye, he was determined to learn more about her.

At the village square, he entered the carpenter's shed. He met the man before at Esther's but never had the chance to speak with him.

Often Esther asked the maid to bring Job to fix hinges on a door or to repair a chair missing a leg.

Out of curiosity, Clint went into the shed and was warmly greeted. The carpenter, who wasn't terribly busy, welcomed the interruption and cleared a spot for him to sit. Clint admired the displays of finished products and commented on their fine craftsmanship.

A bottle of Fanta, an orange-flavored soft drink, was offered. Even though Clint didn't like it much and would have preferred Coca-Cola, he dutifully accepted.

Taking a sip, he turned to Job and asked, "Uncle, have you always been a carpenter?"

Job studied him for a moment. "My father was a carpenter. He served his apprenticeship under one of the few Aro men who studied carpentry at Calabar. You can see his work in many of the houses in Aro Chukwu, including your grandfather's. I was his apprentice. Nowadays, there's no money in it. Local carpenters don't get hired for big jobs in houses, because builders prefer to bring in people from Aba or Umuahia to work on them. We local carpenters make only furniture."

"What are you working on right now?" "I'm making two easy chairs for our chief." There was a short pause.

"I saw you with Da Ndidi. Poor woman has a rough life. Do you know her husband died while she was pregnant? She was very devoted to that child and did everything to nurture him to manhood, but he was killed during the war. Since then, her life has been a mess, and she doesn't have any wish to live.

"Before, she was an active trader and very hard working. Since the death of her son, she feels she has no reason to live. We try to help as much as we can. Poor woman." He sighed.

Visibly upset, Clint was unable to voice his feelings. It was no wonder Esther was good to the woman.

As he walked home, he thought of Da Ndidi, whose life was torn apart by war, and all the others like her who had no luxury of Social Security or someone like Esther to help out. It was terrible that the politicians who made decisions about war never considered the effect on the citizens. Ndidi and the others like her were deprived of any social assistance in their old age. When he returned to Esther's house, he felt he was finally able to understand her kind side.

CHAPTER EIGHT

Clint, riding his newly acquired bicycle early the following Monday morning, was happy. The new bike appeared one week after he requested it. Unbeknownst to him, Igwe, after a call from Esther, called Clint's parents in Washington and asked them to transfer funds through Western Union to purchase a bike for Clint. He argued that, since Clint would be in Aro Chukwu for a while, it would be easier for him if he had something to ride. His own cars were unreliable, and he couldn't entrust any of them to Clint, even though he knew the young man was a good driver. Besides, he needed his one functioning car either to take his wife around or for his personal use. It wouldn't be available for Clint whenever he needed it. Peter acquiesced, and a bicycle was purchased in Aba and delivered to Esther's house.

Clint passed several groups of children entering the primary schoolyard and recognized some from the soccer club, if he could call it that. He saw late stragglers running to reach the school before assembly.

Will they make it? If not, what will their punishment be? he wondered. Everything seemed different to him, because he was seeing it for the first time without being followed by groups of children pestering him for money.

He rode past the village square, where traders were setting up their wares on tables, and the owners of lock up shops were opening their doors. Some recognized him and called his name. He waved and continued riding toward Oror, passing several villagers going to their morning activities. Everyone did his best to avoid collisions with cars, cyclists, and motorbikes, all competing for space on the same narrow, ocher-colored road.

The road from Oror to Obinkita was crowded. On one side shops sold manufactured goods, like plastic cups, cutlery, baskets, basins, and containers of all kinds, along with plates and bowls of many sizes. The number and variety of goods on display amazed him. Since all the stores offered identical items at nearly identical prices, he chose the display he liked best and patronized that stall. He planned to buy a soft drink, but, when he found out he would be charged separately for the bottle, he changed his mind and bought water in a plastic bottle.

The cashier, a neatly dressed young man in khaki shorts and gray singlet, carried out a conversation with other young people standing nearby. They were recent graduates from local high schools who couldn't afford further training or get suitable employment, so they congregated outside shops to trade information.

"Are you the stall owner?" Clint asked.

"No bi so. I de keep am for my uncle. When I kom out from secondary school, dis na the only job I get."

Sipping the water, Clint said, "I see you have a lot of customers. I don't want to disturb you, so I'll leave after I finish my water."

"Dis people no bi customer. De bi my friends." He shook his head.

"De de look for job, too."

As Clint lingered, one of the boys asked, "Where you come from?' "From Ibom."

Loud guffaws came from the young people, which attracted more to the stall, eager to join the fun.

"Ah, no bi so sha ah," someone said. "You de talk like American." "I'm really from Ibom. My parents are from Aro Chukwu, but I was born and grew up in the U.S. I'm visiting my grandparents and learning Igbo."

That seemed to satisfy them.

"You sabi New York? Los Angeles?" "No, no. I'm from Washington, DC."

The young men bombarded him with questions. "One of my uncles ide na Houston. Sabi am?"

One boy pushed the speaker aside, saying Houston was far from Washington, and Clint wouldn't know him.

"Yes, very far," Clint agreed.

"President Bush is in Washington. Do you know him?" another asked.

"Na Black person be president now," another one said.

So many questions were thrown at him, he wasn't able to answer. When he moved to continue his journey, two of the young men volunteered to accompany him to Obinkita.

"No," he said firmly. "I don't want to walk. It's too hot. I need to get to Obinkita soon."

As he rode off, one made a feeble effort to run after him, but, when he looked back, he saw the boy couldn't keep up. He saw two young boys careening down the road, bouncing off the legs of young men carrying furniture for delivery to the next village. Watching them, he almost collided with a woman with a baby slung on her back carrying a load of firewood.

"Look where you're going!" someone shouted. "Are you blind?" He dismounted to make sure the woman was all right.

He was anxious to reach Obinkita square, where Igwe told him Achi first saw the girl he married. Since his enslavement, at each New Yam festival, Achi recorded the passing of years in a small pot in which he placed a pebble to mark each year. Fifteen years after coming to Aro Chukwu, he was an established trader traveling between Aro Chukwu and Calabar, first for his master, then later, after he was freed, for himself. He often sold goods to people on credit, and he spent his spare time chasing down debtors. He was a property owner, and he began to think of acquiring a wife.

One day, he walked along a dirt road dressed in a loincloth and shirt. Arriving at the Amaikpe Square sweaty and tired, he sat under a big iroko tree, which, because it had been standing for many years, had been deified by the villagers.

Sheltering from the evening sun, he watched several pairs of men sitting on the dirt floor, playing Okwe. As the game progressed, the men passed gourd containers of palm wine, laughing and teasing each other. Occasionally, one took out a small tin of snuff, removed a pinch, and stuffed it into his nose, then he pinched his nose and blew it loudly.

Young girls, returning from the stream or market, passed by, and some of the men called greetings to them. Achi noticed one in particular. Small and light-skinned, she had corn-rowed hair and wore only several strings of beads around her waist to cover the lowest part of her body. Her oval face had tiny marks on the forehead. Her entire body was covered with uri designs that were fading, and he was struck by her beauty, but she seemed to be the butt of the conversations among her companions. Her breasts were just beginning to bud.

He turned to one of the men and asked about her.

"She's the youngest daughter of Chief Nwosu," a player replied, pausing to look at the girl between a mouthful of palm wine and wiping his brow.

Standing up to leave, Achi said, "I didn't know he had a young daughter. I'm going to their compound to see Kanu, his son. He bought a bolt of cloth from me and said I should come there today to be paid."

"Do you know his house?" one player asked, his eyes on the game. "We can ask her to take you there."

"No, no. I'll find my way. Perhaps I should be going."

Following the girls, he walked briskly into the compound. It was the evening period, when villagers returned home from day jobs for the evening meal, and children ran and played in the open spaces between houses, waiting for their mothers to call them home for a meal. Several women prepared food on open hearths in front of their houses, flirting and chatting with passersby. The smell of food mixed with the scent of ripe fruit on the trees.

As he walked down the path between the houses, Achi recognized a few men and women, who greeted him warmly and wondered what brought him out of his compound so late in the evening. He wasn't surprised to find Kanu, his debtor, sitting down for his meal. Kanu welcomed him and invited him to eat, but Achi refused. Instead, he accepted the traditional kola nut.

As Kanu ate, they discussed the latest news. Finally, Achi inquired about the girl.

"As I was resting at the square before coming here, I saw a beautiful young girl enter your compound. Her Uri was fading, and her hair had cornrows. No one knew her name."

Kanu waited until he washed his hands before saying, "Oh, yes. That must be Mboro, my sister from my father's young wife. Why are you asking about her?"

Achi let the question go without answering. Both were aware of the taboo against inter-class marriage. Shortly afterward, Achi collected his debt and walked toward home, thinking of the girl. He wanted her as his wife, but, as a slave, though he'd been freed, he couldn't marry into the Amadi class. Many still considered him a slave, and nothing, not even his wealth, could change that. Even in his own compound, many of the Amadi regarded him as beneath them, though they often borrowed money from him. He decided to seek advice from Igwe, his master. If the request wasn't possible to fulfill, Achi would look elsewhere.

As Clint approached the square, he recalled Achi's story. He looked for the iroko tree, but all that was left was a stump where several men sat. It was market day. He found a spot to sit and lingered, joking about the heat with an elderly man who joined her.

"I see today is market day," Clint said.

"Yes." The old man spoke perfect English. "In the olden days, market days rotated among communities. At this site, we had two market days a week. As you might have been told, our week was eight days long. Those market days were called Nkwo Nta and Nkwo Ukwu, Small and Big Market Days." He paused to take a breath. "Nowadays, many communities have their own markets, and things have changed."

As they talked, passersby greeted the old man, calling him Professor. Clint was intrigued. The man was unkempt and looked as if his hair never saw a comb. He wore dirty boxer shorts, but he spoke good English, and many of the people deferred to him. He wondered what the man's story was.

Dr. Nwankwo was the first Nigerian to earn a doctorate in mathematics from Cambridge University. Until the civil war, he taught at the University of Ibadan. Enticed by Ojukwu's rhetoric of a new nation called Biafra, he came to Eastern Nigeria seeking that El Dorado. The war years were hard on him, as he ran from place-toplace and tried to survive. In the end, he suffered a nervous breakdown, from which he never recovered.

On his lucid days, he wandered from home seeking the company of students, writing equations on the dirt floor and making eloquent speeches no one understood. All efforts to get him to medical care failed. His only means of financial support was his daughter, a principal of a large girl's secondary boarding school in Umuahia, who visited on weekends to ensure the servants took care of him. The day Clint met him was one of the man's lucid days.

"It's really hot today," Clint said, looking at the many traders setting up stalls and the customers jostling each other while trying to strike bargains. The produce section of the market filled quickly, as customers rushed to buy fresh vegetables before they withered in the heat.

"Look around," the old man said. "Someone will come soon with ice-cold water in plastic bags. It costs very little."

A boy soon appeared carrying a plastic basin filled with little cellophane packages of water. "Mmiri, zuo mmirir! Ojuru oyi! Water, buy ice-cold water!"

Clint paid for two packages and handed one to the old man, who thanked him. He used his to wash his face and neck to cool off.

Turning to the old man, he asked, "Is it always this hot at this time of year? I still have difficulty getting accustomed to the heat."

Not wearing a shirt, the old man laughed. "I'm dressed for it. I don't envy you young men who insist on shirts and ties."

"I should push on," Clint said, feeling he had to explain why he was in the square. "I have to see what's in the next village. Do you know its name?"

"You aren't from here?"

"I'm staying in Ibom, but I haven't lived here long."

"If I were you, I'd turn back after Atani. The villages are all the same."

Undeterred, Clint rode his bike past several villages indistinguishable from each other. He stopped when he saw the most- elaborate house and wondered if it was the village Mgbala Ekpe, the Ekpe cult house. When he first saw the Ibom Mgbala Ekpe, he mistook it for someone's dwelling and wondered if the decorations on the outside walls depicting leopards in various poses signified the rank of the hut's owner.

"It's the Ekpe cult house," someone told him.

His efforts to gather more information failed. When he asked further, one of his uncles mentioned he was eligible to join the Ekpe cult if he wished.

Emboldened, Clint tried to learn the function of the cult but was stonewalled by his uncle, who refused to answer any questions. Instead, he lectured Clint on the social structure of Aro Chukwu and his place in it. As an afterthought, the man dismissed Clint's interest in the Ekpe cult by saying it was obvious that Mama Esther and Mazi Igwe would never permit Clint to join.

On his daily forays to other villages, Clint saw similar houses in each, but the one in Atani was the most elaborate. Compared to that, the Aro Awada, which he saw from the outside on one of his rides, was insignificant and not very distinctive. The front yard of the Atani Mgbala Ekpe was dominated by the statue of an elephant and a tall palm tree, a statue of an Aro man in traditional dress beating a drum, and other statues scattered nearby.

He walked around the house, wondering if it was possible for him to go inside. Mistaking it for a museum, he asked a schoolboy loitering around about visiting hours, because none were indicated. The boy, staring at him with wide eyes, ran off, calling to an unseen person in a nearby house, who immediately came out.

The man's gaze raked over Clint. "O gen ka inacho? What do you want?"

He must not like my rumpled shorts and batik shirt, Clint thought.

The man held a comb in one hand and wore only a loose wrap tied at the waist. His morning grooming had obviously been interrupted by the schoolboy's call.

"Do you speak English?" Clint asked with emotion. "My Igbo isn't that good." He leaned on his bike.

"What do you want?" the man repeated angrily in English.

"I'm a stranger here. I thought this house must be a museum. I wanted to know what times it was open. I haven't seen a house like this in Aro, and I wanted to see the inside."

"It's the Ekpe cult house, and only members are allowed inside." Turning his back on Clint, he returned to his house.

"Oh."

Clint stopped outside the Atani village square, where there were several stalls, and bought a small bottle of orangeade as a way of facilitating conversation, then he entered a tailor's stall. He hoped the people inside would be friendlier. The elderly tailor's stall was filled with yard goods, and he seemed very busy.

Greeting Clint warmly, he introduced himself as Godson. He had a lady client and was busy taking her measurements before settling down to sew.

After drinking from his bottle, Clint said, "Your village has the most-elaborate Ekpe cult house in all of Aro Chukwu."

"Really? You seen all dem?"

"I've seen many. There's one in Ibom, but it wasn't as well decorated as yours."

"Thank you." He folded material after he cut it.

"I mistook it for a museum and was hoping to go inside." He held out his bottle of orangeade as if offering the man a drink.

Ignoring the outstretched hand, the tailor stared at Clint as if seeing him for the first time. "No be open for public. Na only Ekpe people de go inside. Other persons go if dem get case."

Several young men, noticing a stranger, stopped to join the conversation.

Surveying the small space and wondering if he was making a fool of himself, Clint asked, "Is it a court, then?"

"I no sabi. I no be Ekpe person."

The few people in the shed stared at Clint. "He no belong here," one said.

"How do you become a member?" Clint was intent on learning more.

"Only men fit join," the tailor said. "I don tell you me no belong. I no sabi." Irritation colored his voice.

"Are there any cult houses for women?" Clint seemed oblivious to the negative reaction in the others.

To shut him up, the tailor finally looked into Clint's eyes and said, in good English, over the whir of the foot machine, "My grandmother said that in her time, women had a cult called Iyamba, but that it ceased to exist, because it was associated with heathen practices."

Unable to learn more, Clint rode home. He wondered who he could ask about the role of the Ekpe cult in society. On the way, approaching the square, he saw the market teeming with people. Customers crowded stalls amid deafening noise. Every stall had a radio, each tuned to a different music station. The cacophony of voices and songs—church music, highlife, and other Nigerian music —confused and irritated him.

He walked around the market with his bike until he came to a suya stall near the butcher's section, where the strong smell of roast meat was too tempting to resist. Standing in a long line of customers, one of the young men he met earlier on the road from Oror recognized him and immediately tried to curry favor by asking the servers to give Clint preference.

"No," Clint said. "These people were before me. I'll take my turn. I'm not in a hurry."

Of course, despite the grumbling of other customers, the servers gave him preference, because he was visitor. As a display of gratitude, he bought an extra portion of suya for his new friend, and they sat on one of two benches reserved for customers of the stall.

"I know we met at the stall along the road," Clint said. "What's your name? Are you in school? My name is Clint. I'm visiting my grandparents."

"Nick. I just completed secondary. I should be going to university this year, but my parents can't afford it."

Tired and anxious to get home and away from the relentless heat of the sun and noise, Clint quickly ate his suya, refusing the accompanying sauce and preferring a sprinkle of salt instead. He ordered bottled water and drank half, then gave the remainder to Nick.

As he stood, he asked, "What does your family do?"

"My father is a driver at the government office here. My mother is a trader in the market. I was just at her stall."

Surprised, Clint asked, "Your mother's here at the market?"
"Yes. She would be happy to meet you."

Walking his bike again, he followed Nick to the produce section of the market, where his mother shared a stall with another woman. Clint was amazed at the number of women who were petty traders. Some displayed a handful of crayfish or peanuts or a small quantity of whatever produce they had. He couldn't imagine how anyone could make a living that way. The different types of beans dazzled him—black, white, red, brown, purple, black-eyed peas, peanuts in and out of the shell, bags of rice, and dried peas.

Nick's mother, a small, dark-brown woman, specialized in blackeyed peas, scooping them from the bag with a cup into an enameled basin beside her. She pointed them to a bench while she attended to her client.

After she completed her sale, she welcomed Clint. "I know Mama Esther. We were in the same church committee. You're welcome."

Clint felt awkward, standing there amid the bags of beans and rice. During the ten minutes he visited with her, she had two clients who each bought a cup or two of red beans, and another client who bought three cups of black-eyed peas. He very much wanted to ask about her daily sales and income, but he didn't want to appear rude.

As both young men left the produce section, Clint turned to Nick. "What will you do since university isn't an option?"

"We're hoping that my mother's relative, who lives in Texas, will help. He's visiting this coming December. Even if he agrees, it's too late for me to start this year. God willing, I'll start next year at Abia State College."

"What will you do in the meantime?"

"My father's trying to organize for me to learn a trade at Aba. He's in discussion about it with a friend."

"I hope that works out for you." He felt sad that such a bright young man might not be able to pursue his education.

Before setting off for home, Clint invited Nick to visit him at Esther's. As he rode home, he thought of his high-school days and the Black students who weren't taking advantage of the opportunities for education they had available. He reflected on his father's views that many worthy minds were being wasted in Africa due to the prohibitive cost of education.

—⟋⟍⟋—

At home, Esther paced frantically. Clint left early that morning, saying he wanted to go to Oror to look around. It was well past two o'clock, and he hadn't returned. She was contemplating sending one of her errand boys to find him when she saw the bicycle appear on the path leading to the house.

She was so relieved, she stood on the small upstairs porch to shout at him. Words poured from her mouth in no particular order. "Clint, where have you been? You must be hungry. Okoro Nta brought you some fresh bush meat. It's antelope. He shot it last night. I made a small stew for you. It isn't often we get fresh bush meant. The hunters have to go very far to find animals, since many of our forests have been destroyed. When my father was alive, he loaned his gun to hunters, and we always had a fresh supply of bush meat of all kinds. Do you want to eat now or rest?'

He put the bike away and climbed the stairs to meet Esther. The note of anxiety in her voice made him feel like a little boy who needed protecting. On his way up, he saw a clump of mud on the corner of the stairs, and a wasp came out.

It must be a wasp's nest, he thought. Should I tell her about it?

He considered that for a second, then dismissed the idea. "I'm fine, Grandma. Having a bike is the best thing that's happened to me since I came here. I rode as far as Atani, and can you believe it? There's a really elaborate Mgbala Ekpe there. I wanted to go in, but I was told only members are allowed. I have to learn more about Ekpe society. It might be something I should look into and perhaps join while I'm here. I'm not hungry. I ate some suya at the market."

"What? You have to be careful about where you eat. Those places aren't clean, and you don't want to come down with dysentery. By the way, you should've stopped at Obinkita to see the oldest church in the area where your great-grandfather taught."

"I'll leave that for another day. Grandma, who would I ask about joining the Ekpe Society?"

Ignoring the question, she went to the window to call her maid to bring Clint something to eat. She waved off Clint's attempt to say he wasn't hungry.

CHAPTER NINE

C lint, Man, we miss you. When are you coming back?"
It was Frank, his childhood buddy. Clint, evading the
question, carried out an inane conversation before
finally ending the call.

That was the fourth call from one of his buddies. Except
for Frank, the rest were acquaintances or people he sometimes
played soccer with. Each time he received a call from the U.S.
he recognized as coming from one of them, he ignored it. He
answered Frank's call by mistake, thinking it was from his
sister, to whom he spoke the previous week.

His parents sent subtle messages through his acquaintances
to remind him of what he was missing by burying himself in
the village for so long. He obtained his cell phone at the Lagos
Airport as a way to contact his parents. He hadn't expected
them to make the number available to others, nor had he
expected that he would want to call his friends while in Nigeria.
He didn't want to be reminded of his life in the U.S. He was in
Nigeria for a purpose—to establish a link with his ancestors.

No doubt his parents hoped that by then, he would be tired
of village life and decide to return. Without anything to occupy

him in the village or anything in common with the village youth, he would tire easily from boredom. That should be enough to send him running back to the comfort of Tenley Park, where he had TV, games, iTunes, and many other ways to stave off boredom.

Instead, during the intermittent phone calls with his parents, he gave nothing but glowing reports about his activities in the village.

He also listened without envy to information about the activities of his high-school and college friends.

He surmised that his parents' decision that he stay at Esther's house was motivated by the belief that he'd find life there inconvenient, since the house lacked the amenities of home. In the beginning, food was a problem. He previously ate jollof rice and foofoo, but the foods tasted differently in Nigeria, and he couldn't figure out why. On inquiry, Esther said that most foods were prepared with palm oil, but, if he wished, she could substitute peanut oil instead.

Clint missed the certainties of everyday life, like electricity and indoor plumbing. He couldn't turn on the faucet and have water gush out for his shower, and he particularly resented having to use the outhouse at night. He mastered the art of washing himself with only a pail of water, rationalizing that if he went camping during the summer, as his friends did, bathing that way would be second nature. He refrained from visiting the stream early in the morning to bathe, as did some of his grandmother's servants, because he wasn't comfortable performing his ablutions in public.

He didn't care for the geckos and lizards crawling on the walls, or the cockroaches he encountered whenever he opened one of Esther's fridges to get a soft drink or bottle of water. However, sleeping under mosquito netting on a lumpy, sand-filled mattress was a tolerable inconvenience.

What he found most difficult were the flies and insects attracted by the light of a lamp or candle whenever there was a power outage. The constant outages were disconcerting, especially when he was in the middle of a riveting scene in the book he was reading.

Kerosene lamps or candles made poor substitutes.

In their calls, his parents always asked about power outages and his reactions to them. He often gamely joined in the fun during those conversations. He felt ready to endure an inconvenience, since he was acquiring experiences he could use in the future.

In addition to what he learned from his parents' calls, Igwe occasionally passed on information about Clint's home. He learned that Peace had visited her sister in Toronto, and Sarah went to Jamaica for a few days with school friends.

On the whole, Clint, who never had high expectations about the visit, was happy with village life, even though he was sometimes bored by the inactivity or by not having friends with whom he had things in common. He became acquainted with some of the village men and began to understand how the community functioned.

His thoughts were interrupted by Esther, who announced that the parcel he was expecting could be picked up at the post office. When his mother first asked if he received the parcel, Esther jokingly said it would have been better if Peace sent money through Western Union, since everything was available at the market.

"If you go to Aba," Esther told Clint, "you can buy anything you want. It might not be made in America, but I can assure you the Chinese ones are equally good. The parcel will probably arrive after you return to America."

That morning, Esther handed him a slip from the post office, indicating he had a parcel to collect. He rode his bike but detoured to see Goldie College, and he wasn't disappointed. He wandered the grounds, enjoying the lush, well-kept garden with its many fruit trees. The beautiful old building dating back to 1905 impressed him. The college, which had once been a training institute for missionaries and pastors, was morphing into a university.

As he rode toward the barracks, his mind drifted back to the U.S. He'd been in Nigeria for over two months, during which time many things must have happened in the world he wasn't aware of. Sometimes, he heard world news from radio or TV, but it meant little to him except when it related to the U.S. Whenever things like the floods in the Midwest or the latest budget fight on entitlements between Obama and the Republicans made the news, he shook his head. The big news in Nigeria about the corruption cases involving ex-ministers or someone important only confirmed what his parents said about Nigeria.

In his grandfather's house, he found a copy of a newspaper called

This Day and read about the bombing activities of a fanatical Islamist group called Boko Haram. He wondered what they were fighting for.

After all, he'd been told that the people who wielded the most political power in the country were northerners. If so, why couldn't they stop the violence against innocent people? In the villages, bombings were rarely mentioned. If they were, people just shrugged, more preoccupied with their daily lives.

He knew he was being simplistic in his thinking, after seeing the income disparity problem in Nigeria. Even in an area like Aro Chukwu, the rich lived lavishly. One day, a wealthy man coming to visit his relatives used a helicopter to avoid the bad roads. The cost of the visit, in Clint's view, could have gone toward repairing parts of the road, feeding the poor, paying school fees for bright indigent children, or provide training in the area for the hundreds of unemployed or underemployed youth.

When he discussed the episode with friends at the bar, no one seemed to make the comparison of the cost of the helicopter ride and the alternate use of such resources. They were merely happy that someone local had the money to travel by helicopter. Someone said that, when the man arrived, his big Hummer was waiting to take him to his compound.

Clint couldn't understand such reasoning. His grandfather made him realize that once someone was perceived as being better off, he was expected to care for his extended family, and those financial needs could be overwhelming. "The bad news," as Igwe put it, "is that they'll suck you dry. As long as they think you have money, their demands never cease."

Clint hated the cult of dependency, because he saw the daily parade of relatives streaming into Esther's home to ask for financial help.

Since the helicopter incident, he kept his views to himself, even during conversations in the bars, where the denizens always seemed preoccupied with politics.

As he rode to the post office, he thought about what he missed— the orderliness and plenitude of American life, the privacy and certainty, and the freedom to be oneself. He wouldn't have those in Nigeria, and those were obviously things his parents liked about living in the U.S. Perhaps he should consider returning.

At the post office, while waiting for his parcel, he overheard snippets of conversation among those in line about the current political situation—the marginalization of the Igbos. The whole discussion made no sense to him, because it was all one-sided. He wanted to know about the other side, too. When he was back in the States, he resolved to scour the Internet to learn more about the Nigerian political situation.

He eavesdropped on a conversation between two people.

"Did you read about the latest from that woman who was the exdirector of something in the federal government?" one asked. "I can't remember which agency."

"Yes. Didn't she say the drug cartel sought to kill her the same way they killed Bola Ige? Things happen in this Nigeria, eh?"

"Did you read about the tortoise in her office?" The person laughed.

The listeners laughed, too.

Clint looked from one to the other without understanding the joke.

Trying to restrain his laughter, a young man said, "I saw that. You hear of all sorts of shenanigans by people who feel their livelihood is being attacked, but the tortoise thing beats them all. She's lucky she found it and removed it. Her assistant apparently sprinkled holy water on it to stop its evil from spreading and harming anyone." They laughed and shook their heads.

"It's no laughing matter," someone else said. "That tortoise must've contained some juju. You never can tell."

Clint didn't know what to make of the conversation. Juju? Tortoise? He never heard of such a thing, though once he'd come to Nigeria, he heard the improbable was possible and was usually believed.

His parents were apolitical concerning Nigeria. Although they were avid followers of American politics, they dismissed any bad news from Nigeria as self-inflicted, due to the widespread corruption. Clint finally understood them. He quickly learned that every Nigerian had strong political views, and discussions could get intense. That was why he never expressed his own views in public, just in the privacy of his grandfather's house.

On his way out, he chatted with one of the men who'd been in line, who was a lecturer at the Teacher Training College who urged him to visit the college and the secondary school beside it, both of which were founded by an important native.

"It's the oldest private secondary school in Nigeria," he told Clint. "It was started in the 1930s, and many of its alumni hold important positions in government and politics. You must've heard of Alvan Ikoku, the founder. His statue is the one you see, as you enter Amanagwu."

"I've probably seen it, but I didn't connect it with the secondary school."

Their conversation was interrupted by one of the young women from the post office, who wanted a ride back to the college. Unfortunately, the lecturer had other errands to run and couldn't help.

Turning to Clint, she said, "I've heard of you. You're Peace's son, and you're here to recover from some addiction. Nobody believes the story from Da Esther that you came here on holiday. We would've believed it if you left after a month, but you're still here. As far as I can see, you do nothing."

Shocked by her candor, he stared hard at her. "Do I look like a drug addict?"

"What do they look like? Most of them look normal."

Raising his voice, he asked, "Lady, how dare you accuse me of being a drug addict?"

"I'm just being straightforward. I thought you'd like to know what's being said about you."

"Thanks, but no thanks. Since you know so much about me, who are you?"

Her name was Ifeoma, the daughter of one of Peace's classmates at Queens College. Her grandfather and Peace's father moved in different circles. While Peace's father was a distinguished doctor with an important government position, Ifeoma's grandfather was a steward for a Scottish man in the Colonial service in Nigeria.

His master, who, when the steward importuned him for a wage advance to pay the school fees for his brilliant daughter, agreed to pay for her education as long as she did well in school. He demanded the principal send her report cards directly to him. On graduation, he made sure she was awarded a scholarship to Ibadan University to read English literature, since that was the subject he read at Oxford.

She graduated with honors and went on to teach at the same secondary school she once attended. By then, her sponsor retired to England, and her father retired to Aro Chukwu. While Peace married Peter, Ifeoma's mother married an Owerri man she met at Ibadan. Ifeoma was their only child.

Unfortunately, when Ifeoma was only two-years old, her mother died while being operated on for appendicitis. The situation was even more tragic, because Ifeoma's grandmother was in the waiting room at the hospital expecting the doctor to tell her that her daughter was in recovery. Instead, he brought the news of her death.

All Aro Chukwu mourned when such a brilliant life was cut short. Ifeoma was raised by her grandmother, who still lived in the compound opposite Igwe's. She followed in her mother's footsteps. In college, she excelled in science, majoring in biology. She received a diploma in education, and, at the time she met Clint, she had just begun her teaching career at the Teacher Training College.

"My mother was Peace's classmate at Queens College, Enugu. Their paths diverged when they both went to university. Peace when to Nsukka, and my mother was at Ibadan."

"Ifeoma...may I call you that? I hope you'll disabuse your friends of the gossip about me. I'm not a drug addict. I came here out of curiosity. I wanted to understand where I came from. I hope we meet again."

Mounting his bike, he returned home. The parcel contained some books, a present for Esther in the form of a bottle of hand sanitizer, and insect repellent. Clint was preoccupied, concerned about the rumors of his drug addiction and wondering if his grandparents had heard them. Why hadn't they told him? He missed being in the States and wondered what to do.

The ingrained values of Nigeria were disgusting to him, and he knew they blocked progress in the country. Just recently, a visitor to his grandmother complained that he had to abandon the proposal to build a substation at Aro Chukwu, because with the added 30% due to the Minister and another 30% for the chiefs, the project was too expensive. He implied that was why many overseas organizations were reticent about carrying out improvement projects in the area.

Clint wondered why such payments were taken for granted and just dismissed as the cost of doing business. Everyone complained about them, but no one tried to stop them. He mentioned that to Igwe, who told him that it wasn't like that before the civil war. He added that one couldn't blame the civil servants or the police for asking for such payments. Their salaries were in arrears, and money from bribes allowed civil servants to feed their families. Igwe wished the country would elect men and women who put the country first instead of selfishly regarding the public purse as their private funds to spend as they pleased. It seemed that people went into politics to enrich themselves and nothing else.

With so many young people unemployed, a politician found it easy to buy respect and votes with money. No one cared that such gifts came from money that was allocated for other things, including salaries.

"In America," Clint said, "the press wouldn't allow such embezzlement to go unreported. Many of those people would end up in jail.'

Igwe laughed. "The newspapers often report bribery and the misuse of public funds, but no one pays any attention."

Clint felt troubled. If he wanted to stay in Nigeria, he told himself he would work to change the situation, but would he? He wasn't sure.

CHAPTER TEN

It was one of those rare days since he had the bike that Clint
spent the later afternoon with his grandmother. Stepping out
of his room after a short nap, he sat in the parlor to chat with
her. It was unusual to find her alone at that time of day. Rain
fell outside, and Esther, commenting on the unusual rainfall at
that time of year, seemed happy to have company.

Clint attributed her good mood to the fact that she didn't
have to fight with her daughter-in-law, as was normally the
case each morning. Her live-in son went to Aba and took his
pregnant wife for a doctor's visit while he bought merchandise
to replenish his stock. He owned three stores selling Nigerian-
made batik clothing in Aro Chukwu.

As they chatted about the rain, Clint decided Esther might
not mind explaining the meaning of some of the things he saw
while sightseeing. He was particularly anxious to know about
the symbol on a flag he saw planted on vacant lots. In passing
by one such plot, he asked someone what the flag represented,
only to be told it was an Ekpe flag. The man refused to say
more.

"Grandma, I'm curious," Clint asked. "What does that flag
stand for?"

"It indicates someone lodged a complaint regarding the land against some other person at the Ekpe cult house. The Ekpe council acts like a village court in many cases. Those cases they can't settle eventually go to a council of chiefs."

"That's interesting. Who can join the Ekpe cult?" He hoped that would give him the opportunity to tell her about his interest in becoming a member.

"Let's talk about other things." She squinted in disgust. "I'm not interested in the Ekpe."

"Grandma, I genuinely want to know. I was thinking I might join, so I could learn more from the inside."

"Nonsense, Clint! I forbid it. I watched you visit bars along the road and the slave museum, and I bit my tongue, because you wouldn't listen. Mazi Igwe wouldn't back me up, either, but I draw the line at the Ekpe society."

Clint was shocked by her vehemence. Annoyed that she felt she could tell him what he could do, he wanted to state he was a grown man and free to do whatever he liked, but one look at her quivering lips told him not to pursue the topic.

"Why are you against it?" he asked gently. "From what I've been told, the cult serves a useful purpose. You yourself said they mostly adjudicate cases."

"I've told you the Ekpe cult is a heathen cult," she almost shouted. "In what way?"

Before she could reply, they heard a car horn. Looking outside, Clint saw Igwe casually dressed in khaki shorts and batik shirt, stepping out and unfurling his umbrella, as he walked toward the house.

"Mazi Igwe, what brings you here in this bad weather?" Esther called in concern.

He noted the beautiful tie-dyed caftan she wore with matching head scarf and said, "Mama Esther, I'd like to know what your secret it. You look like a young girl today."

Ignoring his remarks, she looked at him quizzically.

He settled into a comfortable armchair that Esther indicated, as if he wanted to spend time with the two of them. "Since we sent the bike, I haven't seen our young man. I don't know what to tell his parents about his activities. You know how they worry."

"You can see he's fine," she said smugly. "This is the first time he's been here at this hour, and it's because of the rain. I'm glad to see you, actually, because you can answer his question about the Ekpe cult." She called for a servant to bring beer and snacks for Igwe.

Clint, who occupied the entire sofa as if it were his bed, made no effort to rise, since Igwe arrived.

Glaring at him, Igwe asked, "What's this about the Ekpe cult? I hope we won't go through the same nonsense we had with your father. He talked the same rubbish, and he joined against our wishes. We lost that fight, though he eventually admitted he shouldn't have joined, because it served no purpose." He frowned.

Clint uncurled his legs and sat up. "I've seen many Mgbala Ekpe in the villages, and Grandma told me that the cult adjudicates small land cases between neighbors. It occurred to me that it might be useful to become a member, since I can learn more about them from the inside."

Igwe burst out laughing and continued until tears filled his eyes and ran down his cheeks. It was infectious, and Esther soon joined him, laughing even harder.

Collecting himself, Igwe told her, "Soon, he'll be asking to join the Obon secret society, too."

"Don't mention it. I doubt he's heard of that one." They laughed even harder.

They're laughing at my ignorance, Clint realized. "I'm totally confused. What's the Obon society? You're right. I never heard of it."

Igwe wiped tears from his cheeks with a handkerchief. "So, Young Man, you haven't heard of the Obon society?" He laughed again. "It's the most secretive male-only society we have. They meet only at night. No woman is allowed to see the members. I'm not surprised you haven't heard about it, since you stay outside the compounds."

He finally controlled himself. "I have no doubt you're eligible to join the Ekpe cult, but I doubt you'd be able to stand the initiation ceremony, which involves sacrifice and bloodletting.

They'd love to get your money and feast at your expense. However, you don't have to join them to learn how cases presented to them are judged. Anyone can take a case to them, but you have to buy the flag when you lodge your complaint. I don't know what they charge, but, like most things here, it would include goat meat, stockfish, palm wine, and money."

He paused, looking pensive. "I don't know the amount, because I never had to petition them for anything. After lodging a complaint, they set a date for the hearing, and both parties need to be present at the cult house. After the hearing and judgment, you can still opt to take your case to civil court if you disagree with the judgment. That's all there is to it."

Scowling, he stared at Clint before adding, "I'm not a member of the cult, because the initiation process is such that I, as a Christian, can't join. If you want to join, you must consult your parents, who'll send you the necessary funds. You can ask one of your mother's uncles to sponsor you. I don't approve, nor does Esther." He shook his finger for emphasis and slumped back in his chair, tired from such a long lecture.

Clint didn't know what to say. The answers he was given annoyed him. What was so unchristian about joining a society that, as far as he could see, did some good in the community? He wouldn't argue with the elders in the room, but he would reserve the question for his father.

He decided to change topics and talk of something else that might give a reasonable answer. He'd been worried about the rumor of his drug addiction. He hadn't mentioned it to Esther yet, because though she was kind and generous to many, she also always remembered a slight. That attitude came out at unexpected times. He didn't want her to cast Ifeoma as an enemy and dump her with all the others for whom she had contempt. Clint wanted to ask, because he knew Igwe would give him the simplest, best explanation of why such a rumor persisted.

"Since both of you are here," Clint said. "I must ask you about a rumor."

Four eyes fixed on him.

"I understand that people here think my parents packed me off to

Aro Chukwu for being a drug addict."

"Where'd you hear this?" they shouted simultaneously.

"At the post office the other day. I met a girl named Ifeoma, and that was the first thing she told me."

"Ifeoma?" Esther asked. "Who is she?"

"Her mother was my mother's friend. They were in the same school at Enugu. Her grandfather lives in the village opposite Ndi Igwe."

"I wouldn't pay attention to it," Esther said. "People will say anything to explain what they don't know."

Igwe, who prided himself on knowing most of the people in his village and throughout Aro Chukwu, wanted more information about the girl.

Clint gave him what he knew, adding that she was very pleasant and intelligent, and he was glad someone told him what was circulated through the villages.

"I remember her as a little child when her mother died," Igwe said slowly. "Her death was a blow to the family. Her parents took over and raised her child, and, as I understand it, the husband supported them. You say she's a teacher at the Institute here? I'm glad to hear that. I liked her mother. She and your father were close friends and saw each other during the holidays. Then he went abroad and met your mother."

Esther scowled at Igwe. "I heard she was the one you wanted Peter to marry."

"Yes, but let's not go into that now. It's finished, and I now share a handsome and clever grandson with you." Turning to Clint, he said, "I heard the same rumor, but I dismissed it, because I know it isn't true. Esther's right. People here will look for any reason for something they don't know or understand. We know you aren't a drug addict. If I were you, I wouldn't give that rumor any more thought."

As he stood to go, he added, "Come to think of it, there's a man in the compound where Ifeoma's grandfather lives who's a historian and the best source of Aro Chukwu history. He knew Achi, my grandfather. We used to be friends, though I haven't seen him recently. He must still be alive, since I haven't heard of his death. When next you see Ifeoma, ask her about him. Next time you're near Ndi Igwe, try to meet him. He'll tell you things I probably can't remember."

Clint excused himself from Esther, who, as soon as Igwe left, picked up the Bible to read. The table fan didn't work, and there was no breeze, leaving Clint's room hot and uncomfortable. He tossed and turned, sweating profusely. No doubt, the National Electric Power Authority, NEPA, had line problems in Ohafia. He surmised that the lights he saw in the stalls and shops across the road came from generators.

After an hour of being unable to rest, he got up and went for a bucket of water in the courtyard to wash his face. He returned to the parlor, where his grandmother entertained a few visitors who came to visit. He sprawled on the settee, listening to their desultory talk while he tried to nap before going to the schoolyard to see if any of the children were ready to play soccer.

CHAPTER ELEVEN

Clint often admired his grandfather's walled estate. The main house boasted an uncovered courtyard separating the kitchen and storage areas. In addition, there were the boys' quarters at the far end of the yard away from the main house. Both sides of the courtyard had several other small, interconnecting rooms. Fruit trees grew in the yard, and, from where Clint stood, banana plants obscured the boys' quarters from view. Not far from them was the patch of vegetable garden where most of the vegetables used by the household were raised. His grandfather proudly told him that the patch was watered constantly throughout the dry season.

Since his retirement, Igwe said the yard gave him considerable pleasure. He liked to come out early in the morning when it wasn't raining just to walk the garden and check the fruit trees.

On that particular visit, Clint found his grandfather standing in the yard, talking to a servant. Igwe, who usually favored Western clothing, wore a loincloth and short-sleeved shirt.

"What have you been doing since I saw you last week?" Igwe asked. "I'll be calling your dad on the weekend, and I should have something to report when he asks about you. I know you went to Ujari."

With the sun rapidly heating up, the two walked the path to the house, stopping when Igwe gave instructions to his gardener about bringing down some coconuts to be used for Sunday's lunch.

"I hope you'll join me for lunch on Sunday," he told Clint. "The driver will come for you. We'll be having coconut rice, something I'm particularly fond of."

As they approached the main house, his grandfather's current wife came out. A young woman, Igwe married her following the death of his wife with whom he had children. Clint met her several times, but she always shied away from having anything to do with him. When he studied her face, he saw the narrow arc of her eyebrows, her high forehead, eyes as smooth and hard as obsidian and full of unfamiliar light, and her full lips with a trace of a forced smile. She wasn't a good actress, but she had a considerable instinct toward self-preservation.

He shuddered but turned to admire her beautiful damask joji patterned wrapper with matching head tie and blouse, expensive costume gold necklace with matching earrings, and high-heeled black pumps. He heard his father and other siblings weren't close to her, and that was why she tried to be less obtrusive when he visited.

"Auntie, are you going out?" Clint asked in a friendly tone. "I thought maybe I could visit with you today. We haven't seen much of each other."

She looked at him coldly. "My sister isn't feeling well, and I have to go immediately to arrange for a doctor." She walked toward the waiting car. "You'll still be here for a while, so we'll have time to get to know each other."

As the car drove off, Igwe, having watched the exchange, hitched the wrapper to his waist, looked pensive, and walked toward the house, wiping his brow.

Clint tried to read his grandfather's mood. "I hope Auntie is in a better mood when I next visit."

"She doesn't mean to offend, Clint. She really has a reason to rush out today."

They entered the parlor, and Igwe ordered a servant to bring bottles of beer and snacks.

"The heat's too much today," he remarked. "I hope you haven't come to discuss joining the Ekpe cult. I'd rather hear about your visit to the slave museum. Did you enjoy it? Did you learn anything new?'

Sipping his beer, Clint said, "Not really. It was different from what I expected, Grandpa." What had I expected? he wondered. It certainly wasn't a museum with paintings and artifacts neatly exhibited, though I can't tell him that.

He changed the subject. "Uncle Okoro mentioned there's a place near Ujari on one of the creeks of the Cross River where fishermen depart most days to fish along the river."

"He must mean Amasu. In the old days, it was an important port, teaming with canoes laden with goods and slaves meant for Calabar." "At the museum, I saw the rods and cowries used for trading in the old days. Are there still some in our family?"

"My grandparents either sold the rods, or they were melted and fashioned into other things. They may have thrown them away when they became useless. You've gathered by now that we don't care to preserve any old thing. We throw them away as soon as new replacements are introduced."

Clint remembered that when his grandmother visited them in America, his parents took her to visit Jamestown. She was surprised to see old pots and baskets on exhibition, remarking that her parents had similar things but discarded them in favor of enameled pots. At the African Museum in Washington, Esther berated his mother for bringing her to see the carved images similar to the ones that were destroyed by the newly converted Christians in the thirties and forties.

"The rods and manilas seem quiet heavy," Clint said. "I wonder how people were able to transport and store their wealth. Did they have banks? Where'd you grandfather store his money?"

"Did you see the windowless room off the parlor in my brother's house? That was the family bank. Mark you, my grandfather lost it all, but that's another story.

"All our manufactured goods came from Calabar via Itu. There, one could easily obtain cotton material cheaper than the traditional joji, which only the Aro chiefs or men of high social rank could afford at the time."

"What type of cloth is joji?" Clint asked. "Was it made here in the olden days?"

"No, my dear. The type of cloth we had was woven on a single loom and dyed either white or black. Joji has similar designs as madras, and it was the first cloth given to the chiefs when the European traders sought trading privileges. It's called joji, because the traders presented the material as a gift from King George, hence the name."

"Which George?" Clint wondered at the date.

"I'm no student of history, so I can't tell you which of the Georges, but I know one of the big men in the United African Company in those days was someone called Goldie, which, incidentally, was the name of one of the missionaries here then. Traders came back with stories about the various clothes and trousers worn by the chiefs in Calabar, and the parasols and beautiful dresses and hats the women wore to church on Sunday." Sipping his beer, he called for more peanuts.

To Clint, the interruption seemed a long time. He was chafing to hear the end of the story. "I have some more questions, Grandfather." "Fire away, Young Man. I'm glad you're interested in the history of the place. Young people nowadays know very little about the past."

"When I went to Ndi Igwe after the Slave Museum, I saw the old man who lived across from Uncle's house. Uncle implied there was animosity between you and him. What's that about?'

"Don't listen to him. Some people want to re-create the past. They think they own us simply because of an accident of birth. The past is past, and I don't understand why Okoro mentioned that rubbish to you."

The sky darkened, and the rain that had been threatening all day started falling.

"We're a bit tired of this rain," Igwe said. "It's been very frequent this August."

Clint nodded. "Everyone in the village is complaining about it, wondering why there's no August break as in previous years. If we were in America, it would be blamed on global warming."

Igwe called for more snacks, deliberating for a while before replying. "True. We hope this year it'll be dry during Ikeji, but this rain doesn't bode well for a dry Ikeji. By the way, that's another name for the New Yam Festival usually celebrated in September. I'm glad you'll be here during this year's festival. The date has yet to be set by Eze Aro."

As Igwe paused to collect his thoughts, Clint said, "Grandpa, since I arrived, I've been really disturbed by the general untidiness of the place. It's not just untidy. It's trashy. Take the slave museum. It's an important attraction, but the space around it is terrible. You have to pass through all kinds of debris—plastic wraps, broken bottles, and human and animal waste. It's disgusting.

"I'm just using that as an example, but it's the same everywhere. In the market, women sell food next to mounds of rubbish. Little kids were peeing openly. I'm appalled."

Clint shook his head in disgust, then he looked at his grandfather to gauge his reaction. "No wonder typhoid is endemic here. Visitors to my grandmother's house talk constantly of someone coming down with it. I know in America there are places in the inner city where people don't care about their environment, but it isn't as bad as here. Nowadays in the U.S., many communities insist that pet owners carry a bag to put in their pet waste. I don't advocate that here.

"I don't think the problem is just about money, though I know money is important to pay trash collectors, but why can't the village communities pass a rule requiring people to deposit their waste in one area and insist that the local government implement a schedule of trash collection?"

Clint raised his voice a bit. "Don't tell me, Grandpa, that it can't be done. It requires only one or two big plastic containers, similar to the ones people use to collect rainwater. They could be placed strategically, with people instructed to put their trash in it, and fines could be imposed on those who fail to obey the rule."

It was a long speech from Clint. He waited impatiently to hear what his grandfather would say.

Igwe's face showed his unease. He deliberated for a few minutes before answering calmly, "It never used to be that way. People took care of their homes and surroundings. When I grew up, the first thing we did when we woke up was clean the house and yard. Then we went to the stream to bathe. In those days, there were no plastic containers, so whenever we bought anything in a tin, we found other uses for it. Tomato tins were reused as cups or measures. Beer and juice bottles were reused as containers for palm oil or kerosene, to name a few. We wrapped things with leaves or used paper.

"Even now, you can see vestiges of this in the markets, where peanuts are sold in beer or soft-drink bottles. Many of the women in the compound are uneducated. It'll take a lot of time and effort to change their attitudes about sanitation. Since there are no public facilities, you can't fault them too much, but I agree they shouldn't allow their children to use every place as a toilet.

"You know, if I have to attend a gathering in the village, I know I'll have to use the bathroom, but there are no facilities. I often don't drink anything before going to save myself the embarrassment."

Clint smiled at Igwe's discomfort. "Can't the organizers rent portable johns?"

Igwe laughed. "Where would we get them?"

"What happens, for example, at Ikeji, if I need to use the bathroom urgently?"

Still laughing, Igwe said, "You have to find a nearby bush. We still have a long way to go. Trash collection is expensive, and villagers have no money. I agree that the parents of little children should be held responsible for cleaning their children's messes. I'm aware of the situation in the market, but until we can provide public facilities in those areas, I'm afraid we can't fault the men and women."

Clint couldn't let it go. "What do you do with your trash?"

Igwe burst out laughing. "What do you think? Is my yard littered with it?'

"I'm just curious," he said in a subdued voice.

"We have a compost pit out back, where we put all the kitchen and garden waste. The compost is eventually used as fertilizer for the plants. The tins and bottles are collected. The garden boy sells them in the market to petty traders for a small sum, which he keeps. I hope you're satisfied."

As he stood to leave, Clint wasn't satisfied with his grandfather's answers. There are so many rich people in this place, and they still can't get together to tackle the sanitation problem. Living as they do without day-to- day contact with the problem, they just shut their eyes to it.

Resting his bike against a tree trunk to admire a termite mound 300 yards from Igwe's house, he was surprised to hear someone call his name. He walked back to the road to look and saw it was Ifeoma. "How are you?" he asked.

"I'm good. I'm on my way home from a visit to my grandfather."

They walked companionably along the dirt road, with Clint walking his bike

"I'm glad I ran into you," Clint said. "There's something only you can help me with."

"I doubt that's true. I'm sure both Mazi Igwe and Mama Esther will solve any problem you have."

"Perhaps, but I might prefer your help." "What is it?"

"I understand that in your compound, there's an elderly man who's an authority on the history of this place. He knew my grandfather. I'd like to meet him."

"You must mean Mazi Oji. He's very old, and he doesn't come out very often. He lives near my grandfather. With Ikeji approaching, he'll probably be too busy with preparations in our compound. You must know that many people from abroad come home during that time, and his company is highly sought after. Couldn't you ask your Uncle Okoro to approach him on your behalf?"

"Actually, my grandfather thought you were the best one to intercede for me. As I understand it, you're related, and he wouldn't refuse a request from you."

"That may be so. OK. I'll ask him and will send you a message.

You're still staying at Esther's?"

"Yes. Thank you. I hope to hear from you soon. If the arrangements are made, could you accompany me to Mazi Oji's place?"

"I will try."

When Clint returned to Esther's house, he found her sitting in a parlor chair, reading the Bible, with religious music playing in the background. He usually thought it easiest to get her full attention after her morning meal and before the onslaught of visitors. At other times, she appeared preoccupied, dispersing instructions to various people or gossiping about local events with her friends.

That day, however, there were no visitors.

"My live-in son heard from Peace," Esther announced.

"How are they? What did she say?" Clint asked in animation.

"I heard your sister's doing well. When I last saw her, she was just taking her first steps. She must be a big girl now. Your parents took her to the beach in some place called Ocean City. She spent the whole day sunning herself and got sunstroke. I must say, I don't understand why people do such silly things. I see them on TV, lying in the sand to sun themselves. In Sarah's case, I don't know why she wants a suntan. Isn't she already tanned?" She laughed at her own joke.

Clint laughed with her. "Grandma, after the cold winter, we're grateful for the sun's heat. I'm glad my parents took time off work to enjoy the seaside. It's one of the things I enjoy doing in the summer.

What other news did you get? Did my parents tell you she's going to college this fall? I wonder if she decided to live on campus, since she's going to Georgetown University in Washington, DC."

"Your mother never says much during her phone calls. She apparently called to learn how you were, since she was never able to get you on the phone. You should call her."

He made a note to call his mother at some point, but he was still bothered by the nonchalant way Igwe responded to his question on sanitation. He decided to pose the same question to Esther.

When she heard the question, she immediately began ranting. "I don't go to the compound unless I absolutely have to. It never used to be like that, but nowadays, those stupid women in the compound can't control their children. They let them use the whole place as a bathroom. It's disgusting.

"Whenever I have to go there, I always scold them to clean up the place. They have a compound head, and you'd think he should keep the place clean, but no. He doesn't see that as his function. Instead, he spends his time looking for ways of extorting money from the women in the compound for any minor infraction. I really don't want you going there. You might contract some disease."

Suddenly, she changed the subject. "Tell me, how is Chief Igwe? When my husband was alive, we saw him often, but ever since he married that awful young wife, he stays away from his late wife's friends. You haven't said much about her. I presume you've met her." "Yes, I have. She's been very kind to me, and she's always pleasant. Today, she was going to visit her sick sister." "Really? I wonder which one? I hope it's nothing serious."

Mercifully for Clint, a visitor for Esther arrived, so he went to his room.

CHAPTER TWELVE

In the first week of September, Clint decided to leave the confines of his grandmother's house on the outskirts of the village and stroll toward the compounds. He planned to stop at one of the bars along the road to pass the time. It would be fun to hang out and listen to the customers' gripe. Who knew what information he might pick up?

Esther discussed only the problems at her Presbyterian Church or the difficulties of finding reliable help. When she wasn't talking to her village friends, who visited often, or berating the household staff for not carrying out their tasks properly, she sat and read the Bible. Clint felt she must have memorized the whole thing by now after seeing how often she read it and then quoted it to justify or refute something. She seemed uninterested in daily activities except when those events impacted her daily life.

On entering the first bar, he had difficulty focusing his eyes in the dim light. There were no windows, though there was a back door, presumably leading to the kitchen and storage area. The air was suffused with the smell of cigarette smoke mixed with the smell of roast meat, palm oil, crayfish, and paraffin. Smarting from the smoke, his eyes gradually adjusted, and he saw several men sitting on low benches at each side of long tables.

The building was a small hut with two colored electric bulbs hanging on a rope placed along one of the mud-plastered walls. On one wall was a 1999 calendar, while the other held photos of the Eze and members of the cabinet.

A few customers nuzzled their palm wine. They looked at him expectantly, because he was tall for the area and carried himself differently. Someone recognized him and called his name. Two men made space for him to sit down.

When the bar girl came for his order, she made a perfunctory attempt at wiping the table with a dirty rag and offered him palm wine.

"So, you have acquired a taste for palm wine?" one of his new bar friends asked in fairly good English. Clint assumed he graduated from the one of the universities.

"Not really," Clint admitted. "This is my first time. On second thought, maybe I should stick with Star beer. I hear palm wine can be quite intoxicating."

"Try am," a bald man said sitting nearby. "If no good, you fit ask for beer. Make you ask for food. Drink no good for empty belly."

"What do you want?" the bar girl asked in Igbo, looking expectantly at the men. "Goat meat, or, if you prefer, chicken or beef suya?" She looked at Clint and added, "We also have stew of goat innards in pepper sauce. It's very delicious."

"Now you're talking," someone said. "Try it!" another added.

"Thank you," Clint said. "I'll try the goat and chicken suya, if that's all right." He liked the idea of skewered meat.

While his meal was being prepared, he listened to the desultory talk of the customers. More customers came in, and other lefts, and a noisy welcome greeted each new arrival.

"The place will soon be teeming with people," one man said, "since tomorrow is the beginning of Ikeji. Do you know about it?" he asked Clint.

"I've heard of it. Isn't that when the new yam is harvested? I'd like to know what happens during that time. How long does it last?"

"It's when we celebrate the harvesting of the new yam, but it's more than that. For nineteen days, we celebrate the ending of the year and the beginning of the new one. During that time, some activities that we carry out in our daily lives are forbidden." He stopped talking to chew the meat he placed in his mouth.

Conversation was difficult, because of the loud highlife music emanating from the radio mounted in one corner of the room and the loud welcome of newcomers. Speakers had to raise their voices several decibels higher than usual.

Clint leaned forward toward the man who spoke. "Like what?" "Oh, nothing that would affect you."

"Make una no tell am our secret," someone added. "Ikeji be no secret," the bald man said angrily. "Come on," Clint said. "Tell me."

"If you must know," a young man said, "we can't have burials, for example. Other banned activities include farming or buying or selling in the market during daytime." He popped a piece of fried snail into his mouth.

"That's how it was in the old days," a light-skinned man said from the end of the table, his voice loud enough to cause a lull in the conversation. "Nowadays, such mandates, especially about the opening of the market, are difficult to enforce."

"What happens if someone dies during that time?" Clint asked. "The body is stored." The man who replied seemed to think Clint would know better than to ask such a question. The others sniggered, and Clint felt foolish.

"Thank God we'll have a holiday from funerals," someone said, tongue-in-cheek.

"What happens to those who depend on funerals to have a full belly?" asked a man who tore a piece of fried chicken apart with his hands. "Poor fellows will go hungry."

The table erupted with laughter. The radio played a well-known song, and several customers sang along, only to be interrupted by a man sitting at the far end. He momentarily stopped the merriment by shouting in a loud voice, "Nobody goes hungry during Ikeji! There are several opportunities to scavenge for food."

More laughter followed.

When the laughter died down, Clint said, "I thought Ikeji was the time to celebrate the harvest of the new yam."

"Let me explain to our young stranger," an elderly man said, sitting nearby. "Yes, in a way, but it's also the time when we make sacrifices to our family gods and ancestors for a bountiful harvest and for bringing us safely to the New Year. In the past, the last day of Ikeji denoted the end of the year for us. Ikeji begins tomorrow." He gulped down palm wine to chase down a spoonful of jollof rice.

Unlike the other denizens of the bar, that man alone genuinely tried to answer Clint's question. The clatter of plates being removed, the background music, and the loud chattering of customers made conversation difficult. Clint tugged at the older man's sleeve to get his attention.

"What happens tomorrow?" Clint asked.

"First, you must understand we follow the lunar calendar, so Ikeji doesn't always start on a fixed date. You've heard of the Aro-Ibibio War, when we fought for the right to settle here?"

"My grandfather mentioned it." Clint stared at the man, hoping to have many of his questions answered. Perhaps the bar wouldn't be as boring as it seemed.

"If not, ask Mazi Igwe to give you a history lesson. Tomorrow is the day designed for cleaning the Aro Awada at Ugwuakuma. All the Amadis are expected to perform this function. It also signals the beginning of Ikeji."

"I often wonder why the Awada in Ugwuakuma is designated as the Aro Awada. Every compound has its own Awada, after all," someone said.

The others stopped talking. A man at another table overheard the question and began complaining.

"When I was a teacher, it upset me that we were taught colonial history, but nobody bothered to teach us our own. It's a shame we don't know our own history." He paused to let that sink in.

While the others returned to their meal, Clint got up and sat near the man who just spoke, who quietly ate his meal.

"I'm interested in learning as much as I can about the history of Aro Chukwu. I'd be happy if you could tell me about the Aro Chukwu Awada. What is Awada?"

Speaking between chewing his food and belching, the man happily gave Clint a short explanation. "Every village has an Awada, a building where the altar and family gods are housed. Ikeji marks the end of the year and the beginning of the new one on our calendar, just as the other gentleman said.

"The opening of the Awadas and the cleaning and rearrangement of the gods are the first tasks to mark the beginning of Ikeji." He paused to drink from his bottle.

"The Awada in Ugwuakuma was originally the Awada of Akuma Nnaubi, also known as Eze Obin. During the Ibibio War, Eze Obin couldn't personally return in time to clean out his Awada in preparation for the Ikeji of that year, because he was on the battlefield. He sent Okpo, his confidant and close friend, to perform that function for him. In honor of his sacrifice, the Amadis designated his Awada at Uguwakuma as the Aro Chukwu Awada and the first of the Awadas to be cleaned to mark the beginning of Ikeji."

To many in the bar, that was new information, and they congratulated the speaker for his knowledge of local history.

"You should be a professor teaching at university," someone said, as he applauded.

"Make una leave me," he demurred, turning back to his beer.

Clint wanted him to explain who the Amadis were, but he didn't want to sound like a fool, so he asked, "Can I go there to watch the action tomorrow?"

"You fit prove you na Amadi?" someone asked. "If na so, you can go in. If no bi so, you go watch from outside."

Some wag who'd been listening to the conversation immediately added, "If you don't have anything to do. There's really nothing to see."

"How do you know who's an Amadi?" Clint dared ask. "Na them sabi," someone shouted.

"What happens the next day?"

Feeling pestered, the historian said in irritation, "The next day, all the village altars are opened and cleaned. The family gods are arranged and placed in their proper positions, and sacrifices are made to the gods. That's the part of the celebration that's difficult for Christians to participate in."

He was so engrossed, he didn't notice the passage of time. He was only made aware of how long he stayed by the commotion of leave taking, the lull in the conversation, and the shouts of, "Good night!" as people walked out.

He suddenly realized it was dark out. After checking his watch, he called for his bill. "I'd better head home. My grandmother, Esther, will be wondering what happened to me."

—⚬⚬⚬—

Standing outside the house on the evening before the beginning of Ikeji, he wondered how Achi would have felt on that day. Did he accompany his master to the Aro Awada? He heard the faint sound of a drum announcing the beginning of Ikeji and imagined Achi going from compound to compound with the same announcement, reminding the Amadis of their obligation.

—⚬⚬⚬—

Clint awoke to the sound of the cock crowing and the loud voices of servants filtering into his room. He remembered some aspect of what he was thinking, as he entered the house the previous night. During the night, he tossed and turned in bed, anticipating the coming day.

That must have been why, in his dream he relived Achi's life on the first day of Ikeji. It would be his first cultural experience, and he couldn't wait. Would the real thing be as he expected?

He got up hurriedly to dress. On his way from the house, he met Esther at the foot of the staircase, talking to one of the maids. Brushing off her questions, Clint walked to the village square, hoping he hadn't missed anything.

He expected to find the place filled with dancers carrying spears and drums, performing war dances. Instead, he saw crowds on both sides of the road watching groups of five to ten people dressed in traditional Aro costume, with feathered caps, trailed by others carrying baskets of food and kegs of palm wine. They were led by a man who beat a gong, as they walked past on their way to Ugwuakuma. Clint recognized the group from his mother's compound led by one of his illiterate cousins. He was disappointed that there wasn't more to the celebration than a mere parade.

As each group walked past, they called out in unison their clan's name in greeting the crowd, who responded in unison with, "Ayooo." Feeling let down, Clint turned to the person beside him and asked, "Why are there so few from our compound, and the ones in the procession are the unemployed?"

"These are just people who live here year-round. The other family members are in Aba or Lagos or wherever they can make money. Do you think a bank manager or teacher would leave his work to come to the parade today? If he did, it would be during the last day of the festival, when the public events take place."

Clint reasoned that, over the years, Aro Chukwu had undergone tremendous changes. Unlike during Achi's period, when families lived and worked together, the monetization of the economy meant that family members must go to where there were employment opportunities. His own family, for instance, was scattered around the globe and couldn't drop everything to return and see the parade. He shouldn't have been surprised by the low turnout.

He couldn't understand why those family members who lived in Nigeria couldn't take time off for such an important historical event.

Turning to the man beside him, Clint asked, "When these Amadis arrive at their venue, will they perform a war dance?"

Those around him laughed and began chattering loudly about past Ikejis.

Clint felt ignored. He wondered what he would think if the parade were taking place in the U.S. and among them were poor members of the Founding Fathers. Would poor members of the Jefferson or Adams families wish to be identified as the black sheep of the family? Would they be happy in being so recognized? Wouldn't he and his friends scoff at them, as that man did?

Dismissing such thoughts, he walked toward home. He was told the return parade would be that evening, and he wondered what all the Amadis would do during the day at the Aro Awada, which he understood was a big hut. He would have liked to find out if there was a genealogy book tracing the ancestry of all the Amadis. Perhaps it would contain the names of his maternal ancestors, whom he knew were in the group. Perhaps he could ask Igwe or Esther.

Perhaps not, he thought. Neither seems interested in this cultural event.

He decided to follow the processions to Ugwuakuma, anxious to see what happened there. He was disappointed, because the carriers, on arrival, left the baskets they carried outside to be taken in by the Amadis.

"What's happening?" he asked someone. "Only the Amadis are allowed inside."

He went to one of the men he recognized from the Ibom procession and asked, "Why aren't you inside?"

"I'm not an Amadi. I'm a carrier for Ibom Chief."

Feeling let down, Clint imagined Achi as the man carrying for Chief Igwe and having to loiter under the tree until it was time to carry the empty baskets back.

On his way, he stopped at the primary school to join the children playing soccer. He wondered which of them would be in the procession at some future Ikeji celebration.

—◆—

The following day, Clint witnessed the cleaning of the Awada in Ibom. He saw animals being led into the Awada to have their throats slit and blood collected for the gods. The ceremony seemed to have more visible activity than the previous day's. People prepared the animals for sacrifice, and women cooked the ritualized meat. The place teemed with all the activities. Even though he didn't participate in the ritual of sacrifice to the gods and ancestors, he ate some of the food prepared from the slaughtered goats and sheep. Esther was furious with him for that, when one of her friends informed her of Clint's actions.

As they watched goats having their throats slit and blood being taken to be smeared on the gods, Clint felt it wasn't the first time he was present at that ceremony. He saw himself as

Achi, naked to the waist, joining the group slitting the throats of the ritual animals and cleaning them. As he watched, the scene changed, and he saw Achi as an older man wearing a nice shirt with a joji wrapped around his waist, reluctant to participate.

Achi walked away during that part of the ceremony to another gathering of men near a bonfire. All the household gods were flung into the fire to be consumed. The onlookers around the bonfire, unlike at the ritual Clint participated in, cheerfully sang a religious song from an Igbo hymnal, which all held open, to the tune of Onward Christian Soldiers. He saw Achi standing there, his Bible open, reading a passage that prohibited the worship of idols.

The image faded. Clint was back among the families in front of the Ibom Awada, talking and laughing and being questioned about his life in the U.S. and whether they had a comparable festival. He thought of Thanksgiving but decided not to mention it. How could he explain to them about the Pilgrims and Indians? Would it even make sense to them?

Conflicted, he wondered why the two images were juxtaposed in his mind. He longed to find out what happened in the interim. Why did they burn the household gods? Who ordered that? Would he be able to find a date when those events took place?

He needed to find out. Perhaps his grandfather was the one to ask. He couldn't ask Esther, because he felt her disapproval of his activities during the Ikeji period. Whenever he came in from one of those outings, she shook her head.

CHAPTER THIRTEEN

S ituated as the house was on the main road to Ugwuakuma, Clint woke at eight o'clock in the morning on the third day of Ikeji to the beating of a gong and the chiming of bells. The heat in his bedroom was unbearable, and no breeze stirred through the open windows. He dressed hastily and rushed outside.

There, he saw several men dressed in their best joji wrappers with bells around their waists. Some carried gongs, which they beat. Many had baskets of old, dried yam on their heads. He was told they were direct descendants of the original founders of the place.

"Umu Otusi kwenu! Otusi's children, greetings!" someone called from the crowd.

The call was answered with shouts of "Ayooo!" from those in the procession.

Clint asked an elderly man next to him in the crowd of twenty onlookers what was happening.

The man didn't want to be bothered, so he said curtly, "Those men are the children of Otusi. On this day, each kindred head is required to trace his genealogy at the Aro Awada. If he can trace it to the original founders of the town, then his social position is established.

"If you're the head of the Otusi family, you have to prove you're the living descendant of Otusi. Each kindred head is required to prove who he represents. After the ceremony at the Awada, those family heads will lead the holy spirit of the Aros, called Nwaekpe, back to the villages' Awadas."

Clint's natural curiosity was aroused, and he craved more detail, but the informant moved on with other onlookers.

Clint began walking toward Esther's house, but he decided to turn toward the village square to talk to Uche, a cousin he shared the ritual food with during the rearrangement of the gods at the Ibom Awada. The square was unusually crowded, as many people came to watch the parade. He had to fight his way through, pushing and shoving, to the shoe repair stall near the square, where he knew he could find his cousin plying his trade.

When Uche saw him, he waved Clint over. "I didn't expect to see you wasting your time in this fashion. There's nothing to see but a bunch of people parading."

"I'm enjoying it. After all, there's nothing like this where we live." They shook hands.

"What brings you to my stall?" Uche asked. "Do you need your shoes repaired? They look good to me."

"Uncle tell me about Nwaekpe. Will I see it being brought back to the village in the evening?"

Uche, busy applying paste to a heel to put it back onto the shoe, looked up in confusion. The crowd that stood around them held its breath.

Uche looked at Clint, several thoughts passing through his mind. Clint always asked difficult questions. Nobody in his life had ever questioned the presence of the Nwaekpe. It was always assumed that it would be brought back to the village when the head of the clan returned from Ugwuakuma.

Here stood a young man, born in America, wanting to see what was brought back without realizing that it was spirit, not something tangible. He toyed with his loincloth to allay his anxiety.

After a pause to collect his thoughts for a suitable answer, he turned to face Clint. "As a stranger, you won't be allowed to see it." A collective sigh of relief rose from those around them.

Clint looked at them, wondering if they approved of Uche's answer, since no one contradicted it. That wasn't normal in a discussion, because everyone claimed to be an expert on everything.

"I understand," Clint said. "Uncle, what should I expect to happen in the next few days?"

"In the next three days, the kindred heads will visit all the other Awadas in turn to perform sacrifices on those altars. The next big celebration will be on the eighth day, when the two big markets in Amanagwu and Obinkita are formally allowed to open. On that day, traditionally known as Rice Day, people come from all over the area to buy and sell. Husbands and wives are expected to spend their year's savings to purchase everything they need for the celebration. You can say it's our Christmas."

Pausing after such a long speech, he cleared his throat. Clint waited for more.

Lifting his eyes from the workbench, Uche glanced at Clint before adding, "Husbands on that day are expected to buy gifts, especially new clothes for their families. The household gods are offered gin at the family altars." A spasm of coughing forced him to stop speaking.

"Tell me more," Clint said, raking the crowd with his eyes.

Uche took a deep breath. "It's a traditional day of rejoicing and tributes to the ancestors. On returning from the market, each wife is expected to prepare a sumptuous feast for her family." As an afterthought, he added, "It's also the day when wives learn what their status is within the family unit."

The onlookers laughed and giggled.

"If the husband fails to present a gift, that's an indication there's a problem in the marriage."

Clint and his cousin laughed loudly, attracting attention from more passersby, who stopped to share the fun.

"I'm just telling my brother here of Nkwo Nzukoro, because I want him to make sure when he marries, he saves for a big gift to give his wife and family on that day." He laughed again.

"White people don't observe that," someone said in Igbo. "He'll save his money for Christmas."

"Uncle, what recourse does the wife so treated have?" Clint asked. "She can lodge a complaint with the family elders or ask her family to investigate the transgression," a wag from the crowd shouted in Igbo.

"She may," Uche said, "but how many of such complaints are investigated?"

"They aren't, because you men are in control!" a woman called.

Not wanting to start a fight, Clint changed the subject. "When are the new yams eaten?"

A murmur of irritation arose in the crowd.

"Young Man, you're too inquisitive," someone said.

Rather than ignore the question, Uche addressed it. "On the ninth day of Ikeji, sacrifices are made to all the gods to permit the new yam to be eaten. Until the sacrifices on that day, nobody is permitted to eat the new yam."

Feeling he outstayed his welcome and needing to breathe after being squashed in the crowd for so long, Clint stood and prepared to leave. "Uncle, I know I have many more questions to ask, but they'll keep for another day. I've already prevented you from working, so I must go. I have one last question. Which day will the Nwaekpe leave the villages?"

"That's simple. We send him back on the fifteenth day."

By then, Clint felt swamped by the ragtag crowd listening to the exchange. As he stood from the bench and walked home, a large entourage of children followed, asking for money and gifts.

Dripping with sweat, he tried to ignore them, because his grandfather warned him that talking to the children would encourage them to follow him and continue their harassment. Since his arrival, he always attracted such a crowd whenever he stepped outside the house. He hoped by then that his presence would cease being a novelty, and he could move freely without drawing attention to himself.

As soon as Clint could, he went to Igwe's house to find some explanation for some of the things he witnessed. As usual, Igwe sat in his parlor, listening to news on the radio, when Clint arrived.

After the initial greetings, Clint came to the point. "Grandpa, tell me about the Amadis or the sons of the soil. Do they have any specific privileges?"

"Young Man, you always ask questions no one else dares to ask." Igwe laughed and shook his head.

Clint smiled, because those words echoed his uncle's statement. "If your mother married someone from that class," Igwe said, "you would've been classified as Amadi, and you'd be parading with them today, if you wished. We sons of slaves try to keep away from their festivities." He paused to scratch his head. "Seriously, nowadays I see no advantage to being Amadi. Without education or money, being Amadi means nothing. I stay here and laugh at all that prancing about." He smiled broadly.

"I understand that in some Igbo areas, a descendant of slaves can't marry into the family of those regarded as sons of the soil," Clint said. "It used to be so here, too. However, as I told you before, my grandfather married into the Amadi family, but that was an exception. It nonetheless didn't make us, his descendants, Amadi." "Tell me about it."

"For some time, he thought of marriage but wasn't able to find a woman who would fit into his lifestyle. Until then, he was busy traveling to Calabar to buy materials, then come home to dispose of them as quickly as he could. His money room had lots of cowries, manilas, and rods, which he acquired from his trading. All his contemporaries were marrying, and he needed a son.

"He saw a girl he liked, but she came from a different class. He decided to approach his master to seek his advice. He presented Igwe with the traditional gift of palm wine and seven kola nuts, since what he wanted to ask was very delicate.

"He told Igwe he saw a girl who could be his wife, but there was a problem. Igwe listened carefully to what Achi said and wished it were one of his own daughters, in which case, he would readily agree, since he respected and loved Achi as a son. Although Achi was now free and a wealthy man, his slave status could pose a problem in certain quarters. Nonetheless, he agreed to approach Nwosu on Achi's behalf, although he wasn't hopeful about the outcome. He assumed the man would want his daughter to marry into the Amadi class."

Waiting to hear back from Igwe was agony for Achi. It took almost a full moon before he got the answer he wanted. Igwe must have presented him as a person worthy of the daughter's hand, who, because of an accident of history, found himself in a lower social class despite the fact that he rose above even those in classes higher than his own.

"'I told him he couldn't find a better husband than you for his daughter,' Igwe had said. 'I made it clear you're like a son to me, and he should give his daughter to you. Congratulations. We need to proceed quickly with the arrangements.'

"Shortly after the marriage was negotiated, Mboro entered the traditional fattening room for betrothed girls due to come out at that year's Ikeji. The room, which was located within each compound, was a rest house for the girls prior to undertaking the arduous task of marriage. Throughout a period of four to six months, large platters of food were brought for their consumption.

"Pampered, with their bodies washed daily and rubbed with oil and cam wood paste, they weren't allowed to undertake any physical activity. It was the only time in a girl's life that she was expected to do nothing but rest. Isolated in that room, the girls were instructed by elderly family members on what to expect from marriage and their position within the marital household.

"The time of waiting for Ikeji, when Mboro would come out as his bride, was the longest year of Achi's life. He spent the time in an anteroom of his little house, a place where he could have visitors. The house, situated at the entrance to the chief's compound opposite the chief's imposing dwelling, was simply furnished. There was the bed, which he commissioned a carpenter to make shortly after the proposal was accepted, and to that, he added a table.

"Each market day, Achi sent bundles of yam, stockfish, and a bottle of palm oil to Mboro's mother, as his contribution to her upkeep in the fattening room.

"At that year's Ikeji, on the day the brides came out to the Amaikpe Arena to be presented to the public, Achi's bride was there, dressed in several jojis and wearing ivory and coral necklaces. Her legs were covered in ivory bands, as befitted the daughter of a chief. He saw the beautiful body designs on her arms, thighs, and stomach. In his mind, she was the most-beautiful bride of the year. When she was finally brought to his house, his happiness knew no end."

For a moment, Clint, who'd been listening intently as Igwe talked about Achi's marriage thought. That was the outcome I wished for

regarding my high-school prom.

Looking at Igwe, he said, "Theirs really was a love story. It must have taken courage for him to approach the chief with the request."

"Yes, I presume so. He had no expectation when he went to Chief Igwe. As expected, the chief's reaction when Achi said he was ready for marriage was typical. If you came to me today and said you were thinking of getting married, I'd say, 'Good. We should start looking for a suitable wife.' Arranged marriage is the norm. None of this nonsense about waiting to fall in love."

"The chief must've thought highly of him to agree to intercede for him with the other members of his social group."

"Yes. Though he was a slave, his master held him in very high esteem."

"What a story. Thank you for telling me. I thought intra-class marriage was like the British class system, where an impoverished lord can marry a rich merchant's daughter to replenish his coffers and save the family castle."

Igwe laughed so hard he cried. "Do you see any castles here that need to be saved from ruin? Of course an impoverished Amadi can have his daughter married to a lower social class with money, but that doesn't usually translate into wealth for the girl's family. His new in- laws would give the wife's father gifts, but to help him rebuild his house doesn't necessarily follow. If that were true, Chief Igwe's family, who lives opposite your uncle in my father's compound, would be rolling in wealth. That rundown eyesore of a house would be rebuilt. Some of their daughters married men who hold

responsible positions in civil service and industry."

"By the way, Grandpa, did your grandfather's social situation change with the marriage?"

"That was his wish. Because of his marriage to Mboro, his social superior, coupled with his success in trading, Achi hoped his status would change, and he would gain respect within the compound, but that proved elusive. He was often taunted by the Amadis, who found themselves at a disadvantage in their dealings with him. He was conscious of the jealousy and disrespect he received at the hands of Igwe's family.

"Igwe's eldest son always taunted Achi at every opportunity. 'This slave thinks he's someone simply because he has a roomful of money!' he often shouted. Achi tried to ignore the biting words as he walked toward his house.

"The taunting continued. 'Slave, you couldn't buy your way into the highest social class even if you married into it.' His friends often urged Achi to ignore the man.

"The man who taunted him was a thorn in Achi's flesh since the chief brought Achi into the family. He always tried to pick fights with Achi, carried tales to the chief about him, and accused him of all kinds of transgressions whenever he thought he could. As the chief's natural son, he resented the chief's partiality toward Achi and blamed him for his failures.

"At first, Achi tried to be friendly, defending the son when he was attacked by others in his age group and often fighting them off. All his friendly overtures were rebuffed. The master's son eventually sought a public fight to demonstrate who had the real power.

"Achi told us once that he said, 'Nna. I never doubted I'm a slave, but in my house, I'm not. Unless you have something very important to say to me, get out of my way, so I can enter my house.'

Clint remembered the feelings he had toward the old man he met when he visited his uncle. Does that man resent the success of a

slave family? he wondered. Was that why I felt uneasy with him?

Dismissing the thought and knowing his grandfather was in the mood to answer questions, he asked, "Is there a difference in educational achievement between the classes?"

Igwe explained that initially only slaves sent their sons to Christian schools after they were established. The Amadis viewed Christianity as dangerous to their power and refused to participate. Eventually, they came to accept the importance of education and its financial rewards. Participation still depended on one's financial standing, since education wasn't free.

During a short silence, Igwe cleared his throat and asked, "Why bother with the Amadis? Who cares about them? They're just holding onto the past. They can all die for all I care. The Ikeji celebration needs to be modernized." He waggled his fingers at Clint.

"If I were you, I'd stay out of them." His serious tone surprised Clint.

"Wait until the last day and go to Amaikpe to enjoy the traditional dances and festivities." He cocked his head and finally voiced something that had been troubling him. "Clint, I have to say there are some ceremonies I really don't want you to attend."

Clint, taken aback, raised his eyebrows and stared at his grandfather, challenging him to explain.

Igwe returned the gaze with troubled eyes. "Tomorrow is the day when the Aro people are expected to make sacrifices of goats and sheep to their family gods and ancestors. As a Christian family, we try not to participate in that ritual, as well as the following day, when the blood from those animals is added to other ingredients, cooked, and eaten."

Clint flippantly said, "It sounds like blood sausage. I presume Grandma won't be making it."

"No. She won't prepare Osuu paste, even if it's a delicacy loved by the Aro people," Igwe said angrily.

"Osuu paste? What's that?"

"Osuu is the root of s special mushroom found in the forests around here. It's a beautiful pink flower and has the flavor of chicken. The root, however, is ground and mixed with the blood and intestines of sacrificial animals."

Enthralled, Clint pushed his chair forward. His grandfather was telling him something important.

"For lack of a better name, we call it Osuu paste. This mixture is cooked and eaten. The Aro Christians have argued they should be allowed to eat Osuu paste with blood drawn from animals not offered as sacrifices to family gods in the Awadis at Ikeji, but no one seems to have paid attention. I presume it's not the same, since Osuu is associated with the sacrifice to the ancestors at Awada."

As Clint listened, he couldn't understand the disagreement. He watched the ritual ceremony and didn't see how anyone was affected except the animals, and they would have been slaughtered whether a sacrificial rite was involved or not. It was a tradition similar to the ritual of the bread and wine during Holy Communion.

But was it? Probably not, he had to admit. The bread and wine in the Holy Communion represented the body and blood of Christ, whereas in the Awada rituals, the blood was symbolically offered to the family gods. How could his grandfather justify pouring a libation to the ancestors during the kola nut ceremony and not see the other ceremony in the same light?

Clint wasn't a theologian. In fact, he enjoyed the roasted goat and chicken meat and felt it was probably the only time when poor members of the family or compound could enjoy meat, which was very expensive. He was sure other Christians, not as rigid as his grandparents, were happily indulging with Osuu paste without caring about the associated ritual.

He looked forward to trying Osuu paste. His only concern was whether it would make him sick. So far, he'd been spared any stomach problems, because he was careful what he ate.

Having reached the conclusion, he decided to ignore his grandfather's warning.

CHAPTER FOURTEEN

The Ikeji days flew past. Clint cheered his maternal compound team when the Ibom wrestlers rolled out the drums at the square, and twelve teams of young men competed to see who was strongest. In the olden days, that was the day when parents identified the men capable of defending their households as husbands for their daughters.

Fascinated by the wrestlers who circled each other, Clint admired the fluidity of movements of their hands and feet. Oblivious to the scent of the many bodies massed together and the dust the wrestlers kicked up, Clint listened to the crowd shouting encouragement to favorites. He'd never seen a wrestling match before, and it was a novel experience.

If the contest had been in the U.S., there would be judges or umpires to enforce the rules. In Nigeria there were no discernible judges, only the wrestlers and the crowd. There didn't seem to be any rules or points, either.

When Clint asked, he learned that the candidates were selfselected and could issue a challenge only to members of their own age group. Spectators shouted encouragement to their favorites. When a wrestler finally succeeded in dominating his opponent and sending him to the floor, some spectators rushed up to paste naira bills to his forehead. The defeated wrestler left the arena, and a new pair came in.

He watched, trying to envision Achi among the wrestlers fielded by the Amanagwu village, his taut sinews straining to find a weak spot on his opponent's body that would give him an advantage. The image faded, and he wondered if his grandfather ever participated in the sport as a young man. He knew so little about his father's or grandfather's lives in the village. Peter never discussed his life before he went to university. Perhaps after Clint's visit to Nigeria, he would better understand his father's life.

It was a hot, humid day. As sweat trickled down his back, he wondered how the men in the arena felt. He saw them sweating profusely. The colors of the paintings on their chests and faces ran together, and he wondered how it felt to try to grab an opponent only to find him too slippery to hold. How would it feel to know he slithered away?

The people shouting and clapping in the crowd appeared indifferent to the humidity. Clint wondered if he, too, would eventually become accustomed to the pulsating, humid heat.

As dark fell, Clint celebrated at the bar with the winning team.

He looked forward to the thirteenth day of Ikeji, when everyone went to the Amaikpe square to celebrate. Walking eastward, he went to his grandfather's house to ask him about what to expect during the rest of the Ikeji celebration. He saw the outline of the Cameroon Mountain range and the clouds at the peaks, foretelling rain later that evening. He passed several women and children walking barefoot with no fear of ants, thorns, or broken glass. Some, returning from the nearby stream, carried heavy earthen pots.

On the spur of the moment, he went down the path to look at the stream. Groups of naked children splashed around before filling containers with water to take home. Clothes hung on the stream banks, and he surmised some people came to the stream to do laundry. He wondered if his mother had visited the stream while growing up, before her parents moved to the house Esther occupied. Had she horsed around like the children he saw, then later balanced a pot on her head, as she walked home to her paternal compound?

He was told each village had a stream nearby where people could collect water for drinking and everyday use, and all the streams eventually emptied into the Cross River. He wondered how many of his friends knew where their water came from. In the U.S., people took water for granted. When they turned the tap, water came out.

In Nigeria, life wasn't that easy.

One thing I've learned since coming here is not to take things for granted, he thought. These children have to work hard to get those things I have always taken for granted.

After lingering for some time, watching the children trying to impress him with their antics, he walked back down the path to the main road to continue toward Igwe's house in the new extension.

At the junction where the path led to the market, he met Ngwu, one of his cousins, on his way to the government station. Clint was glad for the company. Ngwu, ten years older, pointed out the various new developments they saw. They saw many half-finished houses along the road from the market.

"The owners ran out of money," Ngwu explained, wiping his brow. "They live in London. They only continue building when they visit."

"Why can't they contract out the construction? That's how it's done in America." Clint panted, as they went up an incline, working hard to keep pace.

Ngwu slowed for him. "That would be foolish, since the so-called contractors would just take the money, and the houses would never be finished."

"Wouldn't it be easier to get a mortgage from a bank and have enough funds to complete the building rapidly? It would make things easy. They could repay the money at a convenient pace."

"That may be so, but which bank?" Ngwu looked at Clint as if he came from outer space. "We have only small banks here in Aro.

Besides, banks generally don't lend money for houses in rural areas like Aro Chukwu, where the ownership of the land is uncertain, and people have no proven means of payment. Even in townships like Aba or Umuahia, the banks have difficulty collecting debts."

"If that's the case, I can see why the banks won't lend. Perhaps I'm wrong. I assumed banks operated the same way as in the U.S. It seems the owners must wait a long time before living in those houses."

"You're right. Some die before completing them." Ngwu laughed. Clint shook his head. In the area where his grandfather lived, most of the building were occupied only two weeks out of the year. He wondered how long it took the people to complete the houses, only to live there a few days each year. At least in his grandfather's case, Clint understood that the house had been built for him to live in after he retired.

At a fork in the road, Ngwu halted and pointed to a building on their right. "Have you been to Goldie, where I'm going? It used to be a Presbyterian mission training center, but I understand they're thinking of converting it to a university."

"I've been there. It's a beautiful, well-kept place. I particularly liked the landscaping. I saw only the outside and didn't enter any of the rooms. Someone mentioned it was being converted to a university. Thank you for walking with me."

As they parted company, Clint continued to his grandfather's house. Once there, he waved off an offer of a snack. He was tired of chin chin, the preferred snack, in addition to kola and bitter nuts. His grandfather was on his way out to conduct business in the village, but he invited Clint to tag along.

The rough dirt road outside the estate, covered in some parts with rocks, made driving difficult. The driver tried to avoid broken glass and debris strewn everywhere, as well as potholes in the road. Clint saw old discarded bottles, plastic cups, wrappings, old mattresses, and other household items their owners abandoned.

Oblivious to the surroundings, Igwe said, "This car runs fine now, since the driver went to Ohafia for a new carburetor. If you came yesterday, you would've found all of us at home. Today, my wife went out, because a friend of hers came to collect her. It's funny. I have three cars, but only this one's safe to drive. Our cars break down due to the state of the roads. That's what we all suffer from. In America, you all have good roads."

He stopped rambling to blow his nose noisily into a handkerchief. "Grandpa, why do you all build such big houses in places where there are no streets?" He stared at the debris on both sides of the road. "It's where we can get land. Aren't we driving on a road now? It's just that the local authorities don't have the money to bring the roads up to standard." He stopped and let Clint absorb the new information. "You know, Clint, it was only recently that our town was designated urban. Most of the houses, including mine, were built without permits."

The car swayed, as the driver attempted to avoid a large hole in the road.

Igwe steadied himself. "Although we're now an urban area, there's no town planning department. We don't have urban amenities. We're still required to provide our own water supply and dispose of our own waste. Even though we have electricity, we have to buy generators to ensure a power supply, but at least we're comfortable within our own houses."

"Do you pay local taxes here? If you do, one would expect the local government to use that money for road maintenance. I know I shouldn't expect the same standard as in the U.S., because the local government here doesn't have the same resources, but I still wonder what services the government provides."

Igwe took some time before answering. "We pay poll tax based on the size of our houses to the local government. The state government also allocates resources to it for use in providing certain services, such as payment of civil services and maintenance of government buildings, to name a few.

Unfortunately, due to incompetence, the money collected isn't often used as intended.

"Take this road, for instance. The local government is responsible for its maintenance, but if you ask, they'll tell you there's no money."

"Why couldn't they use all the underemployed youth hanging around the villages to at least pick up the trash and fill in the potholes? If you gave the young people work cleaning the roads of trash, they'd be part of something and would learn useful skills, too. Look at that rusty old fridge and carburetor left beside the road.

Those must've been dropped by rich men who didn't know where to dispose of unwanted items. If, as we discussed before, the local government set aside an area for waste disposal, dumping such things along the road would be unconscionable."

"Don't tell me that in America you don't have people who dump things where they shouldn't?" Igwe became irritated.

"There are, but those are the exceptions." Clint was determined to have his say and didn't care if he gave offense.

As the car turned onto the main road to Amanagwu, Clint calmed and turned to his grandfather again. "Did each family in the old days keep their household gods in Awadas? Once when I visited a friend who was a Buddhist, I saw a figure of Buddha in one room where they occasionally went to worship. Was it the same here?"

"A long time ago, when Awadas were common, we did, but when we converted to Christianity, we regarded such activities as heathen worship. Until the 1940s, converts to Christianity were required to burn all their family idols in a big bonfire."

Clint felt that explained one of his visions. "Really? What a shame the missionaries made you destroy all those precious artifacts."

"They're idols!" Igwe replied sharply. "We're better off without them."

When they reached their destination, Okoro greeted them and was excited to see Clint. "I haven't seen you recently. Come in."

Clint followed his grandfather into the house and sat down, then accepted an offer of beer. It was the first time he'd been together with Igwe and Okoro in that house.

Igwe, recovering his mood after sipping some beer, turned to Clint. "Tomorrow is Eke Ekpe. I'll come with the driver to take you and Esther to Amaikpe to witness the festivities. Tell her I'll be there about ten o'clock. I hope she wants to go. I know how hard it's been for her without her husband, who meant everything to her. I, too, miss my first wife."

"Talking of Eke Ekpe reminds me of the trials and tribulations suffered by our grandfather in the early years of his marriage," Okoro said.

"I remember," Igwe said. "That experience was the reason why, to this day, as I told Clint recently, we should be grateful Christianity came to Aro Chukwu, and we have a lot of be grateful for in this family."

"Tell me what happened," Clint said. "I want to know everything about your grandfather."

"Okoro, you tell him. I'm tired of talking about Achi. He should hear the story from another mouth."

"I don't know how it is in your country, but here in Aro Chukwu," Okoro said slowly, "we want to start a family immediately. Achi was no exception. Early in his marriage, his wife had many miscarriages. On that particular Ikeji, she was almost due, and he was very hopeful."

"Get on with the story," Igwe said impatiently. "We don't have all day."

"I'm coming to it." Okoro ignored Igwe's caustic remark. "On that particular Eke Ekpe, Achi, as you'll do tomorrow, watched his wife among the dancers. Suddenly, she fell down. His heart racing, he pushed the crowd aside in an attempt to reach her. Before he could, those nearby lifted her and carried her along the dusty, ochrecolored path to her mother's house in the nearby compound. He followed and saw her taken inside.

He was restrained from entering. The father already called the priest to offer sacrifices for her wellbeing."

"Those village priests," Igwe interrupted angrily, "what do they know? They probably asked for an offering to the household gods."

"Nnam, if you don't want me to tell the story, tell it yourself. Stop interrupting." Okoro turned to Clint again. "Since it was Ikeji, Achi couldn't get hold of any of the sacrificial items immediately. His father-in-law, Nwosu, offered them instead. The priest offered the libation, and, after invoking the ancestors, he gave his verdict.

"'The child has refused to come out,' he said. 'Where is the husband? We must offer a goat for sacrifice. Where is the husband? Ask him to immediately bring a goat and bottle of schnapps for libation to the ancestors.'"

"I can just imagine him salivating at the thought of goat meat," Igwe muttered.

Okoro eyed Clint. "Ignore him. This is what happened. Achi ran knocking at the doors of traders in an attempt to gather what was required. Most people were at the festivities, and it took some time to find a trader willing to sell what he wanted, but he eventually succeeded. He gave what he bought to his father-in-law, who handed over the items as gifts to the household gods, so his daughter would be saved.

"Shortly after the sacrifices, the midwife came out and said, 'It's a girl, but she was born dead.'

"'Another dead child!' Achi cried, smiting his breast. He hoped one might live. He felt he was cursed and blamed the woman who lived in a house behind theirs, with whom Mboro had an altercation.

"Concerned for his wife, he asked if the midwife told her the news. The midwife felt that in her weakened condition, the information should be without until after the burial. In his confusion, Achi wept like a woman.

"He had to make arrangements for disposition of the dead, because tradition required it be done immediately. With his father-inlaw's permission, the baby was buried under the eaves of Mboro's grandmother's house. He had to break the news to his wife, who stayed with her family until she was fit to travel home. That's the story we remember every Eke Ekpe." He looked up at Clint.

Clint felt saddened. "She must've had other children, or you wouldn't be here."

"True," Igwe said, chafing to leave. "I have other business to conduct in the compound. My driver will take you home. Don't forget to give Esther my message."

———ⱨɱ———

"Grandma, did you get the message I left saying I was walking up to Grandpa's house for a visit?" Clint asked, entering the parlor.

Until then, Esther had been ruminating about her family and her concerns about Clint. Sitting alone in the parlor, she thought of her husband, with whom she hoped to spend her old age. He died suddenly of a heart attack several years earlier.

It galled her that Peace, her only daughter, hadn't returned for the funeral, citing financial problems. True, Peace sent money through Western Union to cover her portion of the funeral costs, but Esther felt Peace's presence would have been comforting. Esther didn't understand her excuse, given that Peace was a doctor, while her husband was a lawyer. Why couldn't she spare the cash for airfare and the time to come to make sure her father had his entire family together to see him off on his great journey to the beyond? That kind of reasoning was beyond her.

Clint's arrival interrupted her reverie. Composing herself, she said sweetly, "Yes, Dear. I got it."

Once Clint sat down, she said, "I was disappointed when Peace didn't come home for her father's funeral. It was most unusual. I'm glad they sent you to stay with me. That compensated for her not coming when her father died."

Clint recalled the many times his mother mentioned her regret at not coming back for her father's funeral. When he pressed her to explain, she always said, if faced with the same situation again, she wouldn't have gone. It was a choice between maxing out their credit cards or foregoing sending Sarah to private school. They agreed early in their marriage to live within their means, and maxing their credit cards for airline tickets was unthinkable. They would rather send the small amount of money they had as their contribution.

"I remember my parents agonizing over the decision not to come," Clint said. "They truly didn't have the money. I was just admitted to university, and they had to make sure there were enough funds for that year. It wasn't easy for them, because Sarah was also entering a private school. As I understand it, they sent money to help defray the burial costs."

"It was long after the burial that I learned that Peter and Peace were strapped for cash at that time due to your college education," she snapped. "Surely you could have secured a scholarship. You appear to be a clever young man. In Nigeria, you would. What you're saying is the same reason your father gave for not employing a full- time maid when I came after Sarah was born.

"No one believes that a lawyer and doctor lack enough money for their father's burial. I'm sure your father prevented Peace from discharging her obligations. Any other husband would've understood the importance of Peace, as my daughter, being here at that time. She could have come alone. That wouldn't have cost as much. I told her to keep her money separate and use it as she wishes."

Irritated by her words, yet knowing the topic had been preying on Esther's mind for some time, he said gently, "Grandma, you really don't understand. My mother has an equal say in their marriage, and they make decisions together.

"I just want to say in their defense that even though salaries are high in the U.S., so are expenses. My parents have no help, because it costs a lot for such help. A driver, for example, would cost twothirds of Mom's earnings. They have to pay the mortgage on their house, pay state and federal taxes, pay for my and Sarah's education, and the upkeep of the house, among other things. In the end, they have very little savings."

Esther wasn't listening. Since Clint came, she had very little to do with her no-good daughter-in-law, who thought the world revolved around her. Why did her last-born son marry that Aba woman, who was a thorn in Esther's side since she arrived? At least Clint's visit made the problem tolerable.

"That's all right, Clint. I don't expect you to understand. However, if I may say so, it wasn't the money but the comfort of her presence we craved. I'm very glad you're here. It was a great day for me when your mother called to say you'd be staying with me. You're a great comfort, even though you've done some things I don't like during this festival. I'm sure Mazi Igwe must've said the same. I wish sometimes you'd accompany me to visit my friends instead of gallivanting all over the place, eating heathen food."

Esther expected him to stay with her, go visiting with her, and be introduced to all her friends and cronies. She planned to explain he finished college and was doing research during his gap year before entering law school.

During the first fortnight of his visit, Clint was happy to indulge her, but, as the days lengthened, he became extremely reluctant to accompany her to the market or to church. He took to hanging around with undesirables, in her view, in the village square or in bars. She felt she had no control over him. She was particularly irked by the fact that Igwe encouraged Clint to go to places like the slave museum, where she, as a Christian, wouldn't go.

Clint's behavior grew worse with the onset of Ikeji. She was sure he'd been taking part in rituals and eating the ritualized meat. She tried to stop him, but she couldn't. She was glad his parents chose her house over Igwe's, though Mazi Igwe's house was more sumptuous and would have been more comfortable. She wondered how Peace convinced her husband to let Clint stay in her house.

She couldn't put restraints on Clint for fear he'd move to Igwe's house with his awful second wife. How could Igwe bear to stay in the same house with that woman, who looked as if she fought against the whole world? She never smiled, and she always dressed as if she were going to church. She wouldn't even come out when Igwe's visitors were his dead wife's friends.

What was wrong with her to be so jealous of a dead woman? She wondered about the woman's reaction to Clint. It was obvious Clint didn't want to tell her anything except that tidbit about her sister being ill. Esther would have dearly loved to ask him what happened in his many visits to Igwe's palace, but she refrained, because she didn't want to pry. Nevertheless, she feared for Clint's safety. That woman could easily slip poison into the food she served him.

When Clint spoke, Esther was still lost in thought. "Grandpa said to tell you he'll be here tomorrow to take both of us to Amaikpe to watch the celebrations. Is that all right?"

"Oh. In that case, I'd better find suitable clothing for you." She pursed her lips and tutted. "You can't go dressed in your jeans and a shirt, as you've been doing. Everyone will be very fashionable, including the men, and they'll wonder where you're from. I know Americans don't care about their appearance, but you're our son, even though you were born in America."

She shook her head in disgust. "Chief Igwe should've thought of that when he planned to take you to the celebrations." A painful thought crossed her mind, but she recovered quickly. "Let's see. I kept all my husband's jojis and traditional shirts, so let's look in the trunk for something suitable for you." She turned to him. "Do you have any sandals with you? I've seen you only in tennis shoes."

Clint followed her to the bedroom without answering. Several trunks were piled on one side of the room. The room was dark, with very little light coming through the drawn blinds. Without any outside air coming in, it smelled musty. He helped Esther lift down some of the trunks until she found the one she wanted.

"Grandma, what's that smell?" he asked, as she opened the trunk. "That's camphor. We use it to prevent mildew and moths."

Inside were several quarter-length-sleeved shirts with various lion or leopard images on different backgrounds. Esther picked one up and handed it to Clint to try on over his clothes.

It fit snuggly, making her smile. She found a matching joji in another trunk. To complete the outfit, she scrambled inside a small box hidden in another trunk and took out a long coral bead necklace.

Tired from her exertions, she welcomed Clint's suggestion that she sit down on the bed while he restacked the trunks and found a place to air out the clothes and remove the camphor smell.

CHAPTER FIFTEEN

On the morning of the appointed day, Esther helped Clint tie his wrapper in the traditional way. He opted to tie it over his khaki shorts. To complete the outfit, he wore the traditional woolen cap with one feather.

He examined himself in the mirror. The shirt was long enough to reach his butt.

Esther, staring at him, said casually, "My husband, your grandfather, was shorter than you, but this shirt fits you very well."

"No one will think I wasn't born to this. I look like all the other Aro men."

"You are, Clint," she said with pride. "Don't ever forget it. I wish your grandfather were alive to see you like this. It would give him great pleasure."

———⚂———

When Igwe arrived, only Clint joined him. Esther declined, using the heat and the crowd as her excuse. Igwe stared at Clint in his outfit.

"My heart swells with pride to see you dressed like us," Igwe said. "No one will believe this is the first time you've worn such clothes. We must take a photograph to send to your parents."

"These are my grandfather's clothes," Clint said self-consciously. "Grandmother Esther insisted I wear them to avoid calling attention to myself today."

"That was a good decision. I'll make sure to tell her." He patted Clint's back.

The car inched its way toward Obinkita. The road was packed with cars, motorcycles, and people bound for the same destination. The drive usually took fifteen minutes, but that day, it took forty-five. When they were almost there, it became apparent parking would be difficult.

Igwe angrily ordered the driver to let them out to walk the last 200 yards and instructed him to return at a specific time.

"I don't intend to stay more than an hour," he said. "I just want to show my face, since there will be many people from abroad I know and who I want to invite to the house tonight. Clint, you can stay as long as you wish."

Walking forward with the crowd, Igwe turned to Clint and shouted, "When I was growing up, the highlight of today was the coming out of the brides from the fattening rooms."

Amaikpe, where most of the important events in Aro Chukwu took place, was packed with people. The Omu Aro, the Aro coat of arms, and various buntings decorated the square. The sky was cloudless, and the sun's rays were relentless without any shade. The Eze of Aro, flanked by Eze Ibom Isii and Eze Agwu, sat on a dais. Behind them were rows of seat for all the prominent people present, including representatives of Aro unions, both in Nigeria and abroad. It was a venue for each village to present traditional dances and other important cultural activities.

Sitting beside his grandfather two rows from the dais, Clint was amazed at the turnout. Thousands of people were in the square, all similarly attired in traditional jojis, with some of the men carrying the traditional multicolored fans common in northern Nigeria.

While the speeches were being made, Clint wiped sweat from his neck and whispered to his grandfather, "Is it always like this?"

"No. Prayers and speeches were introduced after the civil war. This celebration is now financed by the Aro people abroad who wanted to ensure its continuity. Before, it was the time when brides from the fattening rooms were presented and taken to their husbands. That was the main attraction in those days. With education, girls no longer go to the fattening rooms."

"So there'll be no girls today from the fattening rooms?" Clint imagined what it was like in Achi's time, when dance groups from each village performed in assigned spots, and onlookers walked from group-to-group, admiring the dancers. He pictured Achi dressed like some of those men, with a woven cap, making his way toward the assigned spot for his wife's compound, where the showcase was his bride. Clint wished time would roll back, so he could witness the ceremony as his ancestors saw it.

Lost in thought, he started when Igwe said, "It's time to walk around and watch the various groups dance."

As they walked from group-to-group, the rich and prominent among the crowd, tossed naira notes to the dances. Some even joined in the dances. When they reached the Amanagwu group, Igwe jumped in. For five minutes, he performed the traditional dance with the group while his friend tossed naira at him.

The music of the drums resonated with the core of Clint's being. It brought out the dizzying, hallowing, mysterious sounds he heard as a child in his dream. All around were dancers, some with their bodies streaked with yellow or red chalk dotted with white, flashes of light in their eyes, contorting their bodies in response to the drums. Many onlookers urged Clint to join the dance, but he was too shy.

Igwe, breathing hard and sweating profusely, wiped his brow with a damp handkerchief. Panting, he turned to Clint. "You know, in the olden days, the highlight used to be the part when the virgins came from the fattening rooms, dancing and being claimed by their husbands. It was quite a show."

Clint saw the excitement those memories brought to Igwe's eyes. "There's a move by the Aro people of the Diaspora to re-create that part of the ceremony. They're offering substantial sums of money to young girls willing to participate and dance during that part of the festival, but for now, that looks like a big mountain to climb."

Clint had been looking for bridal groups in the crowd. "It would be interesting, Grandpa, to see brides dressed in traditional costumes."

With a twinge of sadness, Igwe said, "My boy, it was quite something. It's part of our tradition that I regret we lost due to education. My grandmother came out on this day during the Ikeji festival, but I ask you, where are the virgins nowadays? It would be hard to find them." In a tired voice, he added, "Clint, look around and stay as long as you wish. I'm tired of the heat. I'll find the driver and head home."

As Clint wandered from group-to-group, he felt weak, sad, and was barely able to stand. Sweating profusely, he wiped away tears trickling down his cheeks. The beating of the drums intensified, as more dancers entered each of the village arenas, determined to make the most of the final hours of the festival. The sun's heat, coupled with the noise, became unbearable.

Feeling dizzy, Clint found a vacant spot on the floor beside some young men and sat. Convulsed with pain and clutching his chest, as tears poured from his eyes, he could hardly move.

When he was finally able to stand, the sun was setting, and the groups of dances were winding down. He stood and wiped his eyes.

Exhausted, he walked home behind the Ibom dance group.

How can I explain what just happened to me? he wondered.

At the Ibom village square, women dancers dispersed to their houses. Clint followed the men into the crowded bars. In the first, he didn't recognize anyone, and the noise was deafening. He left that bar and staggered to the next, where he saw men from Esther's compound who welcomed him.

"We expected you to dance with us," they teased. "Why didn't you?"

Some of them slapped his back.

"We saw your grandfather, Igwe, dancing with the Amanagwu men."

They discussed the day's events, talked about which group fielded the best dance, which women's group was the most colorful, and drank a lot. For the first time, Clint felt he belonged, and he was grateful.

Later, as he walked to Esther's house, he noticed the moon was full, and he could see his own shadow. He felt as if many other shadows chased him—people who were there before he was born. The moon, hanging large and white above the trees, was untroubled. In the U.S., he rarely noticed the moon, but in Nigeria, it seemed particularly bright.

He would always associate the full moon with Ikeji.

—✺—

The sound of many voices woke him the following morning. Through the thin walls, he heard the loud laughter of visitors. Sleep was no longer possible, so he sat up and looked out the window. The sun was up, it rays shimmering on the tin roofs of the houses across the road. There was no indication of the rain from the previous night.

On the road, he saw the usual coming and going of villagers to or from farms, the stream, or the market. His body registered the heat. Stepping out of the mosquito net, he shrugged off his singlet and pulled on his shorts, preparing to face the world. Gathering his clothes and toiletries, he emerged from the room to be confronted by a parlor full of people.

"Hello, Clint," Chima said. "We thought we'd have to leave without seeing you. It's almost ten o'clock."

Clint stared, trying to remember him. Finally, he realized it was his cousin who met his plane at the Owerri airport when he arrived. The last time he saw Chima, he wore shorts, but now he was in a white lace abada and matching cap. Clint saw eight men and six women in the room, eating and drinking from platters of moyi moyi, akara balls, fried chicken, jollof rice, bowls of chin chin, and drinking from bottles of Fanta, beer, and Coca-Cola.

The relatives must have arrived overnight from Owerri, Aba, and Umuahia, where they worked. Unaware of their impending visit, he must have missed them at Amaikpe square.

"I spent the day at Amaikpe," Clint said. "No one told me you were coming for the Ikeji celebration." He moved toward the door leading to the courtyard and backyard, where his pail of water was waiting.

"We were there only briefly," Chima said, "before we went to the new extension for the party at Mazi Uche's house. If we'd seen you, we would've invited you along."

"We came to the house to pick you up," someone added, "but you were still at the square. There must've been fifty of us at Mazi Uche's, and there were folks from Aro Ndizuogu and sons and daughters of Amuvie from abroad."

"Man, you missed a fantastic party," Chima added.

Clint muttered something and slipped away to carry out his ablutions. His relatives continued dissecting the party.

The night before, he came back late from the revelry at the bar with some of the Ibom male dancers and sneaked quietly into the house without waking his grandmother. The servant who opened the door didn't tell him others were in the house. He'd been aware of movement during the night, but he didn't associate that with family members. Finding a crowd in the parlor was quite a surprise.

Clint wasn't a morning person. It usually took him an hour to acknowledge the presence of others first thing in the morning. Since coming to Nigeria, he tried to adjust to early morning visits and chatter. When he reentered the parlor, he was his normal self, anxious to join the party. Many more people arrived in his absence.

Esther was up early, organizing food preparations, and she basked in the praise of those present. She loved entertaining and ordered her servants to replenish platters and drinks. It made her happy once again to have her house full of people. She was glad her close relatives living abroad honored her by visiting during Ikeji.

She bustled across the room, joking with relatives and telling them about Clint. She beamed when he returned to the room.

"I thought by now he would've gotten fed up with me and returned to the U.S. or Lagos, but somehow, he managed to find things to occupy him. The only thing I'm not happy about is his unusual interest in the heathen rituals associated with Ikeji. He seems to enjoy them. Can you believe it? I heard he even tried Osuu paste." She shook her head in disgust.

The others giggled. Clint tried to be inconspicuous.

"Don't laugh," Esther said, waggling her fingers. "When I asked if it was true, he said it tasted good. I'm sure he ate only a little and was being polite." She made a face.

"But Auntie, it's a delicacy, though I, for one, don't like it," Chima said.

"I agree with you," Nkechi, a woman in white blouse said, sipping from her Fanta. "It's an acquired taste that grows on you. Mmmm." She licked her lips.

"Clint, what are your plans?" Chima asked. "Will you be in Aro Chukwu throughout your vacation?"

"I haven't made any plans," he replied. "I still have to explore the different Aro Chukwu villages. I might travel out, but I don't have anything definite yet. I was at Amasu the other day and saw the canoes going to Itu. It might be interesting to be in one, since I understand that Aro traders once went to Itu by canoe along the Cross River."

"Have you heard anything like that?" Esther asked, shaking her head and vigorously clasping and unclasping her hands. "This is the first I've heard of it!"

"Don't worry, Auntie," John, a young man sitting in the corner, said. He was the chief engineer at the Abia State Ministry of Works. "I doubt he could stand the swarms of midges and mosquitoes. Wait until he's eaten alive by the bugs after he leaves Amasu. He'll want to come back immediately." He picked up a napkin to wipe his hands.

"The insects and flies will start sucking his blood as soon as he steps into the canoe at Amasu, I assure you," Flora said, a woman in a green damask wrapper and dangling earrings that swiveled as she spoke. She reached for an akara ball, which she washed down with Fanta.

Esther raised her voice to be heard above the chatter of the others expressing their views on the subject. "I hope Mazi Igwe will join me to dissuade him."

"He'd better carry a lot of insect repellent cream to ward off nasty bites from insects and flies," Flora said. "You, Mama Esther, better make sure he has a big hat to prevent sunstroke." She stood, smoothed her skirt, and walked toward the peanut tray.

"That's true, Mama Esther," added Cecilia, a woman wearing bright-red lipstick. Her plucked eyebrows, outlined with kohl, rose from the bridge of her nose and curved high like the wings of a praying mantis. "When I was in Florida at the beach, I thought my black skin would protect me from sunstroke, as I lay in the sun all day. Man, did I suffer."

Cecilia stood and adjusted her wrap on the way to the door leading to the courtyard. Turning, she whispered to Esther, who sat near the door.

Esther called for a maid to take her to her destination.

"I see Grandma doesn't approve of my intention," Clint said, nonplussed, as he went around the room to shake hands. "I plan to go the old-fashioned way, by canoe. It'll be fun."

Esther was still irritated. "We'll need your parents' permission." "I don't think that's necessary, Grandma."

"Forget all the Oyibo stuff," someone said, waving his hands. "You're still a child, and it would be wrong for your grandmother not to consult your parents. Can you imagine what they would say or how she would feel if anything happened to you?"

Everyone in the room seemed to have an opinion and was ready to express it.

"I suppose you're right," Clint said, "but I'm an adult now, and I'm free to do whatever I wish and bear the consequences." He had no intention of discussing it further.

The place went quiet, with all eyes on him.

An elderly man, introduced earlier as Professor Nduka, broke the silence. "Clint, I hear you're interested in Aro Chukwu history. I presume you know of the Aro Ibibio War, when our forefathers drove the Ibibios away from here. The only remnant of their presence is the name Ibom, our village group, which is on the site of the Ibibio villages. We've been settled in this area since the early seventeenth century."

"Yes," Clint said, glad for the change in topic. "I was told that the first day of Ikeji somehow commemorates that event." He saw two drunk flies making arcs in the air until they landed on the plate of chin chin on the table beside the professor.

"I'm glad you know that much," Nduka said. "Did you know that the city of Onitsha on the banks of the river Niger was founded by an Aro Chukwu group under the leadership of Eze Chima?"

As a professor of history at a local university, he wanted to show off his erudition. A short, thin, brown-skinned man with closely shaven head, he wore rimless glasses, a light-blue eyelet shirt, and matching pants. He had the habit of patting his head as he spoke, as if the words came from there. His sonorous voice gave the impression he stood at a lectern to address a class.

Clint set down his bottle of beer and nodded toward Chima. "I'm interesting in learning about my roots, the history and culture of my family. I told Chima about that when we met." As he gazed around and saw Esther, he said, "The next step is visiting the Ibinukpabi shrine. The father of one of my bar friends might organize that. His son said he would ask."

"How much are they charging you?" Chima asked, looking at Clint hard.

"Nothing, as far as I can tell."

John, a young man in the corner, coughed to get their attention. "That can't be. You don't know those people. They'll find a reason not to do what they say. In the end, you'll need to pay them to make them act."

"Amen," several voices replied.

Esther ordered the servants to replenish drinks, but Chima waved them away and pointed angrily at Clint. "You're too American. You take people at face value. You should've asked Mama Esther or Mazi Igwe to make the arrangements." He paused and looked at Esther.

Esther deliberately looked away, not wanting to get involved in a visit to that evil place.

"I'll ask Uche, my brother the shoemaker, to organize it," Chima said. "Mama Esther!" he called. "You'll probably have to give them some wine and kola first to broach the subject to those in authority and smooth the way for the visit."

Esther, ignoring him, called for more food and drink for the people who just arrived.

Taking advantage of a short lull in the chatter, professor Nduka addressed the room. "Personally, I don't think there's anything to see at the shrine. It was destroyed by the British during the Aro expeditionary war of 1901-1902." He scratched his head.

"What brought about the fight?" Clint asked, looking up from his plate of jollof rice and waving away a fly that wanted to taste his food. 'Why did the British find it necessary to destroy the oracle?"

Only too willing to oblige, Nduka set down his plate and wiped his spectacles with his handkerchief before launching into a short history lesson. "The British administrators felt threatened by Aro Chukwu power in their attempt to penetrate the region. The states east of the Niger were effectively controlled by the Aro through the influence of the oracle of Ibinukpabi."

He went to the drinks table and grinned at an acquaintance who just entered the room. Taking a bottle of beer, Nduka returned to his seat and continued addressing the room. "The priests of Ibinukpabi were backed by military power and alliances with other militarized states, like Abam, Ohafia, Abriba, and Afikpo, to name a few." He paused to sip his beer.

"Please continue," Clint said.

"The power of Ibinukpabi was at its peak in the late nineteenth century. The oracle stewards and their lower members migrated across vast areas east of the Niger and set up a network of emissaries and informants to the oracle. The British called the oracle Long Juju, though I don't know why."

His expression was serious. "Through those networks, the priests administered a socioeconomic and political organization that effectively controlled the area. The oracle became the court of last appeal for many inhabitants. It affected the lives of many."

A car horn sounded in the front yard, indicating the arrival of a newcomer. Those in the room turned to greet him.

Once the hugging and greeting ended, Clint looked at the professor expectantly. "Please finish your story."

Feeling appreciated, he said, "I need to tell you that during the peak of the slave trade, the oracle's power was misused. Those in authority used its influence to profit from the transatlantic slave trade." He resumed eating. The others in the room began chatting among themselves, while more food arrived in the parlor.

Clint, feeling confused, went to Nduka. "How can that be? I didn't know the Aro people participated in the transatlantic slave trade. My grandfather talked only of house slaves, which were common at the time throughout the world. At the Ujari slave museum, I saw the chains and wondered why it was necessary to chain the slaves if they were only for the domestic market." Nduka looked at him with pity.

Before he could speak, Ngozi, a young woman in a gorgeous long skirt and matching blouse, entered the conversation.

"Well, they did," she said. "With the oracle network in place, trading posts and satellite shrines were set up in different villages throughout the region where small litigations were handled. Those found guilty were sent to the temple here for sacrifice to appease the oracle. Instead, though, they were invariably sold to the European slavers. So, my dear, our forefathers contributed big-time to the exportation of thousands of people to the Americas."

Everyone stared at her in amazement. She sat beside her husband, who wore colors that matched hers. His right arm rested across her shoulders.

"She knows her stuff," he said. "She's a lawyer. I thoroughly agree with her."

"But when the slave trade was abolished," Clint asked, "wouldn't it have been good for Britain to use such a network to its advantage?"

All eyes went to the professor. Another bottle of beer was set before him. "You'd think so, but the British traders and administrators viewed the Aro political and economic power as threatening their quest for colonial power east of the Niger. Tension between the two led to the decision to mount 1901 expeditionary force against the Aro and to demystify the Long Juju. The Aro people put up a strong defense, but the British eventually defeated them." He ate a bite of meat from his plate.

"Come on, Doctor," John, who had sorrowful eyes, said. "They were bound to be defeated. The British had superior power, and they were able to incite surrounding tribes to fight with them."

"That's true. The Aro people were overwhelmed."

"I bet they thought Ibinukpabi would protect them from disaster, the poor souls." Flora's eyelids fluttered. "Little did they know the power of the bullet."

The professor waved her aside. "It was a three-pronged attack led by Colonel Montanaro. His orders were to destroy the Aro Chukwu, reduce the city, temples, and altars to nothing, and to kill all the men and their sons. He came down the Cross River from Afikpo and Unwana in a steamboat with eighty-seven British officers and thousands of African soldiers and bearers."

A young man across the room, reaching toward a plate of akara balls, said, "Professor, that's the first time I heard those numbers." "It's a matter of record. Another attack was mounted from Calabar via Itu. The third came with cannons on land through Ohafia." He paused to let his words sink in.

Esther reached for a bowl containing the remnants of fried chicken, which the server carelessly left uncovered. Waving away flies, she replaced the cover. After retying her top wrapper, she sat heavily in her chair.

"On November 27, 1902, the colonel bivouacked at Amasu, where he could see the smoke from the houses and hear the muffled sound of the war drums of the Aro people. His Black soldiers were ready to panic, and he feared mass desertion, so he decided to attack five days earlier than planned."

"I'll bet the natives feared the wrath of Ibinukpabi," a man said, refilling his plate.

Nduka waved that aside. "That may be so, but on December second, Aro Chukwu was surrounded, and the cannons, which by then were near Amuvie, went into action. It was an unequal fight."

"Of course it was!" another man shouted, slamming his hands on a table. "The Aro warriors had only bows and arrows, spears, and swords. How could they withstand cannons and guns?"

"I agree with you. At two o'clock on the afternoon of December third, the troops entered Oror and approached the palace of Aro Eze.

This is the saddest part of the whole tragedy."

The room became quiet, and all eyes were on the professor.

"The palace had been destroyed by the cannons. The walls were in shambles, and the throne, covered by a leopard skin, was empty. Beside it was a frightened ten-year-old boy named Kanu Oji. Can you imagine how he felt?"

He paused to let those words sink in. Many present had tears in their eyes. They knew the young boy as an elderly man who died only a few years earlier.

"What happened next?" Clint asked, full of emotion. "Did they kill him?"

Nduku's tired voice was tinged with sadness. "No. He stood there, without crying or panicking, and went outside to join the men and women who'd been rounded up as prisoners. All were emaciated. You must remember it was the dry season, and food was scarce. It had been a long, drawn-out battle. He was ordered to lead the soldiers to the oracle."

Many in the room wept openly.

"What did they find?" someone finally asked.

"What do you expect they found?" Patrick, a young man who'd been listening silently, asked angrily.

Ignoring the outburst, the professor continued. "Kanu Oji led them to the ravine called Ibritam. There they entered the large abyss and found several small altars surrounding a bigger altar in the form of a pyramid. It had assorted offerings to the Ibinukpabi. The British set out to destroy the area. Historically, that was the beginning of the waning of Aro Chukwu."

The professor stood and walked toward the courtyard. "What happened to the young boy?" Clint asked softly.

Pausing at the door beside Esther, Nduka said, "He became a prisoner of war. There is a theory he was sent to an island, where he stayed until he could be safely brought back and installed as Eze. We hope one day his family will write his biography, and we'll know what happened after the destruction of Ibinukpabi."

"What a sad story. I'd like to read more about it."

"There are bits and pieces you can find in books by Dike, Nwogu, and Afigbo. The story is also told in a book by a Frenchman named Clezio. The details came from him. I can give you the reference when I see you again. No one has written a truly definitive history of the period."

"Doctor, that was quite a story," Flora said. "I hope one day you'll do some research on this."

"I doubt it. There's no money in research. I'd like, however, to say that the destruction of the oracle opened the way for Christian missionaries to penetrate Aro Chukwu, but that's another story. Whether or not that was a good thing remains to be seen."

Esther, who'd been sitting quietly, stood. "I for one am glad that evil thing was destroyed. My husband's great-grandfather was the chief priest, you know. My husband said his father was the first son of the priest of the oracle to become a Christian. His father sent him to the very first mission school that opened in the area."

"My young brother," the professor said, patting Clint's back, "You'll probably hear more about the Christian influence on your lives from your grandfather. I've given you enough on Aro Chukwu history. Your head must be reeling. I'm going to the compound to see about my application for a plot in the new extension."

As the sun dipped toward the west, a small breeze came in through the open windows. Those in the parlor began drifting away, and maids cleared the remnants of the party. Esther went to her room to rest.

Clint walked out with the professor. After lingering outside a short time, he decided to accompany him to the compound. He wanted to visit the shrine to the oracle. Clint felt the explanation of the invasion was unsatisfactory. There had to be more to the story. At the earliest opportunity, he would seek his grandfather's view.

CHAPTER SIXTEEN

Clint's effort to visit the shrine of Ibinukpabi was filled with frustrations despite the optimistic suggestions by the crowd at Esther's house. Promises were made, only to be broken at the last minute. Esther finally stepped in and made a short trip to the compound, which she rarely visited unless it was unavoidable, and presented her brother-in-law, the head of her husband's family, a bottle of schnapps and seven kola nuts. She urged him to intercede on behalf of Clint with the chief, the titular keeper of the oracle, to permit the visit. She received promises but no action.

Why is it necessary to gain permission? Clint wondered. Couldn't I just ask anyone in the village to direct me to the site? It must be widely known.

He complained to his grandfather, who explained that despite all the talk about the oracle, the actual site was known to only a handful of people in the village. Even so many years after its destruction, its powers were still feared by many, who refused to set foot in the area. Some visitors were deliberately directed to a clearing in the forest and were told it was the place left by the British after the destruction of the oracle, when it wasn't anywhere near the site.

In the end, Igwe made an appointment with the chief. He didn't reveal his plan to Clint in full, but he told him clearly that if he failed to convince the chief to permit the visit, he would urge Clint to abandon his plan and seek direction to places that were fully under Igwe's control.

"There's no point trying to dislodge a big boulder, if, once you succeed, there is nothing that compensates you for all the energy you have expended." At least he was willing to try to help.

On the appointed day, Igwe and Clint arrived at Peace's chief's village. They were accompanied by a house servant, who carried a bag of gifts—a bottle of schnapps, assorted kola and bitter nuts, and a dried leg of goat.

The last time Igwe had been there was during the funeral for Esther's husband, Clint's grandfather. Much to their chagrin, they were told the chief was currently out of the house. Since they were expected, they could wait in the parlor where visitors were received.

Shortly afterward, the chief's spokesperson rushed in to welcome them, while a young boy was sent to find the chief and inform him of their presence.

The room they were in contained a chair on a raised platform, where the chief normally sat while conferring with village elders or meeting important visitors to the community. It also had a long table with chairs. Assorted calendars of important people in Abia State and Aro Chukwu hung on the walls, along with photographs of chiefs performing various ceremonies.

Igwe and Clint had a long wait. Just as Igwe began mumbling that he had more important things to do, they saw the chief come in from the back door and go to a room off the corridor. Other members of his cabinet arrived, and the long table quickly filled.

On entering the hall, the chief greeted them perfunctorily, sat in the chair, and coughed his order to begin the meeting. "Who is this stranger in our midst?"

Clint saw he changed into official regalia—a leopard-patterned long shirt, several long necklaces of large-cut coral, a woolen cap with one feather, and a staff with a golden handle.

After the traditional salutation, Igwe introduced Clint, who was struck by the formal nature of the visit.

Even though Clint's presence in the village was widely known, he hadn't been formally presented, and the chief pretended it was the first time he saw him.

"My grandson, Clint," Igwe said. "I call him that, because it's the only name he understands as his. Even though he has an Igbo name, his parents chose not to use it. What can I say?'

As if on cue, the village men shook their heads in disapproval of the actions of Clint's parents.

"However, our chief," Igwe said, folding his arms as if in prayer and wiping his mouth, "this young man has been commissioned by a Black American newspaper to write a travel article on important places of tourism in Nigeria. He's starting with Aro Chukwu, where his parents came from and where he is a son of the soil. His maternal grandfather, as you know, was Mazi Okoro Oji, whom we lost last year. He wants to visit the Ibinukpabi site to see for himself what the British did to it. As you know, this is an important part of our history. His article will put Aro Chukwu on the map."

Clint was startled to hear about the article. Igwe patted his thigh with his left hand to prevent him from contradicting. He stopped himself from speaking just in time and kept a stone face, staring at the chief, who looked impassive despite the fly hovering over his head.

"Just imagine the money tourists will bring and spend," Igwe continued. "We'll probably have to build a large hotel for them and spruce up the oracle site, perhaps restore it to what it was before the destruction."

At the mention of future money flowing into his coffers, the chief suddenly seemed interested.

"That's all we want," Igwe said, coughing gently. "We've often wondered what the Nigerian Tourism Board has been doing. We haven't seen that many tourists here.

"Mazi, that will change when my grandson's article comes out. To show you how important this is for us, we've brought you a little gift." Igwe beckoned to the boy with the basket of gifts to step forward and present them, to which he added 5,000 naira.

The chief, suddenly energized, welcomed them more warmly. He turned to an elderly man from an adjacent compound who sat quietly in the corner, dozing, and instructed him to organize the trip immediately. It was the same man Clint had spoken to earlier without success.

Next, the chief ordered his spokesman to bring kola nuts and palm wine for his guests. The ablution to the ancestors was poured, glasses of gin distributed, and kola nuts broken and shared. The rest of the visit was spent arranging when the men who knew the area would accompany Clint to the oracle site.

Outside, Clint waited beside the car, parked under an udara tree, for his grandfather to finish conferring with the chief. He looked at the hodgepodge of mud houses with thatched roofs interspersed with a few houses made of cement blocks and zinc roofs. Small vegetable plots grew beside several houses, along with a few pawpaw trees. On one side of the chief's house, the grandest in the compound, were several coconut trees.

As he waited, a crowd of children and some adults came from their homes to gawk.

The small children, in different stages of undress and dirt, starting tugging at him.

"American give us money to buy bread and Fanta? We're hungry."

He wasn't surprised at being called "American," since it wasn't the first time. After all, he spoke mostly English. Still, he felt uncomfortable and wanted the car to move, so he would feel safe.

When Igwe finally arrived, he asked, "Grandpa, why are there no trees inside the compounds?"

Igwe was taken aback by the question, having expected Clint to comment on the children pestering him. "It's because we associate trees with forests and wild animals. Only wild animals live in the forests. We feel that what makes us human is that we don't live in the forest but go there to kill or hunt for food. Besides, trees attract snakes, and many of us fear them."

Clint felt that was a lame excuse but didn't pursue it.

After they were both in the car, Igwe said, "It was a successful meeting."

"Why did you say I was a journalist?"

"I had to give them a reason to make them act. Money is the only thing people understand nowadays. I was right, too."

Early one morning before the sun's heat became unbearable, Clint found himself and four others on a narrow path deep in the Ibritam forest, en route to the shrine of the oracle of Ibinukpabi. His grandfather and three elderly men from the village chief accompanied him. Igwe's car deposited them on a roadside three miles from the grove. The Ikeji festival was over, and the Nwaekpe had been returned from the villages to Aro Awada, the place where it would sleep for another year. That signaled the beginning of the Aro New Year and the resumption of normal activities.

At first, the party of five passed through cassava farmland crisscrossed with defined paths created by generations of bare feet trampling the area, exposing the ochre-colored earth beneath, as they walked to and from their farms. Soon, though, the paths disappeared, and they reached the edge of the forest

There were no defined paths in the forest. It seemed to Clint they walked on an incline. Grunting, the old guides zigzagged from space to space, avoiding boulders or stumpy shrubs and shoving aside thickets of branches blocking the way. They passed a dead log covered with butterflies, and their movement made the butterflies disperse upward in a cloud of red and yellow.

They must be walking by instinct, Clint thought. I hope they know what they're doing. He hopped over a fallen branch blocking the way.

All around them, the sound of unseen animals filled the air. He heard the caw of birds from the treetops, the hissing of snakes, the buzzing of mosquitoes, wasps, and bees, and the incessant sawing of other insects. Under their feet, thousands of ants, some carrying twigs while others were loaded with dry leaves, scurried to their nests. Tortoises and porcupines hurried past them. Birds flitted among the branches, disturbed when the men made sudden contact with the trees or shrubs where they temporarily perched.

Occasionally, Igwe warned Clint to watch out for snakes, tortoises, or any crawly animal lurking in the undergrowth. The old guides moved on, seemingly unaware of the dangers around them, occasionally swatting swarming gnats and mosquitoes with the fans they carried. In contrast, Clint and Igwe had only their hands as weapons against the millions of flies and insects determined to eat them alive.

It rained the previous night, and occasional droplets of water trapped on the leaves above were dislodged by the movement of animals, birds, or the slight breeze that penetrated the forest and fell on the men.

When they'd been walking up an incline for what seemed to Clint like a lifetime, they came to the rim of an abyss. There, the forest hadn't taken over. It was a valley of tall grasses and short, stubby trees, with the contours easily discernible. The guides followed the rim for a short distance to find an easy descent.

"This is where supplicants waited to appear before the altars," one guide said, spreading his arms to indicate the extent of the abyss. "As you can see, it's been in disuse since the oracle was destroyed."

In his mind's eye, Clint saw hundreds of men and women with only a yard of cloth, if any, to cover them, huddled in the dirt, some with animals they brought as offerings, while others carried yams or different food items. They waited in agony, not knowing what the verdict would be when it was their turn. Clint shuddered.

"Are you all right?" Igwe asked. "Should we go back? You look unwell."

The sun's rays intensified since the men came out from under the shade, and Clint felt hot and sweaty. His short-sleeved shirt was soaked, and he felt physically sick.

Determined to complete their task, the old men pressed on, oblivious to Clint's discomfort. They walked around the rim of the abyss until they came to an opening in the hillside.

"This is where supplicants were supposed to enter the cave after making their offerings at the altars," one man said, pointing toward the escarpment. "There's an opening on the other side of the hill where they would come out."

Clint, being intrepid, was determined to continue the adventure. He wanted to go into the cave, thinking it might provide a short respite from the sun. Just wait until my parents hear what an

adventure it was to see the other side of the cave.

"I wonder what's on the other side." He moved toward the entrance, pulling aside branches in the way.

"No, Son!" Igwe shouted. "No one has been in there for a long time. It's inhabited now by pythons and other horrible, wild, creepycrawly creatures. We don't want to lose you. You'd be good food for them."

"Foreigners," an old man muttered. "They aren't afraid of anything."

Clint, flinching at the warning, felt angry. Despite all the fuss and talk and money expended to get him to the place, there was nothing to see or to differentiate it from similar jungles in the area.

These people are all talk and no action, he thought, thinking he'd been on his way to a site similar to the Civil War sites in America, where the fields were well-maintained, and plaques were strategically placed to tell visitors what happened. Instead, he was in the jungle without a single artifact and no visible evidence of whatever happened there. How did he know it was the site of Ibinukpabi? Perhaps, if he'd been allowed into the cave, there might be something to see.

"I'm upset that you expended so much money and effort to get me here to see nothing," he said.

"I thought you knew the British destroyed everything," Igwe said. "Grandpa, that's no excuse. If this place is as historically important as you all think, why let it revert to jungle? Don't blame the British. Nigeria gained its independence a long time ago. During the time since, you could have preserved your historical sites. If nothing else, clear it and place markers to tell people what once existed here. I'm feeling a bit annoyed right now, Grandpa."

Not sure how to respond, Igwe joked, "Your article will enable us to obtain money to maintain this place."

They continued walking along the rim, and soon, Clint heard a loud noise.

Shivering, he asked, "Is there a waterfall nearby?"

"Yes," a man said. "You're coming to it. That's what completes the mystery. The supplicants waiting below in the abyss would look up for the answer to their prayers from the colors of the falling water. Depending on the color, they could tell if their offerings were accepted and their prayers answered."

I can hear it, Clint thought, but I can't see it because of the jungle.

"How ingenious," Igwe said. "Of course, during the slave trade, the priests would substitute animal blood for human blood and give the impression that those who were led into the cave had been sacrificed to appease the deity. Instead, they loaded them onto canoes and transported them to Calabar to be sold," he said in disgust.

"Where were the temples?" Clint asked.

"Over here." A guide pointed to a place in the abyss.

Recovering his composure, Igwe laughed and said, "Clint, my son, use your brain." Overcome by coughing, he stopped for a moment. "These men will point anywhere. They weren't born during the time. The British destroyed the temples long ago, so anyone alive today who tells you he knows precisely where the temples were placed is a liar."

Clint observed a group of birds fly over in an arc. He watched them for a minute before asking, "If the temples were to be recreated as you suggested to the chief, does anyone have a copy or photograph of the originals?"

"There are no templates," Igwe said. "In those days, no one wrote things down, and there are no photographs of this place in existence. The people were illiterate. The original founders must've reconstructed the structures they built from memory, or they might have carried them to this place. Who knows?" He scratched his head and continued walking.

The elderly guides were getting restless, anxious to return to civilization, and Clint felt very tired. On one level, he was happy he'd seen the place, even though there was nothing but forest. The waterfall was interesting, and he was happy he heard it immediately after the rainy season when the water was full.

The return journey to the car was slow. When they finally left the forest for the farms, Clint noticed that although the predominant crop was cassava, there were several yam plots with okra plants in between, and egusi, or melon, plants spread over large areas. Igwe told him it was natural for yams to share the same plot as okra and egusi.

Clint wanted to ask more questions, but Igwe seemed tired and unwilling to have a serious discussion. When they finally reached the car, Clint was glad for the air-conditioning.

Igwe asked the driver to drop them at his house, so he could offer drinks to the elderly men before taking them to their village.

When the car arrived at his house, Igwe turned to their guides. "One thing you forgot to tell us is that there are many paths leading to the real oracle shrine that you didn't show us. The British destroyed the visible elements of the oracle, but they failed to realize that the big stone obelisks were just for show. The real oracle altar was known only to the clan priests, and it's still intact and can be reached from several interconnecting caves." He stared at the men, daring them to object.

They looked away sheepishly.

Gesturing with his hands, Igwe said, "When I was a young boy growing up in Amanagwu, I was friendly with the son of one of the minor priests. One day, we followed his father, Kanu Nta, when he disappeared into the forest. We thought he was going to gather medicinal leaves at the Iyi Eke area. His son wanted to know where he got the leaves he prescribed to his patients."

Warming to the story, Igwe discarded his wet shirt. "Kanu Nta had a live cock with him. We saw him enter an opening in the side of the hill. When he came out, the cock was half-plucked and dead. We waited until he departed, then we went in and saw an altar where the cock had been sacrificed. We followed an opening on the other side of the cave, and that took us to the abyss we saw today."

They men looked dumbfounded for a second, then one said timidly, "You're right. There are seven or eight caves around the area. If you turned to a different opening, you would have reached the great altar of Ibinukpabi." He covered his mouth with his hand and whispered, "We're all sworn not to let anyone know where it is. Obviously, you didn't expect us to expose our hidden secrets to your grandson, who hasn't take an oath of secrecy."

"I understand," Igwe said, nonplussed. "I don't fault you, but I wanted my grandson to know that the altar of Ibinukpabi still exists and is known to a few. He wondered how it might be reconstructed for the sake of tourism." Remembering his responsibility to be hospitable, he said, "Come in and have something to drink to cool off."

"Thank you, Mazi, but if you don't mind, we'll take the bottles of beer with us," one of the men said. "We'll come in next time."

To show his gratitude, Igwe tipped them 1,000 naira, and they thanked him.

As the car sped away, Clint shrugged off his wet shirt, walked into the house, and sat on the nearest sofa. The whirling ceiling fan in the parlor felt good, even though it was merely recirculating warm air. He needed time to absorb what he saw and heard, so he silently drank the cold water placed before him.

Later, when he felt cooler and slightly rested, he went looking for his grandfather and found him in the kitchen, having an intense discussion with his wife. Clint heard his name mentioned, and, from their movements when they saw him, he surmised he'd been the subject of their discussion. He went back to the parlor to wait.

When Igwe finally reappeared, he chuckled and said, "Thank you, Clint."

"For what?"

"Just to let you know, I've never been there before from this end."

Clint returned to his main preoccupation. "I presume that with the destruction of the Ibinukpabi, the conquering troops were stationed at the barracks."

"I never associated our barracks with the troops, but come to think of it, that was why the government station here is called the barracks. You're clever."

"What I said has nothing to do with being clever," Clint said, irritated. "Ever since I came, I wondered why it had that name. When someone said a large army was sent to destroy the Long Juju, I put two and two together."

Contrite, Igwe said, "The troops must've been kept there until the British administration could be established."

"Grandpa, why didn't the British work with the existing power structure, as they did in other parts of their empire?"

"I believe they would have, if it were possible. Son, there's more to the story." Scratching his head, he walked to the window, staring out lost in thought.

"From the bits of history I've read," he said slowly, "this is what is said to have happened." He sat down and cleared his throat. "By the end of the nineteenth century, the British established a protectorate in northern Nigeria, governing by indirect rule though the emirs. Sir Ralph Moore was commissioned to explore and pacify the hinterland of the south. It was said that Aro priests of Ibinukpabi, who controlled southern Nigeria, were in his way. I understand that one of the British vice consuls came within fifteen miles of Aro Chukwu trying to open the area for trade. He was driven off and barely escaped with his life."

Igwe stood up and walked toward the fridge in the dining room to get cold water for Clint and a beer for himself.

Clint accepted the water. Horrified at Igwe's words, he said, "One would've thought the Aro people who traded so frequently with Calabar would've welcomed him."

"It would appear that way, but the Aro people, ironically, considering what happened later, viewed such penetration as the first step toward domination."

"There was a lively discussion at my grandmother's the day after the ceremony at Amaikpe about the expedition."

"Did they tell you what finally precipitated the invasion was witnessing over a hundred tribesmen, part of a larger group who came to consult the oracle, arriving half-dead at a British post? The British were morally outraged by their tales of cannibalism, enslavement, and exploitation.

"One thing is certain: the British occupation made it possible for the missionaries to feel safe to proselytize."

He looked around and shouted, "John, where are you? Come at once and remove these bottles. We need fresh ones."

He paused to listen to the sound of running feet. "I'm parched." Clint, who had dozed off, didn't reply.

Igwe shook him gently. "Clint, my dear boy, you must be tired. You're nodding off. The driver's here and will take you back to Esther's house. We'll talk more another time."

CHAPTER SEVENTEEN

"You're up early today, Clint," Esther said, surprised to see him up so early. "Where are you off to this time?" "I'd like to see the old Presbyterian church you often mentioned." "Remember also to visit the school where my husband's father taught," she said, as he rode off.

Approaching Oror, Clint saw the statue of the old king blocking the palace entrance. He got off the bike and leaned it against a tree. Several people were going about their business. Some women returned from the spring, where they collected water, while others were setting out for the farms or leaving their homes to attend to business. All stopped whatever they did to speak with him. Some did so out of curiosity, because they never met him, while others seemed genuinely interested in what brought him out so early that morning.

"Is Mama Esther well?" they asked. "Are you having a good time?

We saw you during the Ikeji celebration. Do you have a case today with the chiefs? Are you looking for someone?"

As he gazed at the statue, trying to ignore the litter of rubbish strewn all around, goats scampering around, and the hordes of chickens strutting and pecking for food in the dirt, he remembered the story of the expedition. He imagined Colonel Montanaro, supported by his troops, entering Oror and destroying everything in sight.

He probably thought the Oracle was at Oror, Clint mused. Why'd he have to destroy the palace?

He imagined the five-year-old boy, sitting amid the rubble of the old palace, wondering what his fate would be, knowing his father was already dead. If that had been me at five, how would I have felt? I was in kindergarten at that time, angry at being there and thinking only of when we'd break for lunch, so I could eat my sandwich.

He was so lost in thought, he didn't hear his name being called until someone touched him. Startled, he realized he was looking at the chief of of his mother's village, who came to Oror for a cabinet meeting. He had several men with him, wearing the woven cap Aro men favored.

"What are you doing here, Kanu?" the chief asked. "Should I call you Kilinti?"

It took Clint a moment to collect himself and frame a response. "Chief, I'm continuing my research, and today I'm visiting Oror. I was hoping to see the palace."

"How was your visit to Ibritam?"

"That went very well. Thank you, Sir, for arranging it. I'll visit Iyi Eke later, because that will complete my knowledge of the oracle. I should be able to write a good piece." I might as well perpetuate the

myth of being commissioned to write about this place, he thought.

"Let me talk to the big chief. Perhaps we can let you see the cabinet room before we begin our deliberations."

"Mazi, ime ele. That would be nice." Clint used the little Igbo he learned since arriving in Nigeria.

The chief led him down a long corridor into a cavernous room with a long table and chairs. Photographs of the dead king in various poses with visiting dignitaries lined the walls.

Emphasizing Clint's journalist role, the chief introduced him to the waiting cabinet members.

Murmurs of appreciation passed through the room. Anxious to begin their deliberations as soon as the current titular chief appeared, the spokesperson addressed Clint.

"Young Man, did you know there was an official treaty between us and the British king? When our beloved Eze Kanu Oji died, the British queen sent her condolences."

"I didn't know that. Thank you for giving me this piece of information."

He lingered in the room a short time, trying to shake the image of the boy sitting on the throne, calmly accepting his fate, facing the English warlord by whose hand his father died and who was bent on destroying everything he cherished and knew.

Clint silently left the room and went out into the yard, gazing at the statue. Picking up his bicycle, he rode toward Obinkita, passing the stalls, where he stopped briefly to talk to Nick and arrange for Nick to visit him. Nick offered to accompany him to Obinkita, but Clint refused. He wanted to visit the school and look around.

—m—

At Obinkita, he noticed it wasn't market day. He wandered around the square, looking for the church, then he spied the old man he met on an earlier visit and hoped the man could direct him.

As he approached, the old man stared. "Young Man, what brings you here at this time of the morning? Today isn't market day, and the place is a little quiet."

"I'm looking for the Obinkinta church."

"It isn't here. Just keep going down the road, and you'll see it. It's the very first church started in Aro Chukwu. You won't miss it, even though it's a bit neglected and is surrounded by buildings and shops.

You'll see many young schoolchildren around there."

"Thank you." Clint remounted his bicycle and pedaled away.

Five hundred yards from the square, he found an old cement

building with a steeple and gazed at it. "This must be the church built by Rankin. I wonder where the rectory he built is."

Luckily for him, the door was open, and he went inside. It was cool and smelled musty. Glad to be away from the heat even for a short time, he sat in a pew and looked around. It seemed vaguely familiar. When he thought about it, he realized it resembled the church in the photographs of his parents' wedding.

They must've been married here, he thought.

His parents had no affiliation with any congregation, but they went to church whenever the spirit moved them. They spent most Sundays reading the Washington Post, shopping, going to museums, or watching football on TV. Clint and Sarah were baptized, but he couldn't remember which church they used. He once visited a Presbyterian Church with his parents for the baptism of a child of someone they knew. The inside of the church reminded him of that one.

It had a simple design, with bench pews arranged on both sides of the aisle and a plain lectern up front. He gazed at the stained-glass window with the images of two White women, one of whom he presumed was Mary Slessor, surrounded by many Black children. An inscription below in Igbo read Sita na obe Jisus ay ge enwe meri. He wished he had his notebook, so he could write it down and ask his grandmother to translate it. She would be happy to know he visited the church that meant so much to her family.

Hearing steps, he looked up to see a man in a clerical collar walking up the aisle. Oh, my God. He'll ask me to leave. I must be trespassing. Clint stood.

The man had cropped hair, and his hands were clasped as if in prayer. He wore a dark-purple shirt tucked into black trousers and black loafers. He waved Clint down again. "It isn't often we have someone sitting in the church contemplating. Please continue. I'm sorry if I disturbed your prayers."

"Thank you, Pastor. My name is Clint Igwe. I'm visiting my relatives for a few weeks and staying with my maternal grandmother, Esther, in Ibom."

"Yes, yes. Welcome." He patted Clint's back. "I've heard of you from Esther, who's one of our loyal parishioners. I'm Pastor John Ibekwe. How long are you staying with us?"

"I'm not quite sure how long I'll stay in the country. I may travel to Lagos to visit my uncle before heading back. I suspended my education to come here, and I need to get back to finish."

"I'm glad you came to visit our church. I've often asked Mama Esther why you never accompany her to services. Is there anything you'd like to know?" He sat in the pew beside Clint. "Perhaps we should start our conversation with a prayer to thank God for your journey so far and ask for a safe journey in the future." Surprised, Clint nodded.

When pastor Ibekwe knelt, Clint followed. They observed a short period of silence, then Ibekwe said, "Amen," and rose. "Let's sit in this pew, so we can talk."

He sat, and Clint joined him.

"The church was built between 1905 and 1906. For a long time, it was the only church in Aro Chukwu. The Catholics came later. After the civil war, several villages sought to open their own churches, so that's why we have another Presbyterian Church at Amanagwu to cater to the religious needs of the people in other villages."

"I know where that church is. I often pass it when I visit my father's uncle."

"Of course. Nowadays, there are many denominations fighting to claim the souls of our people. Sadly, we now have many different types of evangelical churches and other nonmainstream churches." He waved his hands, as he spoke.

"Competition is good, isn't it?" Clint asked, wondering how to respond.

"I'm not sure."

"I was looking at the beautiful stained-glass window. One of the women is Mary Slessor, isn't it? Who's the other?"

Ibekwe followed Clint's gaze. "I understand her name is Mrs. Arnot. She came with Mary Slessor and lived here among us. In those days, we practiced human sacrifice, particularly at burials of important persons. Twins and their mothers were often killed or cast out. Mary Slessor stopped all that. She brought us Christianity, and, through her influence, the first big primary school was opened here in Obinkita by Reverend Rankin. We also had Reverend Wilkie, who visited but didn't actually live in Aro Chukwu."

He placed his hand on Clint's shoulder. "Go visit the school. Before it was built, our young men were sent to Calabar for education.

Many returned and taught at that school, and many of our important historical figures attended. At present, it's no longer affiliated with us but is part of the state system. The school near Esther's house came later. That was always a government school."

Clint listened impassively. "Sir, what does the inscription in the window mean?"

"It means, Through the cross of Jesus, we will have victory. Did you know that on the anniversary of Mary Slessor's death, the Scottish Clydesdale Bank created a ten-pound note in her honor? On the back was a map of the Cross River villages associated with her. We've heard of it, but I haven't seen it myself."

"So much history," Clint murmured. "Thank you. I'll visit the school."

Clint walked to the door, and the pastor came with him. Outside, Clint turned to him and said, "I know you said this building was built around 1905, but before that, what happened? How was Mary Slessor able to persuade people to abandon the old ways?"

"By her example. They saw her collecting abandoned twins who weren't killed at birth, ministering to the sick even when they were on death's door, and preaching forgiveness. She didn't do it alone. After her first visit, she came several times. You must've heard that she convinced the chiefs to allow Efik and Ibibio evangelists to live in Aro Chukwu unmolested. Apparently, past attempts to use such people proved disastrous. Many were killed, and only a few escaped with their lives."

"Did the chiefs agree? I presume they must have."

"Yes. Why wouldn't they? They were anxious to please her and repay her for her support during the pacification period."

"What happened next?"

"From what I gather, the other woman depicted in the stained glass who worked with her came to live among us. They both saved the lives of many children who would normally have been killed, though that didn't stop human sacrifice. That continued for a long time, albeit in secret, since it was generally known the British wouldn't tolerate it."

Clint silently digested that information.

"Eventually, the chiefs met and decided to grant the mission this land for the opening of a school and the construction of this building. A man called Reverend Rankin came to stay with us permanently. The lower portion of his big, two-story house wasn't enclosed, and that was where services were held until the church was built. Of course, his house was demolished, and, as you can see, the area is different from those times. Many modern houses have sprung up."

"Many thanks." The area surrounding the church looked chaotic and unplanned. Clint saw jumbles of modern buildings interspaced with old mud buildings with tin roofs. Stalls outside the houses offered everything imaginable, from peanut oil in bottles to akara and moyi moyi. Oranges, peeled and unpeeled, were arranged in rows on the tables outside the stalls. On the side of the houses stood a gas station with one broken pump, currently inoperable due to the power outage, though the proprietor sold kerosene from a big tank inside the station.

Taking in the chaos and noise around him, Clint tried to imagine what the building represented in the past and the White man who risked his life to live among the people while supervising the construction of the church. Were his forebears part of the building crew, or did they contribute only funds? Did Achi come there for his catechism classes, learning the Igbo alphabet and eventually being able to read the Bible?

So many questions fought in Clint's mind. He would try to get answers from Esther, who surely would be willing to discuss that part of Aro Chukwu history.

He bade the minister good-bye and picked up his bike. He would skip the school. Approaching Amaikpe on his ride home, he noticed some locked stores at the perimeter of the square were doing a brisk business. Every store and the few stalls operating each had a radio tuned to a different station. The cacophony of voices and songs— church music, highlife, and other Nigerian music—confused and irritated him. He was glad he had a quiet moment in the church, however short.

CHAPTER EIGHTEEN

Esther had a synod meeting at the church, and Clint had nothing particular to do. Ikeji days were busy. He met many of his relatives who lived outside the area, and all invited him to visit them.

The house was quiet, so he sat in the veranda, trying to decide whether to travel outside Aro Chukwu or continue staying there while he figured out the next phase of his life. He had to decide soon. He needed a career, but the question that was uppermost in his mind was whether to seek that career in Nigeria or the U.S. His grandparents never mentioned his future, though he assumed they were wondering about it. He'd been living with them for three months, but he never told them he had any plans, not even an inclination to return to the States. He didn't feel like visiting Igwe that morning, even though the visit at the Presbyterian Church left him with many unanswered questions.

His thoughts were interrupted when a messenger brought him a note. He opened it and saw it was from Ifeoma, the girl he met at the post office. She wanted him to meet her at the Presbyterian Church near Igwe's compound at ten o'clock that morning. She had business at the church that would be completed at that time.

Apart from Nick, Clint hadn't connected with anyone from his age group. When he first met Ifeoma at the post office, he was struck by her candor and intelligence. She became a person he could ask for information about things he didn't understand or that his relatives wouldn't give candid explanations for.

During one of their encounters, he asked her if she was his sister, because everyone who came into Esther's house was introduced as sister or brother. She explained that traditionally, compounds were made up of descendants of the original founders, and, in some cases, close friends. The term family included all the extended family no matter how far removed. There was no word in Igbo for cousin, nephew, or niece. Everyone related, no matter how far removed, was a brother or sister.

He mentioned his disgust at the pervasiveness of corruption in Nigeria. He heard his grandfather decry the fact that it was so endemic one had to factor in the extra amount whenever one had an issue with a government officer or when traveling between cities. Clint wondered what would happen if everyone refused to pay.

Igwe dismissed the comment with a laugh. "It's the way of life here."

Was there a cultural explanation for it? Ifeoma believed corruption owed its origin to the importance of family in an agrarian society. "A person's obligation is first to his family, then his friends, and no one else. When preference is given to family members or close friend's family, that's culturally correct. When one offers money to someone to have him favor his family or friend, that, too, is traditional and expected. It's part of our culture."

"The system might have worked well in an agrarian economy, but it can't work in the current system, where there is a multifaceted family structure, and there's more industrialized, competitive economy and politics."

She nodded. "You're right. The old norm must go to avoid the situation where people use political advantage to enrich themselves and their families."

She felt petty corruption was the result of poor salaries, which, in many cases, were in arrears.

"When workers with families aren't paid for six months, they have to seek other means to feed their families. That's why we have petty corruption."

He looked forward to seeing her. She promised to arrange a meeting for him with a man whose family was closely associated with his great grandfather. He felt the meeting was important, and he hoped she could make it happen.

—⚇—

Walking toward the church, he saw Ifeoma talking to a young man on a bike. She wore a fitted batik caftan with head tie of similar material, long, dangling beaded earrings with a matching necklace, and sandals.

She introduced the young man as one of her students at the teacher training college. He was doing his teaching practice at the primary school near Esther's house. They chitchatted about the after- school soccer practice Clint continued coaching, though it was sporadic, depending on having enough children to form two teams.

He saw several knots of people talking to each other in the square. "What's happening?" Clint asked.

"A village meeting just ended, and those are the remnants of the attendees."

"What was it about?' "Something to do with land."

Soon, they entered the compound, walking along very narrow passages about the span of their outstretched hands. Sometimes, a passage ended, and the next began around the corner of a house. It looked very unplanned. Most of the houses were made of mud with thatched roofs, but occasionally, he saw a cement house with corrugated sheet-metal roof.

As he walked with her, Clint realized that, apart from his uncle's house, he'd never been inside Igwe's compound. Peace's father's compound was different, because it had less people, and it was possible to still see the contours of the horseshoe from the original plan.

"A stranger would get lost here," Clint commented.

"True, but someone at the square would always be willing to show whoever the way." She swatted a fly that settled on her forehead.

Deep inside the compound, they reached a small opening in which there stood a chief's house. Several yards away, she pointed out her family house. Her grandmother, on the veranda, waved at them.

Mazi Oji's house, at the very end of the compound, was an oldfashioned house that belonged to his mother, where he lived since her death. There was an outer room in front with short walls and mud benches for visitors to sit. Directly in front, a doorway opened into a corridor with rooms on both sides and a door at the end leading to the backyard, where there was a small vegetable garden with banana and plantain shrubs at one end.

When Clint and Ifeoma arrived, they saw four old men sitting in the anteroom, conversing.

Ifeoma hesitated. "Did you remember to bring a gift for Mazi?"

When Clint told Igwe he might meet Mazi Oji, Igwe gave him an envelope that held 3,000 naira for a gift. "Remember this," Igwe said. "He'll expect a gift from you. That's how he can survive." Clint was very glad he brought the envelope.

Mazi Oji, the oldest man in the room, was once a driver for successive British district administrators in Aro Chukwu. For the fifteen years of his working life, he lived in his employers' servant quarters. With independence and the departure of most British civil servants, Mazi Oji lost his job and returned to his village house. With no pension, he survived on the small amount of money his employer's children sent him and his wife's income from her petty trading when she was alive. Since her death, he became totally dependent on the goodwill of his visitors.

As a respected elder statesman in the village, he was often consulted on matters relating to village tradition and history. That day, Mazi Oji had with him Mazi Nwosu, a retired produce trader who came from a long line of traders who plied the route between Aro Chukwu and Itu on the Cross River. Both Nwosu's father and Achi were friends, and while Achi traded in yard goods, Nwosu's father traded in produce. With the demise of the oil palm trade, Nwosu also became totally dependent on his children's handouts.

The third man at the meeting was Ume, who, until he could no longer hold a tool due to arthritis, was a pirogue builder. His father was known as the best canoe man of his generation. He knew all the bends of the creeks and the Cross River. Ume learned the trade from his father, and, until a few years earlier, he was still fishing the Cross River.

Clint, sweating profusely from the heat, noticed the old men wore long-sleeved shirts hanging over their jojis and knitted wool hats.

Ifeoma entered the room and genuflected before Mazi Oji the oldest person in the room. At the age of eighty-five, he was barely five-feet tall, with wrinkled, sunken eyes and teeth stained by tobacco. She introduced Clint as Mazi Igwe's grandson from Peter.

Welcoming Clint, Mazi Oji spoke in a strong voice that belied his appearance. "If I hadn't been told, I would've mistaken you for Achi. You resemble him. He died in the 1950s."

After the customary pouring of a libation to the ancestors and breaking of kola nuts, Clint handed his gift to Mazi Oji. "I hope I'm not interrupting an important meeting."

"I can see why you'd think so because of the other men. We normally spend our days telling stories of the past to keep our memories alive. These men will help me answer some of your questions."

"Mazi, I suspended my education in the U.S. to come here to learn the history of this place where my parents are from and my family's part in it. Since coming here, I've heard about the expedition to bring the Aros under British rule, the reason for the destruction of Ibinukpabi, and the death of Eze. I haven't been able to discern how the ordinary people in the villages felt about these events or what happened to the other chiefs, especially the high priest. Did they all go underground to regroup and plan to restore Ibinukpabi?

"When I visited the Obinkita church, the reverend told me how Mary Slessor was instrumental in converting the Aro people to Christianity. Was Christianity imposed on the Aro people by the British ruler? I'd be glad if you could provide me with some of the answers."

Mazi Oji, sitting up, rubbed his hands together, and after a moment, he looked at the other men. "We'll try to answer your questions. We weren't born then, though we may look that old, but our families lived through it. I anticipated your question. That's why I asked Ume, whose grandfather traveled to Itu many times with Achi, as well as Nwosu, whose grandfather was Achi's close friend, to join me today. There's another person who should have joined us, but he has malaria. He said he would talk to you some other time." Mazi Oji began to relate his story.

The occupation by the British began many changes in Aro Chukwu that ultimately affected the lives of ordinary people like Achi, though at first, their lives remained unchanged. Before a formal administration could be set up, minor chiefs still enforced native laws and customs within their communities. People worshipped their ancestors, and, in their Awada, the usual human sacrifice was widely practiced. Slaves and women were treated inhumanely.

Rumors abounded about the activities of the strange-looking people with the native troops. People gathered to watch the White soldiers, as they supervised laborers who were setting up tents. Later, they molded clay blocks for permanent houses.

Such activities attracted many onlookers, including your greatgrandfather, Achi, who came back each day to the villages with tales of what he saw. The minor chiefs and priests never had contact with White men and didn't know how to behave during the early part of the occupation. The Eze, the only authority who could have mediated between them and the new people in charge, had been removed. With the Eze killed during the war, and his son who should have succeeded him sent into temporary exile, there was no longer a central native authority that could adjudicate any differences between communities. That authority was supposedly vested in the Englishman in charge of the occupation.

Witnessing the new kinds of buildings springing up in the barracks areas, many minor chiefs coveted such houses. In exchange for their loyalty, the administration provided each village head or priest with a spacious house with zinc roof. Achi and all the other young men and women watched such a building being constructed in their village. Achi and others of his social class became part of the building crew for the construction of Igwe's new house.

Our people listened to tales brought back by traders along the Cross River of another God said to be more powerful and more forgiving than their household gods or Ibinukpabi. Many of the converts to the new God in and around Calabar and the outlying Ibibio communities on the Cross River talked of how the White men and women who worshipped that God presented Him as a God who was equally accepting of all social groups. This message of love for all mankind appealed especially to the slaves and the destitute members of the communities where Christianity was introduced." He stopped and coughed loudly and drank from a gourd of palm wine on the table before continuing.

"In and around Calabar, missionaries set up schools where young men learned how to read and write as the White men did. Were you told that Achi was a big trader? He and my grandfather traded between Aro Chukwu and Itu on the Cross River. Our traders also heard rumors of the new God and of a White woman who performed miracles in several communities along the Cross River. Whatever God she worshipped gave her the power to save the lives of sick people when the local priests gave up. They never saw her, but Achi told me that he longed for her to come to Aro Chukwu, so she could cure his wife who couldn't carry a child to term.

—❧—

Mazi Oji paused. "Does anyone have anything to add?"

"I can tell you how Achi met Mary Slessor," Nwosu said. "My

Grandfather Nwankwo was with him during that trip to Itu."

All eyes turned to Nwosu, who sat in a corner drinking palm wine, as he gave his story.

—❧—

On the first Ikeji after the destruction of Ibunkpabi, Achi met my Grandfather Nwankwo at Amasu. Achi recently bade his wife goodbye at the dawn of the New Year to take a canoe to Itu. Frustrated, he thought of returning home to his wife. He wasn't happy about leaving her, given her state of mind, but she said she'd stay with her mother during his trip. He needed to stock up on inventory.

Amasu teemed with many traders working between Itu and Aro Chukwu. Some went farther down the Cross River to Calabar to buy yard goods. Achi specialized in yard goods, with an occasional purchase of stockfish, though he sometimes bought kerosene for resale. Traders bought fresh fish and smoked fish from the arriving fishermen. Men unloaded tubers of yams and bunches of plantain, as well as manufactured goods, such as machetes, iron pots, and bolts of cloth from Calabar.

On other parts of the beach, women and children bathed or collected drinking water. It was a busy beach, and the noise was deafening. At least ten canoes were leaving for Itu when he came.

Nwankwo, my grandfather and a friend of Achi, was bound for the same journey, and they agreed to share a canoe. Nwankwo had bags of palm kernels to take to Calabar for sale at the United Africa Company depot. They both wore loincloths and the long-sleeved shirts that set them apart from their fellow countrymen as rich traders able to buy foreign-made shirts. Inevitably, they discussed recent events while wondering what the future might hold for Aro Chukwu. Nwosu stopped to have a drink before continuing his story. Achi envied Nwankwo for his carefree attitude, especially since Achi was worried about his wife's childless condition. He hoped the journey would take his mind off his travails. He asked why his friend would want to go as far as Calabar to dispose of his goods, since he could easily do that at the depot at Itu.

My grandfather, a no-nonsense, taciturn man, said, "I'll get a better price there than in Itu. Besides, I have things I want to buy in Calabar." He waved his hands to indicate he didn't want to discuss his reasons.

Achi persisted, believing that since they'd be spending the day together, it would be nice if they had something to discuss.

"Will you be taking the launch to Calabar from Itu?"

"I have some business at Ikonetu. From there, I'll take the pontoon across to Itu, where the new launch to Calabar sails.

It'll reduce the hours I'll spend on the river."

The journey to Itu took almost a whole day by canoe. That particular day, it was rough going, because the canoe was overloaded, and the rower had to be careful it didn't tip.

After two hours, they reached the first of the Ibibio villages on the water's edge. Men with baskets of fresh fish begged them to stop. The thought of freshly roasted fish was too tempting to resist, so they paddled to the small beach of the tiny hamlet and stopped to eat before continuing to Itu.

As they approached, they saw the fishermen were unduly excited.

One of them helped them moor their boat.

"Man, what a day we're having!" he'd said. "The White woman has just arrived and gone to the village. Her canoe came from Itu this morning."

"Where is she?" Achi asked.

He paid for a whole fish and sat on a nearby trunk to watch the fishermen tend their nets. Others came to listen to the story, too.

"I told you she was going to the village. Did you see how many canoes are here? Ten came with her. The women wore long dresses. She wore a voluminous skirt and long-sleeved shirt tucked into it, and she had a big hat." The speaker used his arms to demonstrate.

Achi looked at his friend in anticipation. "Let's go to the village to see what's happening."

Nwankwo hesitated, because he wanted to proceed to Itu immediately to conclude his business.

In the end, Achi persuaded him to stay a bit and go watch the event in the village. He reasoned they wouldn't have many opportunities to watch such a thing. They set out for the village of Chief Okon.

On arrival, they saw a huge crowd in the middle of the village square, but they didn't see the White woman. It looked as if Chief Okon was in the process of passing judgment on a naked woman held by two men. Achi and Nwankwo learned that the woman was a witch who'd been eating babies in the stomachs of village women.

My God, Achi thought. It's possible my babies have been eaten by a similar woman in our village. We have to find her!

"Woman, you've sinned against your ancestors, and we will hang you," the chief said.

There was a commotion. To Achi's horror, a White woman in a voluminous dress and hat burst into the center of the square, walked up to the chief and said loudly, "No, you will not!"

There was dead silence. People recovered their voices, and all started shouting in Ibibio, urging the chief to kill the White woman, too. Achi was petrified. It looked as if the crowd would take matters into its own hands and attack her.

After what seemed like eternity, Chief Okon rose from his dais and approached the White woman. "Mama Etubom, we didn't expect you today."

The people held their breath. Achi understood that the chief had invited the White woman into the area to set up school similar to the ones she set up elsewhere along the Cross River.

"Chief Okon, you may take my life in the place of this woman's," the White woman said.

Achi and my grandfather were stunned. All expected the chief to insist the judgment be carried out, or that the White woman should be driven from his land. Achi saw the chief was in a quandary. Saving the woman would be a sign of weakness.

Chief Okon conferred with his advisors. He told the White woman to take the sinner as her slave, since she wasn't wanted in the area.

Achi and my grandfather were amazed. It was too late to start off for Itu, and both had to return to the canoe to sleep and wait for dawn.

In the morning, when they were ready to pull out, several men from the village arrived with more tales of what the White woman did during the evening.

"There was the question of where she should spend the night," one said.

"I wondered about that, too," Achi said. "What happened next?" Nwankwo asked.

"The chief gave her one of his wife's houses to sleep in, but you haven't heard the worst thing she did!"

At that point, Ume, the third man relating the story, joined the conversation. "My grandfather owned the canoe that took them to Itu. He told us that the three of them from Aro wanted to know what happened and urged the speaker to continue the story, which he did."

Ume took up the tale.

In addition to letting the witch sleep in her hut, the White woman told the chief it was wrong to kill women who gave birth to twins or to kill the twins themselves. To everyone's dismay, she went around collecting all such abandoned children who'd been left to die. She talked about the God who forgives every wrongdoing and doesn't expect human sacrifice.

Achi and Nwankwo vehemently doubted that.

An elderly fisherman who'd been mending nets nearby said, "A miracle happened last night."

The others fell silent to listen.

"A woman was having a difficult birth. The midwife tried every medicine to get the baby out, but to no avail. You know how it is. The priest asked for sacrifices, which the husband performed, also to no avail. The woman was known to be very wicked, and people said she deserved to die in childbirth.

"The White woman, seeing the crowd outside, learned about the problem." He paused to turn over the fish roasting on an open fire. "The White woman went into the woman's hut. We don't know what she did, but whatever it was, the baby turned and came out alive. The woman's life was saved. Everyone was amazed, and it has been discussed often."

He stopped and looked at the faces around him. "The chief wants her to stay longer and even gave her one of his daughters to travel with her and learn about her God."

That was a strange tale. My grandfather and the others who heard it were skeptical. However, my grandfather said that of the three of them, Achi was most affected by the story because of his domestic situation. Before leaving, they learned that the strange woman was expected in Itu later that day.

Their canoe arrived in Itu late in the evening. Hundreds of people milled around, but there was no launch.

"Where's the launch?" they asked someone.

"An important White man from Aro Chukwu came and commandeered it to take him to Calabar."

"Just my luck," Nwankwo whined, his expression gloomy. "I didn't plan to spend the night in Itu. Now I either have to sell my goods at the depot here or take the canoe all the way to Calabar. I'm not sure

what to do. First, I'll need accommodations for the night." Achi didn't reply.

As they walked around the beachfront, where many canoes were lined up, they saw a large crowd on the hill and went to see what it meant.

"It's to see the White woman," someone told them. "She arrived. She also missed the launch and has been offered accommodations at the mission post up the hill. The crowd is here to see her, because they've heard so much about her efforts regarding twins and indigents."

Skeptically slapping his thighs, another man said, "By the way, her God gave her the power to cure diseases that even our priests can't cure." He laughed.

Intrigued, they walked up the hill in the hope of seeing her, but the crowd was too dense.

The following day after completing his business, Achi stood on the Itu beach, looking for the canoe that would take him home. It was a busy place, with hundreds of canoes of all sizes loaded with produce. Some carried tins of palm and palm kernels bound for Calabar. Others were going to Oron, and many others were on their way along the Cross River to Unwana and beyond, carrying all types of manufactured goods.

Achi walked to the area where canoes bound for Aro Chukwu anchored, hoping to see my grandfather. Nwankwo told him he would either continue his journey to Oron or hopefully find a Calabar-bound canoe in Itu.

"This part of the story was told to me by my grandfather," Ume added, "because Nwankwo didn't travel back the same day as Achi." He continued his narrative.

After looking around, Achi found my grandfather's canoe about to push off. He recognized the passenger in the canoe as Chief Kanu Nta of the Amasu village who had only recently assumed the chieftaincy after the death of his father. His pockmarked face showed he once suffered from smallpox.

"Nna, I'm also Aro Chukwu bound, so maybe I could share your canoe," Achi said, walking up to the chief. "I don't have much, just two tins of kerosene and a bale of stockfish."

"What do you think, Nna?" the chief asked my grandfather.

"It'll be tight, considering how much you both have. I can take you both, but I'll charge extra for the goods."

They haggled for a time until they agreed on the fare.

As soon as the canoe left Itu and was on the river, Achi looked up the hill toward the mission past. "Yesterday, this area was full of people intent on seeing the fabled White woman."

"I was there, too," the chief said. "You were? I don't believe it."

The chief laughed. "I came to invite her to visit Amasu. My mother's been ill since my father died. I heard the White woman can cure all sorts of diseases, even the ones our priests can't cure, so I invited her. Perhaps she can find a cure for what ails my mother. She promised to come to Aro Chukwu if the man in charge, Montanaro, can assure her it's safe."

"How were you able to get close to her given the mass of people in the area?"

"I've met her before. During the war, a group of us, which incidentally included your chief, found our way to Akpap, where we hoped to hide until things calmed down." He continued solemnly. "You remember how the man in charge was hunting for all chiefs and priests, determined to wipe us out? When we got to Akpap, we sought out the chief and asked for his protection. She was at the mission post and helped protect us. She never told anyone we were there."

Achi gazed at him with his mouth open. He wanted to hear more, but the boatman indicated he wanted to push off. He was anxious to get home and urged them to finish storing their goods.

Hurriedly securing his kerosene tins with a rope, Achi said, "I remember there was a time when Chief Igwe was missing. We thought he was killed during the fight. We rejoiced when he appeared several days later. He kept his whereabouts a secret."

"Yes. We were all together." The chief settled down for the journey home. "Since then, we've stayed in touch with her. We wanted her to teach us how to deal with the White man in charge.

This time, however, I went to invite her to help us start a school to teach our children how to read and write, as is happening in Akpap." "When will she come?" Achi thought of his wife's condition.

"I don't know the exact date, because she's very busy." The chief shrugged. "She promised to come once it's safe. According to her, the launch's absence at Itu today was because of that man Montanaro. He was traveling to Calabar and needed the launch. It'll come back with him when he returns."

"Are you sure she's coming?"

"As sure as I can be." The canoe moved toward Aro Chukwu. "It all depends on Montanaro."

———❦———

Ume completed that part of the story and stood to refill his cup.

Clint, who'd been listening intently, said, "I've often wondered what happened to the minor chiefs. I thought they'd all been rounded up and killed. Now I know some escaped and returned only when they weren't in danger. However, I don't understand why Chief Okon easily acquiesced to Mary Slessor's demands. Wouldn't he lose face among his people by deferring to a woman?"

Mazi Oji raised his hand to stop Clint. "Young Man, you must remember that Mary Slessor had the full support of the British government. Anything that happened to her would bring the wrath of the British administration in Calabar down on the chief. Besides, my grandfather told me that Okon was in Calabar and saw all the new schools and health clinics set up by the missionaries. Chief Okon desperately wanted to open his district to the new things happening in and around Calabar."

"Thank you, Mazi. The occupation must've been very hard on the ordinary people, given that they were left on their own without even the presence of the chiefs, who ran to save their own lives."

"The beginning of the occupation was very hard for our people. You must remember it was during the dry season, and normally, food would be scarce. It was particularly bad that year, because the preparations for war preempted the usual period when families prepared the land for planting the next year's harvest.

"In the year with the war, many people were starving. My grandfather said that most people were reduced to one meal a day, perhaps only plantain. I remember him saying they went to the barracks to see the new building being put up by the soldiers. The activities attracted a lot of onlookers who returned to the compounds, regaling everyone with stories. The lucky ones were hired for the building crew.

"To get the cooperation of the minor chiefs, the administrator built a house for each of them. My grandfather and Achi were in the building crew for Chief Igwe's new house, which is that dilapidated structure in front of Okoro's house in the village. It used to have two stories with verandas all around. I can't remember if they were paid for the work, but at least the men who worked in the barracks were paid.'

Clint turned to Mazi Ume. "Being told of the pregnant woman saved by Mary Slessor must've reminded Achi of his own predicament, wouldn't you say? The other day, my Uncle Okoro told me of Achi's wife's miscarriages."

Mazi Ume nodded. "Achi said he sometimes felt that the ancestors were punishing him for marrying outside his social class, but he also knew that his current status was imposed on him by circumstances. He wasn't born a slave, and, looking around, he saw that he and his wife lived better than most of the Amadis he knew."

"He wouldn't be a man if he thought the situation was normal," Mazi Oji added. "My father said that for a while, Achi looked very sad. Everyone felt his pain, but no one could help."

"Poor Mboro," Ume said. "Can you imagine how she felt for being unable to give her husband the one thing he craved? He couldn't blame her, because seeing her cohorts from the fattening rooms, who by then had three children, reminded her of her failure. He often said to her, 'It's not your fault. We've done everything we could possibly do.'

"You should consider taking another wife who'll give you a male child,' she said.

"He stopped discussing the situation with his male friends, because he knew they'd say the same thing. 'Get rid of her and marry someone who'll give you a son.'"

"They probably had a point," Mazi Oji said. "He was a successful trader and could afford as many wives as he wanted."

"But deep inside," another man argued, "he loved his wife and couldn't imagine bringing another woman into the household." He turned to Clint. "Is this of interest to you?" Clint nodded.

The men were anxious to leave. As they stood to go, Mazi Oji said, "Mazi Igwe should be able to arrange for you to meet Mazi Mkemdirim at Amasu, who can tell you more about Mary Slessor."

As Clint left, Ifeoma suggested they stop at her grandmother's house for a meal before heading home.

CHAPTER NINETEEN

S omething very important must have brought you here today," Igwe said. "Whatever it is, I'm glad you're here to keep me company. I was on the phone with my son in Finsbury Park in London, trying to persuade him to come back home. I miss my sons, and I can't understand why they won't return to establish themselves here."

Igwe was surprised to find Clint outside on such a rainy day. The rain, which began the previous afternoon, showed no sign of abating.

Clint furled his umbrella and stepped into the room, closing the door behind him.

"Don't mind me," Igwe said, still thinking of the phone call. "I understand their situation. They have to go where they can find employment. It's just that old age makes you want to be surrounded by family. Sit down. I'm glad to see you. By the way, I saw Oji at the village meeting last week, and he said you went to see him."

"I did. Ifeoma arranged for me to meet him and some others."

"He said Ume and Nwosu were with him when you visited. I went to school with one of Ume's brothers. The one you met was the only one who followed in his father's footsteps. He was a good boatman. I remember his father taking us in his canoe to Itu during the Christmas holidays. Nowadays, you can hardly find anyone in Aro who practices the art of canoe building. He's the last of them.

"By the way, I'll be leaving you shortly. I have a meeting in the compound I must attend. One of our daughters died, and we're meeting to organize the funeral. The wake is tonight. I hope the rain ends soon."

Igwe went to the window and looked out. "It looks like it's ending."

"I'm sorry to hear someone died," Clint said. "Was she sick?" "Oh, yes. Before her retirement, she was the Chief Matron of the

government hospital in Enugu. I'll be gone for only an hour, so I

hope to see you here when I return."

After assuring Igwe he wasn't planning to return to Esther's house so soon after his arrival, Clint settled down to watch a replay of a soccer match between Nigeria and the Cameroons. The video was a present from Igwe's friend at Aba, whose son was one of the players.

—⚡︎—

When Igwe returned, Clint looked at him expectantly, as they settled down to lunch.

"Grandpa, I was a bit shaken when Mazi Oji pointed out my resemblance to Achi, your grandfather. Why would that be unusual? I'm his grandson."

"Think nothing of it. You probably don't know that we Aro people believe that death is not the end of life. We believe everyone returns after death to live again. When you die, you come back as a child to some member of your family, and your next life is better than the previous life. If your current life is rough, you hope that in your next one, you'll have the things that were denied you.

"When a child is born, we always try to find out which dead member of the family has returned to live again. When I first saw you, you reminded me of my grandfather. The way you held your head, the way you walked, the shape of your head, the curve of your eyebrows—all were very familiar. I mentioned it to my brother, who agreed, but we didn't want to say anything to you. Don't be upset by what the old man said. Achi was a good man who was loved by many people."

"Thank you. Tell me about your meeting."

"We meet to ensure everyone would gather outside the compound when the hearse arrives late this afternoon and to decide what we, as her family members, will contribute toward the funeral."

"Was she your sister?"

"In a way. We all belong to the same compound, and everyone in a compound is related, but we aren't from the same parents."

"I should leave, since you'll be taking your usual afternoon nap soon."

"Stay and watch TV if you wish. I see the sun has come out, and the rain has stopped. If you wish to go, the driver will take you."

At Esther's house, it was gloomy. Unlike her usual self, she looked disheveled. Her blouse didn't match her wrapper, and her head tie was askew. Mba, her live-in son, held her and tried to comfort her.

Clint was surprised to see Mba at that time of day. He usually left the house at the crack of dawn and returned late at night. He'd been spending weekends at Umuahia, where his wife stayed until the birth of their child.

Alarmed, Clint asked, "Grandma, are you all right?"

Mba hustled Esther into her room. When he returned, he explained, "We lost an important person in our compound. She was very close to my mother. The wake is tonight, and Mama has been busy organizing the women to gather firewood and cook for the wake and the meal tomorrow. She's tired."

"That's funny. My grandfather told me he also had a funeral and a wake to attend."

"Yes. It's the same person. She came from their compound and married into ours, just as your mother came from our compound and married into theirs. The husband died a few years back. You can see the tents for the wake being set up across the road."

Mba pointed out the walled house across the way, where Clint often bought peanuts from a vendor outside the gate.

When Esther reappeared, Clint sat with her awhile, but she seemed very nervous, frequently calling to the servants to perform urgent tasks.

"I spent the whole day helping with the arrangements for tonight and tomorrow," she muttered.

Clint was at a loss what to do. "Are there any errands you'd like me to run for you, Grandma?"

She managed a smile. "Thank you, Clint. I've done most of them and designated a maid to carry out the rest. She'll help fetch water and firewood for cooking. Everything has been prepared for tonight. Early tomorrow morning, the designated cooks will prepare for the funeral celebration, which starts immediately after the church service."

Clint noticed how tired she was. "Before he left, Mba told me to make sure you rest for at least an hour. I'll go to the wake with you. Promise me we'll stay only a short time, since you'll need a good night's sleep before the funeral tomorrow." Esther nodded and went to her room.

Not having been to a funeral of known someone who died, Clint didn't know what was expected of him. The person who died must have meant a lot to Esther, given her behavior. He realized Esther's gloom had descended on the other occupants of the house, too. Often at that time of day, the house was full of laughter, as the maids and house servants traded friendly insults.

Later, when Clint reentered the courtyard after his evening wash, he heard shouts of welcome. Esther was up and receiving visitors.

It was completely dark outside by the time Clint entered the parlor, and the light from the single bulb hanging from the ceiling cast a shadowy haze. He saw several people in the room, some of whom he recognized from the Ikeji period. Some of the gnats coming through the open windows pelted the visitors, while the rest ended their lives against the naked bulb.

The air was filled with the endless pings of insects on the wall, as Esther introduced Clint. After explaining that all the people were there for the funeral the next day, she called a maid to bring food and drink. Clint realized that while he was lounging about at Igwe's, Esther was busy organizing food for the visitors.

The talk in the parlor centered on the grandeur of past funerals. Clint learned that the body had been kept in cold storage for five months after the woman died, so the family could gather enough money to give her a fitting funeral. The official announcement was made only three weeks earlier to give friends and relatives time to make arrangement to attend.

That came as a surprise to Clint. Judging by Esther's behavior, he assumed the death was sudden.

"Is such a delay normal?" he asked.

"Of course," Chima, who came from Owerri for the event, replied. "The family is scattered around the globe, and they must have time to make travel arrangements and discuss what is needed for such an important person. They know much will be required of them."

Clint learned that each of the woman's grandsons donated a cow, and seven had already been slaughtered for the wake and the repast the following day. The family decided to give each visitor a mug engraved with the dead woman's photograph and age. There were announcements on the radio every hour for a week preceding the funeral, and a huge crowd from throughout Nigeria was expected.

"This will be something," Esther pronounced.

Clint felt uncomfortable during the discussion, thinking of the average villager who had trouble buying more than one meal a day. "I still can't understand why funerals are so expensive here. In America, it would be unusual to keep the body so long before burial. The cost for storage would be exorbitant. Besides, we have funeral homes."

"Of course it's expensive," Nduka said. "We spend too much on funerals. It means nothing to the dead."

"She's worth every penny the family will spend!" Esther said angrily. "I don't agree with those who say we spend too much on funerals. It's a time when we celebrate the life of a loved one. Our expenditure is supposed to match our love for that person." She stood to adjust her wrapper.

"Mama Esther," Nwankwo said, who arrived in time to hear her final statement. "I don't wish to argue with you, especially at a time like this, but I always feel it would be better to use the money to make sure the person is taken care of during her lifetime, rather than bankrupt ourselves giving a lavish funeral. I know cases where men borrowed money they couldn't afford to repay, just to meet what was expected of them."

"If that family had money to waste," Nduka said, "why can't they donate a portion of the money to charity in honor of the beloved dead?"

"That's usually the case in the U.S.," Clint said.

Esther shook her head vehemently. "We aren't in the U.S. That reminds me, Clint. I got you a shirt and wrap, too, since you're family. I took one of your shirts to the tailor for measurement."

Clint frowned, knowing how often Esther changed subjects when it was something she didn't understand or like. He had no intention of going to the church for the funeral. Why must he wear a uniform when he wasn't a family member? All the formalities he was experiencing made him fed up. Sitting there, confused and irritated by the conversation, he felt mosquitoes biting his ankles. One dug into the back of his neck and flew down his shirt to a place where he couldn't scratch.

Many more people stopped by. It was only then that Clint realized that the wake was actually being held across the road. The dead woman's husband's house was a two-story building, where Clint went many times to buy roasted corn in season. He saw chairs arranged outdoors and strings of light bulbs hanging across poles placed at the perimeter of the yard.

"I hope NEPA won't choose this night for its regular power outage," Clint said. "If there is one, what happens?" The others laughed.

"We managed before we had NEPA lights," Nduka said.

"The family can't trust NEPA during such an important event," Esther said. "They must have generators."

The conversation veered to events at recent funerals. Clint tuned it out until he heard Esther say that the group responsible for digging the grave wanted more than food and drink.

"They said that cutting through the cement foundation in the room was too much effort," she added.

"I don't blame them," Nduka replied. "I think it's high time we designated an area for a cemetery. Soon, in each house, coffins will be on top of other coffins."

"What do you mean?" Clint was puzzled. "I was told at Ujari that the custom here is to bury the dead in their homes."

"That's true," Nduka said. "We don't have cemeteries here. From time immemorial, we've buried our dead in our houses. I remember recently that a friend of mine was replacing his mother's house by building a bigger one. Several skeletons of long-dead relatives were dug out during the laying of the foundation.

"In the past, if you didn't have a house, your body was stored until your family built one for you, so you could have a resting place. Why do you think we have all those mostly empty houses in the new extension? That's why we all try to build houses, even when we spend only two weeks a year in them."

Disgusted, Clint remembered all the incomplete houses along the road to the barracks. Unnecessary expense even when you can't afford it, he thought.

"We have a cemetery near the barracks," someone said.

"That's for prisoners. No Aro man of worth would agree to be buried there."

Clint almost choked on his laughter. Being buried in a cemetery would be better than wasting all one's assets building a house just to be buried in it.

"There are several cemeteries in places like Aba," Chima said. "I presume one can always be buried there if you live in the city. We have a saying, Nobody goes on a journey that they won't return from. That's why even when someone dies overseas the body is brought home for interment."

In a satisfied tone, he concluded, "When I was in the U.S., I often resented being asked to contribute to the expenses of repatriating people to their homeland after they died. It seems that this custom is universal among Africans. We always want to return to our land. I suppose if, in the end, there wasn't enough money for an airplane, the family would eventually succumb and bury the person in the U.S."

"It would be cheaper to cremate the person and take the ashes home, but I assume that would be sacrilege, because it's the body that must be returned," Flora said.

Clint shuddered. I'd better make sure my parents don't subscribe to that view. Their home is in the U.S. "How long is the wake tonight?"

"The dancing and singing will go on until early morning," Chima said. "The funeral itself will continue as long as there's food. Funerals help keep a lot of the poor alive. A rich man's funeral even more so."

As they talked, more people arrived at Esther's. She soon had to send someone to the nearest bar to fetch benches for people to sit on outside.

To Clint, it appeared that the whole neighborhood was participating in the wake. Certainly the music was loud enough to cover the whole area. At an appropriate time, he slipped away to his room to rest. He surmised, judging from the number of people arriving and the pre-wake party at Esther's house, he wouldn't get much sleep that night.

—〰—

When Esther called to him that it was time to pay their respects, Clint left his room and walked across the road with her, holding her hand. The crowd was such they had to push past people to get near the house. Finally, they entered the parlor, with walls papered with joji, and the dead woman lay in a collapsible coffin on a double bed with a white canopy. Beautifully made up and dressed in an expensive joji, a damasked matching blouse, and head tie, wearing her gold jewelry, she looked as if she were sleeping, though she wouldn't have dressed that way for bed.

"Grandma, is it like this for all funerals?" Clint asked softly.

"Only the rich can afford such lavish decoration," she whispered. "You should've seen your grandfather's funeral. This doesn't even compare. Let's pay our respects to the family."

The dead woman's daughters and sisters sat on the floor mat opposite the bed. As visitors arrived to pay their respects, they sobbed and cried out praises for the dead woman. Wiping their eyes, they thanked the guests for coming.

Occasionally, a group of dancers entered the room and circled the bed, dancing and singing the dead woman's praises. The band blared loud music the entire time, pausing only occasionally when the players needed a drink before continuing. Young girls served drinks, chin chin, and akara balls.

Everyone appeared to enjoy the festive atmosphere, and there was nothing apart from the corpse itself to show this was a funeral. If he hadn't known better, Clint would have thought the party was to celebrate a family event.

I guess death is an event, he thought.

Esther had timed her arrival to coincide with that of the pastor, who went to the DJ and asked for selections of church music. During the pause, he offered prayers for the dead, and everyone sang the selected hymn. Shortly after, the dancing continued.

Esther lingered, speaking to mourners and acquaintances before walking with Clint to a home filled with the overflow of people from the wake.

"I'm surprised we've been spared rain for tonight," Clint remarked. "We've had a downpour every day this week. Where are the mosquitoes? I haven't been bitten once."

"The family spent a bit of money to spray DDT over the yard," Esther explained. "I wish the daughters of the family could have a little rest before their obligatory run around the different villages with their age groups early tomorrow to sing their mother's praises and announce her death. Maybe they'll forego that part. Who knows? It's up to them. They'll have time to rest after the church service tomorrow at Amanagwu."

She became nostalgic. "When your grandfather died, my daughter and daughters-in-law who were present went out early in the morning to announce to all the village that their father died. I like that tradition."

Clint realized she was hinting at her regret that Peace hadn't honored her father by being present at his funeral.

He thought of his mother. Esther wanted Peace to be physically present at her father's funeral and perhaps at this one, too. Since Esther mentioned the duties Peace would have performed, Clint imagined her on the floor all night, facing the body of the deceased, then getting up in the morning to run to the villages to announce her father's death. He wondered if she would have done it and shook his head, knowing the strong views his parents had about Nigeria.

He'd been staying with Esther over three months and was still trying to make up his mind about the country. Would he want to live there forever? He appreciated the cultural heritage, but there were many customs and practices that he, as an American, found difficult to embrace. The toll that such an elaborate funeral took on the bereaved family was something he didn't appreciate or accept.

After the funeral service the following day, the feasting and celebrating continued. Clint was amazed by how many people showed up. It was as if all of Aro Chukwu came to bury the woman, who, as far as he could gather, owed her prominence to her husband's position as a judge and to being the mother of several high-achieving children.

Upon leaving, each guest held a mug, the thank-you gift from the family, for helping them bury their mother. Once all the mugs were given away, unfortunate guests received plastic bread baskets instead.

Early the next morning, Esther dragged Clint to the dead woman's house for a compound meeting. It began raining hard, as they left. Every drop struck the ground with great force and bounced back as if striking a hard surface. When they arrived at the house with their umbrellas dripping water and shoes soaked, all the important men and women in his grandmother's compound, as well as the male members of the bereaved family, were present. The meeting— clothing of the dead— was traditionally held the day after the funeral for two reasons: first, for the families to give the community an account of all donations from friends, and second, for the extended family members to present their own gifts, as prescribed by custom.

As the extended family members presented their gifts in turn, attention focused on Clint, who, as his father's representative, was asked to present his father's gift, since he was an in-law who married into the compound. He was taken aback. He hadn't anticipated such a request, and he hadn't even mentioned the event to his father.

Luckily, Esther rescued him. "My in-law sent his gift through me. I should have given it to Clint to present, but I wasn't thinking. Forgive me. Here is his gift." She presented six yards of joji as Peter's gift.

Gifts from other members of the extended family were recorded. All were tallied and divided equally among the immediate family and the compound.

Baffled, Clint turned to his grandmother, as they left the meeting. "The family should have kept the gifts to defray part of the cost of the funeral."

Esther shook her head. "They didn't have to hire people to cook, fetch wood and water, or dig the grave. This is the only payment the members of the compound will receive, so I think it's fair. Remember, too, that everyone who gave them gifts expects them to reciprocate when the same event occurs in their own family. That's the way it is here."

"Why didn't you warn me, Grandma?"

"Sorry, Clint. They didn't mean to embarrass you in that way. They knew I had the gift for the family. I sometimes wish we would have, as in America and elsewhere, firms that take care of all the funeral arrangements." She wiped her brow to indicate what a tiresome business it was.

"What happens next?"

"A memorial service will be held on Sunday, after which the family members can return home to their places of employment. My hope is you'll attend the memorial service. Your grandfather, Igwe, will be there."

From her mocking tone, she knew Esther didn't expect him to go.

CHAPTER TWENTY

C lint made arrangements with Nick to walk the slave route the next dry day. The maid knocked on Clint's door early one morning to say that Nick arrived. Clint got up and welcomed his friend, who drank a Fanta, which Esther graciously offered while waiting for Clint.

When Clint was ready, they set out for the Ibom village square. Clint rode his bike, while Nick walked alongside. At the square, Clint left his bike at a carpenter's stall to be retrieved later, then they continued on foot.

Armed with a new can of insect repellent, Clint plunged onto the bush path leading from Ibom to Amanagwu. Several paths were available, and after some wandering, they finally found the right one.

The path was uneven and narrow. Low shrubs grew on both sides, behind which the forest extended as far as they could see. The smell of rotting leaves intermingled with that of bush flowers. The incessant calls of birds nesting above the trees joined with the buzzing of bees and humming of insects. They passed groups of tappers carrying calabashes of fresh palm wine, as well as people on their way to the farm.

It was hard going through the muddy, difficult path, but they persisted. By the time they came out at Ujari, having decided not to branch off to Amanagwu, the sun was high, and their feet were caked with mud. Scraping as much of it off as they could, they took an undulating path that led to the beach at Amasu. Halfway there, the path rose sharply before descending toward the river.

Reaching the beach, both were tired. Clint couldn't help imagining how the slaves felt, as they were led on the path toward the river. Once at the river, there were probably canoes waiting to transport them to Calabar. All Clint saw were fishermen mending their nets and men sitting on logs, talking with the fishermen.

How many slaves passed over this beach? he wondered. I wish the beach could talk.

Clint removed his sneakers and washed them thoroughly before pulling them on for the next phase of their walk from Amasu to Amanagwu, then to Iyi Eke.

They stopped at a stall in the Ujari village to get something to eat and drink. They must not have cleaned themselves of the mud, because the owner asked in Igbo, "What have you two been doing? You look as if you've been rolling in mud."

They discussed the heat before continuing to Amanagwu, where Clint hoped to talk to his uncle and get directions to Iyi Eke. At the village square, she sought out the statue of Alvan Ikoku, which he'd seen many times but hadn't associated with a school.

While he stood in the square, someone beckoned. It was Pastor Ibekwe, the man he met at the Obinkita Presbyterian Church, though he didn't have his clerical collar. Clint, glad to see him, introduced his friend.

"Are you admiring the statue of our famous person, Mr. Alvan Ikoku?" the pastor asked.

"I've often walked past this place, but I never really looked at the statue before. Sometime ago, I met someone at the post office who told me about the association of this man with the secondary school here."

"He was a great man," Ibekwe said expansively. "He not only founded the school, which I, too, attended, but he represented Aro Chukwu for a long time in the eastern Nigerian legislature before the civil war. I think someone said he was among those who translated the Bible into Igbo, though I'm not certain of that. There's a teacher training college at Owerri named after him."

"My grandmother told me he was a distant relative of my grandfather, and my family members attended the school."

"Oh, really? Before independence, there were several students from the Southern Cameroons in the school. There's an alumni organization in American, and I'm sure your father must belong."

Clint looked at the passersby for a while, then said whimsically, "If he belongs, he never said anything about it to me. This is all news to me. I'm sure when I get home, he'll have a lot of explaining to do."

Laughing, Pastor Ibekwe said, "I wouldn't want to be in his shoes when you confront him. Are you going back to Esther's house now, or are you going somewhere else? I could give you a ride."

"I'm on my way to visit my uncle. I wanted to go to Iyi Eke today, but it looks like it's getting hot, so I might do that another day. Why are you here?"

The pastor's expression became somber. "One of my parishioners died, and the funeral will be this weekend, so I came to Amanagwu to consult my colleague on the arrangements. Funerals take up a lot of our time here, especially since it was decided that all funerals should take place on weekends. In fact, the celebration begins Thursday or Friday with the wake. You must've witnessed a few funerals since you arrived."

"A few weeks ago, I was at the wake of my grandmother's friend, but that was an exception. She never expected me to attend funerals with her, since I don't know the families of the bereaved."

"She's right," Ibekwe said solemnly, "although, in our culture, knowing the dead is immaterial. Unfortunately, many regard wakes and funerals as a time to enjoy themselves at the expense of the bereaved families. I often marvel at the amount of money spent on funerals for entertainment, but in our culture, the amount spent shows how much the dead person was appreciated and loved." Before Clint could frame a suitable reply, Ibekwe's attention was distracted by several men who wished to speak with him. Clint and his friend slipped away and walked toward Igwe's compound.

As they approached, Clint saw Ifeoma standing in front of the tailor's shop. He went to talk to her, saying he was hoping to visit Iyi Eke, but he needed directions from his uncle.

"Do you still want to see Mazi Nkemdirim?" she asked.

"Yes. That's my next project. My grandfather was supposed to arrange it, but, with his mind preoccupied with so many things, I haven't reminded him."

"I saw Mazi Nkemdirim at church on Sunday, and I told him of your interest. He would be glad to see you at any time."

"That's good to know. I'm really here to get directions from my uncle. I want to go to Iyi Eke."

"Do you mean the stream where we get our drinking water? It's on the way to your grandfather's house. You've passed the road to it many times."

"No. I mean the one associated with the Ibunkpabi."

"I'm not aware of any such stream. If you find it, perhaps you'll tell me about it."

He saw his uncle in animated conversation with two men. "There's my uncle," Clint said. "I'd better try to catch him in case

he's on his way out."

Okoro greeted Clint warmly, asking, "What are you up to these days?"

"I actually came to ask you for directions to Iyi Eke, since I wanted to go there tomorrow to explore the caves."

"What?" Okoro shook his head. "You can't go there by yourself. Amanagwu people have someone designated to look after it. If you want to go, as soon as I'm back, I'll consult the keeper of the caves and get someone to go with you."

Clint groaned. Nothing is easy here. "I'm not going alone. My friend who was with me will come, too. He left, because he had to go home. He lives at Oror."

"Even then." His uncle waved him aside. "You need to go with the keeper of the caves. Iyi Eke isn't a problem. It's just a stream where we get our drinking water. If you want to go to the caves, you have to be accompanied by a designated person. Besides, there are rituals you have to perform."

Another hurdle! Clint thought. These people create hurdles where there should be none. I'm getting tired of this. I can't imagine being told I have to get permission to visit Mount Rushmore or any other historical site in the

U.S. "So, Uncle, when do you think I should do this? Next week, I'll be going to Calabar, and I really would like to do this before then."

"I don't see any problem. You and your friend should come the day after tomorrow. By then, I'll have made the arrangements.

Come early."

"I have one other request, Uncle."

Bemused, Okoro looked at him in anticipation.

"Do you know Mazi Nkemdirim? I'd like to visit him, too."

"That's funny. I saw him about an hour ago, and he said he has

business at the tax office in the barracks tomorrow, and he hopes

to have lunch with your grandfather."

Relieved, Clint went to retrieve his bike. He would try to intercept Nkemdirim at Igwe's.

Leisurely relaxing in the house and listening to Al Jazeera's newscast, Igwe wasn't surprised when Clint arrived.

"I hope you'll have lunch with me," Igwe said. "I have a guest arriving any minute. The driver went to bring him from the barracks. You'll be glad to know he's Nkemdirim, the one you're anxious to meet. I must warn you that he's very entertaining and dramatic."

Shortly thereafter, a mild-mannered, precise man with loincloth and khaki shirt, who, unlike most people, spoke in a soft voice, came through the door. Igwe, welcoming him profusely, sent for the gourd container of palm wine for him.

He introduced Clint. "This young man is asking for information on the coming of Christianity to Aro Chukwu. I told him as much as I can, but it would be nice if he could hear it told as only you can tell it." He turned to Clint. "Nkemdirim will make Achi's story come alive."

After making himself comfortable and drinking palm wine with lunch, Nkemdirim settled in the sofa and began his tale. He was a raconteur, very theatrical and gesturing to make a point, changing voices to portray different speakers.

He began by saying, "I presume you told Clint that even though Achi was a free man, he was still under Chief Igwe's domain, so Igwe could call upon him to perform a task at any time."

"Of course," Igwe replied. "He knows that Achi first heard of Mary

Slessor when he went to Itu to purchase goods." Nkemdirim settled down to tell his story.

One month after Achi's return from Itu, the chief sent for him. Achi sensed something important happened, because he found the chief pacing his parlor in excitement.

Before they could sit down, Igwe said, "She is arriving this evening."

Achi stared at him blankly. "Who?"

"Who else but the White woman you saw at Itu?"

"Nnam Ukwu? Is she really arriving?" It was one month since he saw her in the Ibibio village on the Cross River. He could barely contain his excitement.

"Go immediately and round up a group to accompany me to Amasu. Kanu Nta expects us to come with our drums and gong.

Hurry. It will be a festive day."

While Achi went to look for men in the compound to form an entourage to Amasu, Chief Igwe quickly donned his ceremonial gown.

Nkemdirim paused to make the sound of beating drums, then he gulped a mouthful of palm wine before continuing.

In all the adjacent villages, the chiefs rallied their subjects to proceed to the Amasu beach to welcome the White woman they called Ma Etubom. Achi, as part of Chief Igwe's entourage, was present when the launch approached.

First to come out was the hated Administrator, who couldn't hide his surprise at seeing the chiefs. As soon as they saw him, the chiefs turned their backs to show their feelings toward him. Achi wondered what the White man thought of such behavior. He had to know he was hated. His comings and goings in the past were usually unnoticed.

When Mary Slessor came out, the chiefs moved as a group to welcome her, rejoicing that she finally came to visit. The sound of drums and gongs filled the air. Achi, seeing the administrator's face turn red in amazement, asked her to explain. Chief Igwe later told Achi that they understood, through the interpreter, that her response was, "These chiefs are my friends, whom I've known a long time."

It was quite a scene with half-naked men and women massed together on the beach.

Kanu Nta, addressing Mary Slessor, said, "Ma Etubom, welcome to our village. We're glad you kept your promise."

"Thank you for inviting me to come," she replied through her interpreter. "I have wanted to come for a long time, but the timing wasn't right. I have come to bring you the good news of a new God greater than your god."

A murmur went through the crowd, and many shifted their feet. "This God whose words I bring created heaven and earth and all the creatures in it. He loves everyone equally."

"We already believe in one god who created the world," a chief shouted. "We only believe that we cannot see him, but we can worship him through Ibunkpabi and our household gods."

"The God I bring you is not worshipped through any carved images. He sent his Son a long time ago to live among us. His Son gave His life, so that we who live will have eternal life."

"Mama Etubom," Kanu Nta interrupted, "we'll have time to discuss your god later. We invited you here to ask your help in establishing schools, so that we, too, can learn how to read the White man's book and understand his ways. Come, let us show you your abode for your stay."

The party moved from the beach to Kanu Nta's compound, where Mary Slessor was not only shown a place to rest but was entertained with dances for the rest of the day.

That day, our people had a lot to think about. Rumors abounded about the activities of the White woman and those who accompanied her. They heard that in and around Amasu, she was berating the men for the ill treatment of women. One particular man aroused her wrath when he called a compound meeting to sentence his wife to death for producing twins. The midwife killed one at birth, hoping to hide its existence and spare the mother's life, but the husband found out through other members of his family. He wanted her dead, saying she was no different from an animal that gives birth to several babies.

Igwe jumped in to say, "Achi told us he knew this man. He consulted him regarding Mboro's condition. Now the White woman showed she was strong enough to stand against the most-feared healer in Amasu. Not only had she confronted him, but she ordered the wife taken to her abode for protection. The White woman reportedly said, 'My God forbids the killing of an innocent person. This woman did no harm."

"Yes, that's true," Nkemdirim replied. "They said that people from adjacent villages, including Achi's flocked, to Amasu to listen to her. My grandfather, too, was there.

"The men standing by were miffed, but what could they do?

She was under Chief Kanu Nta's protection, and besides, any harm to her would bring severe punishment from the hated administrator.

"When she finally left, she extracted a promise from the chiefs that they would allow Efik catechists to live in Aro Chukwu to preach the gospel. She left a White woman, Mma Arnot, who came with her to live among us, to work for the protection of women."

"Thank you, My Friend," Igwe said. "I heard the same story. It was afterward that Reverend Rankin arrived to set up the Presbyterian Church. At first, Achi and the few converts met with him every Sunday under a tree. He needed land to build a church, and the chiefs were reluctant to provide it for a God they didn't want and who would take away the prestige of the gods worshipped by their ancestors.

"In the end, Reverend Rankin got his wish. A large piece of land was given to him by the Obinkita chief. Achi, as one of the converts, worked on the construction of the rectory, where Reverend Rankin lived while he supervised the building of the church. Until the church was completed, services were held in the lower level of the rectory.

"Every Sunday, Reverend Rankin urged the new Christians to travel to all the villages to preach the good news of the gospel. Converts, led by the Efik catechists, marched to the villages singing Onward Christian Soldiers and urging onlookers to rid themselves of their household gods. New members were encouraged to collect all their household gods to be burned in a bonfire in the village squares. Many Awadas were desecrated in that way.

"The message was simple: 'Christ is the son of God. He died on the cross for our sins. Through Him all sins of the world are forgiven. God loves everyone equally. He commanded us not to take the lives of our fellow men.'

"Before they could be confirmed as full members of the church, Achi and his fellow believers were required to memorize the Ten Commandments, the Lord's Prayer, and Psalm 23, which began, 'The Lord is my shepherd.' A fervent Christian,

Achi attended the adulteducation classes required of those who showed the most promise of becoming future leaders in the new religion, and he learned to read the Bible in Igbo. He was the first one confirmed, and, upon confirmation, he was presented with the Igbo version of The Pilgrim's Progress and the Bible. Those two books became his mostprized possessions."

Clint, who'd been listening closely, finally found his tongue and turned to Mazi Nkemdirim. "Reverend Ibekwe said the same thing to me when I visited the Obinkita church. Sir, how did the newly converted Christians feel about Ikeji with all its Awada rituals? It must have been hard for them not to be part of the celebration."

Nkemdirim wiped his brow with his handkerchief before answering. "Ikeji and its rituals presented problems for the new Christian converts. On one level, the church ordered them to renounce all things from Satan, but on the other hand, Ikeji was in many ways a cultural event, so it was difficult for them to remain totally apart from it. Many new converts still participated in the ritual of eating the ritualized animals at the Awadas, but the most-fervent of them, of which Achi was one, resisted. Instead, they used the period to intensify their evangelism. On such occasions, they tried to ward off temptation by standing in the middle of the village square, surrounded by adherents of the new religion, and urging people to let go of the old ways, refuse the ritualized meat, and let fire destroy their household gods."

Igwe pointed at Clint and shook his hand to emphasize his words. "Now you can understand why Christianity is part of our family and why I've been telling you not to participate in heathen ways during the Ikeji period."

Igwe sighed. "It wasn't all peace and harmony in Achi's home, because his wife was reluctant to accept the new God. She was finally persuaded when she gave birth to a healthy daughter. Achi threw his body and soul into the new religion and ascribed the addition to their family to his embracing the Christian faith. He was eventually rewarded by the birth of two more daughters. In that regard, Christianity was good to him.

He still longed for a son, but that wasn't to be. Though his line continued, it came about in an unforeseen way, and that's a story for another day."

Clint, still mesmerized by the story, reluctantly brought his mind back to the present. He was grateful for the thoughtful way his grandfather answered his questions about the past and especially for the contributions of Nkemdirim, who made it seem alive.

Igwe, elated that Clint was a good listener, offered the driver who was taking Nkemdirim to Amasu to also take Clint to Esther's while it was still daylight, since the sun was already setting.

That night, Clint repeated in his mind all that he heard. He still had questions, and he wondered if Esther would be willing to indulge him and join in a conversation about the early period of Christianity, given the prominent part played by Peace's grandfather.

Igwe's visit the following day provided Clint with the opportunity to ask about the things that troubled him. As he listened to Esther and Igwe argue about Aro politics, the rift in the governing council, and who was to blame for it, Clint couldn't help but interrupt.

"Grandfather, I'm sorry to break in. I can't thank you enough for devoting so much time telling me about the history of the place. I'm sure you're fed up with my questions, but I really need to know when the Bible was translated into Igbo whether your grandparents were able to read it. I'm curious, because the pastor at Obinkita said that before the church was built, the services were held in the lower floor of the Rankin parsonage."

Breathing deeply as if to keep calm, Igwe said, "My grandfather was among the first converts. He learned to read the Bible. I believe I mentioned that the other day."

He paused, then continued in a more congenial tone. "Until the Bible was translated, converts depended on the interpretation of the Bible as told by the catechists. I mentioned previously that the early converts were drawn from the ranks of slaves and the disaffected members of the society who found Christianity's inclusiveness appealing.

He paused to eat something from the plate a servant boy brought in.

With pride, Esther said, "Your great-grandfather on your mother's side was among those selected to go to Onitsha to work on the translation of the Bible. He was among those who represented the Presbyterian mission at that time."

"Which year are we talking about?" Clint became more animated. "I think Mary Slessor came to Aro Chukwu around 1902, and it was after that date that the Presbyterian missionaries began arriving."

"I'll have to check the exact date for you," Igwe said, "but I'm sure

it was between 1902 and 1910 that the Bible was translated into Igbo. However, I'm not a historian, so my dates may be off." He sipped from a bottle and coughed. "I understood there was discussion as to which Igbo dialect should be used. It was a fight between the Aro and Onitsha dialects, but, in the end, the Onitsha dialect was selected. The Pilgrim's Progress must've been translated into Igbo, because I can remember Grandfather Achi reading bits of it and telling us children that his life was like that of the pilgrim. He had to overcome many temptations to finally arrive at the gate of heaven."

He turned toward Clint and looked into his eyes, waggling his right hand. "You see, your family on both sides has always held an important position in the Christian Church in Aro Chukwu. We want to continue that with your generation.' Clint listened intently.

"It's all very well for you to learn about the culture of the place you came from. I applaud that, but we must draw the line. You can't join the Ekpe society. That's that." His voice brooked no contradiction.

Clint wisely remained silent.

Igwe stood and walked toward the door. "By the way, I came to tell you I'll be going to Umuahia tomorrow on business, and

I wondered if you'd like to come with me. It would be a change of scenery. Umuahia, as you know, is the capital of Abia State."

Clint reasoned that a change of scenery would do him good. He'd been cooped up in this place for almost nine weeks. While Igwe conducted his business, the driver could take Clint around Umuahia in an air-conditioned car.

Then again, what would he see? There was no museum in Umuahia or any interesting tourist places. In Clint's experience, Nigerians, even in the U.S., weren't interested in visiting museums, though his parents were an exception, sometimes going to museums on Sundays. Most people spent their spare time shopping and visiting friends.

Clint would consider Igwe's offer if it meant he could visit a cultural center in Umuahia. From what he knew, there were none.

Before he could make up his mind, though, Esther killed the idea, by muttering an aside about the unnecessary time spent in traffic in Umuahia. "Unless you're visiting a friend, there's nothing to see that's different from what's here at home."

Raising her voice, she said, "Mazi Igwe, you'll probably be visiting your friends in the government offices or their homes. What would Clint do? Sit around eating and drinking while listening to old men talk politics? I wouldn't go if it were me."

She turned to Clint. "Don't listen to me. Go if you want to look around, but don't expect anything extraordinary."

Clint tended to agree and decided he'd rather ride about on his bicycle, visiting nearby places and learning more about the other villages.

"I'm disappointed," Igwe said. "I hoped to show off my grandson to my friend at Umuahia, but if that's how you feel, I must be going.

I have business in Amanagwu."

Clint and Esther walked him out to the car.

"By the way," Esther said, "I meant to ask how your family land case was decided."

"It's still pending. That's one reason I'm going to Amanagwu. I want to find out when the case will be heard."

"It's been dragging on a long time. Perhaps the village elders feel you haven't paid them enough. You know how greedy they are."

"They won't get another naira from me," he said in a determined voice.

Clint glanced between them, wondering what was going on. "What's this about? I didn't know Grandpa had a case before the village council. Has it already been decided in the Ekpe house? What was the decision?"

"It was never presented to them," Igwe said sharply. "They have no jurisdiction over it."

Clint, seeing his grandfather was avoiding the discussion, wondered why. Esther raised a hand to make Clint stop speaking, and he subsided.

"You and your Ekpe cult," she said. "Not every case is taken to them. Igwe's case is with the chiefs. They have no right to use

Igwe's land to settle a debt with the lawyer."

"That's true," Igwe said reluctantly, "but I can't stay to discuss it.

I'm fighting to get a substitute for it." He got in the car and left.

Clint tried to continue the conversation by questioning Esther on land ownership and registration, but she lost interest and began hunting for a Christian radio station. It was one of those days when NEPA had continuous service. Soon, church music filled the house.

Outside, the rainwater on the roads was almost evaporated, and many people went about their business. At the stall on the opposite side of the road, a line formed, and their neighbor's charcoal-roasted plantain, maize, and native pears enjoyed brisk sales. Clint briefly considered walking there to get away from the house, which was totally engulfed by loud church music.

He decided instead to walk to the bar, where the loud highlife music favored by the proprietor threatened to blast a hole in the customers' eardrums.

Oh, Nigeria, Clint thought, loud is inescapable.

CHAPTER TWENTY-ONE

Three days after his visit with Nkemdirim, Clint rode his bike alone to Slessor Memorial Primary School to meet the party going to the caves at Iyi Eke. Nick, Clint's friend and a fundamentalist Christian, begged off at the last moment, feeling uneasy about visiting such an ungodly site. The designated priest for the caves led the party, accompanied by a gray-haired man and a young boy with a lamb on a leash.

After leaving his bike at the gas station across from Slessor School, Clint joined the party for a half-mile walk from the main road. They veered off to one of the many paths crisscrossing that part of the forest. The path was rough, full of rocks and pebbles, and, at the priest's suggestion, they broke off branches from low-lying trees to use for support.

"I should've brought my cane," the priest grumbled. "In my haste, I forgot it. I had forgotten about this visit and was only reminded this morning by your uncle."

Clint found a suitable dead branch to use as a cane. Looking around, he observed that on one side of the path was a steep drop to a ravine. Trees of low quality bordered the path, and the scenery was inferior, suggesting that the whole forest was continually being robbed of all fallen branches and dead wood for firewood. They passed several women carrying bundles of firewood, walking back toward home. Occasionally, they passed young children and women balancing water containers on their heads, indicating a stream was nearby.

"We won't go down to the stream here," the priest said, anticipating a question from Clint. We'll cross at another point, just before the caves."

Soon, they passed deeper into the forest, where there were denser trees and very little sunlight. The air was suffused with the smell of rotting leaves and dead animals. The ground was covered with thick undergrowth, masses of leaves, and fallen twigs. Clint worried about what might lie underfoot.

Occasionally, the priest called a warning. "Watch out for snakes!

Look out, there's a wasp nest nearby. Don't fall into a ditch."

After trekking for about a mile, they came to the meandering Iyi Eke stream and stopped to consider the best place to cross to the other side. Looking pensive, the priest said, "When supplicants arrived here in the old days, they knew there was no return." He waved his hands expansively.

The stream at that point was about three feet deep and three yards wide. They waded it easily.

"If you came here during the rainy season, you wouldn't be able to cross," the priest said, shaking water from his legs. "It can be quite

deep. People have been known to drown."

The road became steep, and Clint fell behind.

At a suitable spot, the priest paused to call back to him. "You know, Kilinti, I wouldn't have been able to take you here today if your uncle hadn't already performed the required initial ritual. Hurry up, Young Man. I don't have all day."

That elicited guffaws from the others.

"How far are the caves?" Clint opened his knapsack, took out a bottle of water, and swallowed.

"Are you already tired? I thought your eagerness to visit the site ever since you went to the Ibom side would be enough to outweigh your qualms." The priest shook his head in irritation at Clint for being such a laggard.

"I'm not tired, just thirsty," Clint said, fortified by the water.

Eventually, they reached a gully filled with thick shrubs. They went through an opening in the shrubs that led into the cave. Clint remembered that when he was on the Ibom side, he was forbidden from going into a cave because the others said it might be full of wild animals and snakes. Sweating profusely, he hesitated, his throat constricted in fear. He heard the loud beating of his heart, but the priest had already gone in, so Clint had to follow.

They came to a small circular room eighteen feet in diameter and eight feet high. Many layers of scent were inside. Clint caught the strong smell of dampness and mildew mixed with the smell of dead mice and lizards and the smell of the outside world. Those scents would soon be joined by the smell of a wood fire.

Clint saw another opening at the far end of the room. It was a dark dank place with the only light coming from the entrance. He was overcome with fear there would be other openings in the cave, and, when it was time to leave, he wouldn't be able to find an exit and would be lost in the tunnel.

As his eyes adjusted to the darkness, he saw several palm fronds hanging on an altar erected on one side of the room. Several carved wooden figures were prominently displayed on the top. In one corner of the room, dry twigs had been placed on the hearth in readiness for a sacrifice. Pieces of colored cloth and the heads of dead animals hung on the walls.

The priest struck a match to light the fire in the hearth, and the flames brightened the place a bit. He made an incantation, as the lamb was led to the altar to have its throat slit and the blood smeared on the wooden figures.

"This is our sacrifice to show you we have come in peace," the priest said. "This man with us is not a stranger but one of us." He slit the lamb's throat, spilling blood. Some was collected in a calabash container, as the priest addressed whatever spirit he invoked.

The lamb struggled, bleating pitifully, and died.

Turning to Clint, the priest said, "As you can see, the blood from the lamb will be given to the gods. Usually, the lamb would be roasted here on the hearth, but we'll omit that part of the ritual. Normally, before you could proceed to the next most-important shrine, you'd be expected to make some sacrifices, but your uncle paid for you to see everything." He coughed gently. "We'll come back without you and complete our oblations."

They went to the opposite opening and entered a tunnel into the next cave. The shrine there was decorated similarly but was larger.

Sniffling and coughing loudly, the priest said, "There are at least seven more caves, shrines, and streams in Aro Chukwu, all interconnected to the abyss you saw from the Ibom side. They're all different. There's one thing I didn't mention, though I probably don't need to, because your uncle assured me it doesn't apply to you. In the old days, twins were prohibited from crossing over, but nowadays, we permit them after they make the required sacrifices to the gods."

Clint tried to calm his pounding heart, as he looked around the second shrine and saw human and animal skulls piled in the corner. He wanted desperately to convince himself he had nothing to fear.

As they proceeded toward the entrance, the priest pointed to a mound on one side. "This was where the supplicants, who were about to be sacrificed, left the rags they wore before facing the final judgment."

Chills went down Clint's spine, and his body shook. He thought of the thousands of people who lost their lives there. He remembered his grandfather talking about the supplicants who fled and stumbled into the British station, telling of the horror they experienced at Aro Chukwu when they went to consult Ibunukpabi. Clint earlier dismissed the story as false information released by the British to justify the Aro expedition, but perhaps that part of the story was true after all.

Soon, he heard a waterfall and knew they were on the other side of the abyss.

They took a different path out of the forest. At the main road, Clint realized he was one mile from Igwe's house. He decided to part from the group and walked to his grandfather's estate. He would collect his bicycle later.

Having misjudged how tired he was, he had difficulty walking up the hill before the turnoff to Igwe's estate. To recuperate, he sat on a fallen log on the side of the road. Longing to discuss the day's events with his father, he felt alone and drained. He tried to fight off his torpor and the fear of being stung by wasps or other tropical insects.

A sense of hopelessness overwhelmed him. He felt Achi's pain at the loss of another child, especially since he specifically appealed to the Christian God to grant him the gift of an heir.

He saw Achi weeping uncontrollably, holding a dead child while surrounded by mourners who tried to comfort him. Then the scene shifted to Achi standing at a church altar with his wife, presenting a baby girl to be baptized. Christian converts surrounded them, singing hymns of praise for the happy occasion. Achi knelt at the altar in fervent prayer.

———m———

A blaring car horn abruptly ended that joyful scene, much to Clint's sorrow. Jerking upright, he realized a car stopped in front of him, and Igwe stood there.

"Clint, are you all right? Where's your bicycle? Why are you here at this time?"

Clint didn't know which question to answer first. When he was fully awake, he wiped his brow with his handkerchief. "There's nothing wrong. I spent half the day at the Iyi Eke caves, and I feel a bit disoriented. I was on my way to your house and wanted to rest before going home."

"But where's your bike?" Igwe feared it was stolen.

"I left it at the gas station opposite Slessor. It's quite safe."

"Come. We'll drive you home, and you can rest. I just hope you aren't overdoing it."

On the drive, Igwe talked about the funeral of the chief's matron and what a grand affair it was. "Everyone said it was grander than her husband's funeral five years ago."

Overwhelmingly tired, Clint didn't have any reply. When they arrived at his grandfather's house, he revived a bit. "Grandpa, I need to talk to you." They went inside.

"You're talking to me now." Igwe laughed, wondering what they'd been doing except talk.

"Seriously."

"All right. What's up?"

"Tell me more about your grandfather Achi. I need to know everything about him. From what you said before, he had no male son from his wife. Did he remarry? Is your father from a different wife?"

"What's there to tell? He was brought here as a slave. The circumstances of his capture are immaterial. Family lore has it that an important chief in Ibom died, and, as part of the funeral obligations, the Amanagwu chief had to provide him with several servants in the afterlife. The chief didn't want to part with one of his own slaves, so he sent out a hunting party to capture men from outside the area. Achi was lucky in that Chief Igwe bought him instead, and his life was spared."

"Was that how the family got its surname of Igwe?"

"Yes. During his lifetime, he was known as Achi. Family names weren't important then, because everyone knew where other people came from. When families sent their children to school, the missionaries expected them to have surnames, so Achi gave his children Igwe as a surname. That's how it happened.

"As Achi aged in Christianity, his oldest daughter married the son of a well-placed Amadi who was a Christian, educated in the newly established training institute, Hope Waddell, in Calabar. He was a teacher in the primary school she attended. Achi saw her married in the church he helped build.

"With the help of the missionaries, his two remaining daughters received their primary education at Slessor, but they tested his faith. First, the White woman in charge convinced him to send the youngest, a brilliant girl, to a nursing school in Calabar.

"His wife disagreed. She wanted her daughter to settle down and marry. I think she feared for her daughter and didn't want her leaving the area to study. Achi told us he was convinced by the missionaries in Slessor, where the child was, that further training as a nurse would also benefit them, because she could support them in their old age. He reasoned that she would be able to marry an educated person. Against Mboro's will, the daughter left home for Calabar.

"Late one night in her second year at the nursing school, Achi and his wife heard frantic knocking on their door. They rushed to open it and found their daughter outside, drenched from the rainy evening. She said she didn't feel well. Achi thought nothing of it, believing that whatever the matter was, his wife could deal with it. He had several errands to run the next day.

"In the middle of the night, they heard their daughter calling out in pain, and, when Achi went to her room, he found her bleeding profusely. They couldn't stop the bleeding, so she died.

"It was then that his wife, in tears, confessed that Mary was pregnant and in danger of being expelled from school. She feared if that became known the church would excommunicate them, because the church forbade adultery. They would lose face, so she resorted to abortion."

Igwe faced Clint. "You must remember that the church at that time was very strict. Adultery was a mortal sin. In telling us this part of the story, Achi said he couldn't believe that the God who'd been portrayed as a kind God would allow such shame to befall him. He had to tell his kinsmen of his shame, and he had to bury his daughter. "Eventually, he got over it, believing that as with the pilgrim, this was one of the many ways God chose to test his faith.

"A few years later, his other daughter, who was training to become a seamstress, came home to announce she was pregnant. At the family meeting, Achi asked for the name of the father, but his daughter refused to say. I can imagine him shouting at her and calling her a harlot.

"She remained adamant. Family members begged her to divulge the name, but she wouldn't. She bore the taunts of others in the villages without shame. Achi was the one who had to bear her shame. It was his fault he didn't have enough money to give her a dress or trinkets when she wanted, and she had to get the money the only way she knew how. He couldn't turn away from her despite his feeling she erred against one of God's commandments by committing adultery. He tried again to find out who her lover was, so he could get the man to take responsibility, but his daughter stubbornly refused to give him the information.

"The pastor of the church preached about the sins of the fathers being visited on their children, and Achi told us he felt the sermon was directed at him. It was easy in the old days when children weren't sent to school to control their actions. It appeared he was being punished for agreeing to educate his daughters.

"He felt as if he were on the cross, and, like Christ, he cried, 'My God, my God, why have You forsaken me? I'm being punished for being a Christian.'"

Clint felt overcome with sorrow. "It must've been very hard for him, since he put all his trust in the new God."

"Yes, it was," Igwe said. "As a good Christian, he felt his faith was being tempted, and he must persevere. He lived with the shame of her pregnancy, and, when she gave birth to a son, he gave the son his name. It was through that son that Achi's line continued."

Igwe paused. "Achi witnessed great changes in Aro Chukwu, not always for the better. His business didn't do well following the changeover from manila, rods, and cowries to modern currency. He also made a bad investment decision following an eclipse and lost money. He never recovered from that loss. He witnessed the change to self-government in the country and was able to cast his ballot in the first election in his adopted town.

"Before his wife's death, he was often seen walking with her to the farm, market, or stream. He tried to be a good husband,

and, unlike many of his contemporaries, he had no difficulty keeping to the Christian restriction of only one wife. In a place where the number of wives was a sign of prestige and wealth, many new Christians circumvented the rule by presenting one wife at the church as the official wife while still living with many more in their homes. Achi decided that Mboro would be his only wife.

"The Bible was a great comfort to him in his old age. He never missed a church service or catechism. He became an elder in the church and was often seen in his parlor, reading the Bible despite his remorse.

"His grandson was a great comfort, too, and Achi prayed he would accomplish great things despite the nature of his birth. His remaining daughter cared for Achi in his old age.

"When he died, his coffin was taken to the church he helped build, and he was buried in the little room where he kept his money during the time he had it."

Enthralled, Clint wondered if that was the end of the story. "So it was through this grandson whose father wasn't known that his line continued. Now I know."

"Yes," Igwe said, lost in thought. "When I first saw you, I thought I was seeing Achi in his youth. You look like him, you know. Have I mentioned that before?"

"Many old men in the villages have commented on the resemblance." Clint still felt very moved by what he heard.

The gate bell rang, indicating a visitor, and Igwe called for someone to answer. When he didn't hear any movement, he became agitated.

"These boys," he complained. "They're never around when you need them. I can't understand why I have to feed so many people in this house, yet no one's around when I want him."

Clint offered to go to the gate, but Igwe wouldn't hear of it.

Instead, Igwe went through the corridor to the courtyard.

"Are you all deaf?" he shouted. "Don't you hear the gate bell?" Clint heard the skittering of feet, as a young boy ran to the gate.

The visitor was a professor at the teacher training college. Clint met him several weeks earlier.

"Welcome, Professor," Igwe said. "I'm sorry we kept you waiting at the gate. You know these houseboys. They're never around when you want one." He spread his hands in despair. "Can you believe it? There are four servants in this house, and I can't find one when I need one." He turned and shouted, "Obed! Come here to get beer for the professor immediately!"

Clint, bemused, wondered why it was necessary for Obed to come from the kitchen to get a beer that was in the fridge in the next room.

Drinking his beer, the professor said, "Igwe, you're lucky you have help. I have two boys at my home whose school fees I pay in exchange for helping me around the house, but they're completely useless. Can you imagine?" He glanced at Igwe for support. "My wife has to scream and yell at them to wash the dishes or sweep the floor. When I complain to my friends in Enugu, they say I'm lucky to have them, because houseboys are getting scarce. When they have them, they sometimes steal everything a man has."

"I know what you mean," Igwe said angrily. "I'm having problems with my driver. I had to drive myself today, because he wasn't anywhere to be found. I'm pondering if I should sack him."

"I suggest you just give him a warning. It's difficult to find an honest driver these days."

Listening to the two men grouse about their servants, Clint couldn't help smiling at how middle class Nigerians tended to regard it as their privilege to have a constant supply of the underclass to cater to their needs. Esther was constantly shouting at her helpers, berating them for small inconveniences.

Clint didn't understand it. His parents had no help. They once had a woman come in to clean every two weeks, but they stopped when their children reached adolescence, preferring to have the children help with housework.

He remembered one area of conflict between his parents. When it came to household repairs, his father was incompetent and couldn't even change a hose washer. When Clint was small, his mother complained whenever she had to call a handyman to make minor repairs. As Clint grew up, he became the handyman by default.

He remembered that in his first year in college, he often came home to be presented a list by his mother of all the things that needed fixing around the house. That irritated him. During his third year, he started ignoring such requests. That forced his parents to hire outside help. His mother often complained about paying over ninety dollars for a repair that took only a few minutes. Thinking it over, Clint realized that his services enabled his parents to provide him with pocket money during the time he was home.

At least the plumbers and electricians in the U.S. were competent. In Nigeria, his grandparents constantly complained about having to pay repeatedly for shoddy work. When Clint first arrived, he had trouble getting used to the length of time it took to complete a simple task and take action on something that needed to be done. He finally learned to be patient and in less of a hurry for results.

When he listened to the discussion in the room, he realized they had moved on to Nigerian politics and the problems in the Delta and the Northeast. When the older men finally ended their conversation, Clint was able to get a ride from the visitor to go pick up his bike.

CHAPTER TWENTY-TWO

That night, as Clint lay in bed in his room at Esther's house, his mind returned to the day's events until he couldn't sleep. Looking out the window, through the crudely attached mosquito netting, he was astonished at how soft the night was. Through the foliage of the coconut trees, he saw the zinc roofs of the neighbor houses illuminated by the light of the full moon. At home on such a night, when so many thoughts chased themselves in circles in his mind, he would've turned on his bedside lamp and try to read to settle his mind. He couldn't do that in Nigeria, because of NEPA's imposed power outage, so he tried to still his mind as best he could to fall asleep.

He must have succeeded. The next thing he knew, it was morning, and he was awakened by the usual sounds of Esther giving instructions to the servants, the car and bicycle horns from the main road, servants shouting to each other, the bleating of goats as they were chased by the chickens, and the early morning visitors.

He had to get up to face the day, though the days were becoming boring. His mind was frequently full of thoughts of returning home. He was at a crossroad, and he needed to decide whether he should stay in Nigeria or go back to the U.S.

It was a beautiful, less-humid day, and he decided to visit Igwe to make an unusual request.

When he arrived, Clint said, "Tell me about Calabar, Grandfather.

The other day when we talked about Amasu, you said traders went from there to Itu and on to Calabar. I'm interested, because my parents spent their honeymoon in Calabar."

"I'd forgotten that. Now that you mention it, there was talk of their having been involved in an accident. We thank God it wasn't serious."

It was only after his first sip of palm wine that Igwe continued the tale. "From time immemorial, Calabar had an important place in the psyche of the Aro people. The Efiks seemed sophisticated, because they'd been dealing with White people longer than the Aro. Calabar was a big port, and ships from around the world docked there."

He looked hard at Clint. "I presume you know of our involvement in the slave trade." Clint nodded.

"Calabar was where the Aro exchanged slaves for manufactured goods. With the waning of the slave trade, it became a major port for exporting raw materials like palm oil, rubber, and hardwood. It was through trade with Calabar that the Aro people shifted from barter to money in the form of rods of different shapes, cowries, and gradually, to money as a means of exchange. Those kinds of money were introduced by the European traders."

With a twinkle in his eyes, he added, "I presume they found it more convenient than barter, which would require so many trinkets or bales of cloth as payment for, let's say, one slave." He laughed uproariously.

"Grandpa, how can you make such a comparison?"

Igwe laughed even harder. "Exchanges with rods and cowries were preferable to barter, and the Aro traders loved it. I told you before that Achi was a great trader. He traded between here, Itu, and Calabar."

Igwe's voice grew distant, as he remembered. "Calabar was a sophisticated city. Women covered their bodies, unlike the majority of Aro women, who walked around wearing only strips of handwoven rough cotton material tied around their chests and waists."

Clint had questions, but he held back, because that was the first time Igwe mentioned that.

"Many foreign ships visited Calabar carrying many manufactured goods, and, of course, taking away large numbers of slaves brought there by Aro traders. It had the first schools, and it was from there that Christian converts were sent to proselytize along the Cross River and its creek. The Aro chief fought the incursion of Christianity and White rule.

"When they were subjugated, missionaries brought Efik tailors, who taught the Aro how to sew. They were teachers in the first primary school the church opened. Bright boys were sent to Calabar to train as teachers or clerks. Oh, the food!" He smacked his lips in nostalgia. "Traders would salivate about the various foods they ate, describing the different seafoods and the methods used to bring out the flavor. Until independence, many upper-class Aros spent Christmas vacation in Calabar."

"You talk as if that relationship was severed. What happened?" Igwe studied the remnants of his beer. "I have often felt that at independence, the Aro people made a bit mistake when they agreed to be part of the Ibos. Aro chiefs should have insisted they wanted to be part of the Cross River. After all, that's where they lived. Our people fought the Ibibios to settle here. Culturally, they had more in common with the Ibibios and Efiks than with other Ibos. Indeed, the Aro people adopted many Ibibio customs and made them ours. The Ekpe cult and the premarital fattening rooms for girls were some of those shared customs."

He began to excoriate the Abia State government. "Look at the state of our roads compared to those in adjacent Ibibio states. Many of their small communities have good roads, whereas in ours, contracts are awarded, and the contractors use the money for other purposes." He frowned, shaking his head in despair.

Recovering quickly, he turned to Clint. "By the way, this should interest you, since you come from a country where women compete for everything. Do you know the only woman in what was then the Eastern Nigerian House of Assembly in the 1950s was a woman from Calabar named Margaret Ekpo? I heard the Cross River State recognized her contribution in some form, but I've forgotten what they named after her.

"Perhaps if and when you go to Calabar, you'll find out for me. I really liked that woman. She stood her ground in the assembly and fought for women's rights."

Clint, who had heard nothing good about the Abia State government since he arrived, asked vehemently, "Grandpa, why don't you become a politician and fight for the rights of the Aro Chukwu?"

"Not me. One of my relatives was a big politician. As a member of the opposition party, he fought for the rights of the Aro Chukwu against the Azikiwe government. Where did it get him? Nowhere!" He banged his hand on the table. "As a politician, I would have to sell my soul. I don't want to soil myself."

He shook his head vigorously and waggled his fingers. "You think politics here is like in your country, America. We organize things differently. Wait until the elections. Then you'll understand what I mean."

I doubt I'll be here that long, Clint thought. I'm getting tired of this place. I miss my parents and would love to see them and discuss some of my experiences.

"Where were we?" Igwe asked. "We were talking about Calabar. You seemed interested."

"Yes. I thought I'd get there the old-fashioned way, taking a canoe from Amasu."

"Hmmm. You make me wish I was young again. I remember making that journey with my father when I was a boy. Seriously, I would suggest you go by road. It's much easier."

"But, Grandfather, I wouldn't be able to experience traveling on the Cross River as Achi, your grandfather, did."

"I'll bet Esther will have a convulsion when you tell her of this plan, though I tend to agree with you. I'll find an experienced young man to accompany you. When did you want to go?"

"Perhaps soon if you help with the arrangements."

Arriving at Esther's, Clint used the phone to call his mother, whom he hadn't spoken with for almost a month.

"Clint? I don't believe it! How are you?" she asked. "OK, I suppose." He tried to hide his loneliness.

"Are you having a nice time? Have you traveled outside Aro Chukwu? How do you spend your time? Is my mom driving you crazy?"

So many questions, Clint thought. Which one should I answer? "I actually called to say I'll be going to Calabar and to ask if there's any place you would recommend I visit. I know you spent your honeymoon there."

"I recommend the slave museum, but I warn you, it's not for the foolhardy. Stay away from Ikom Fall!"

Before he could reply, he heard noises in the background, indicating Peter had come home.

"I'm talking to Clint!" Peace shouted.

Clint heard his father's footsteps, then he took the receiver. "Hello, Clint. Is that you? How's the old place"

"I don't know how it looked when you were last here, but I doubt it has changed much. The people appear relatively well-off despite the lack of employment opportunities and the inability of the state government to meet its obligations to its workers. Do you know that salaries are in arrears for three months, sometimes more? I heard that from a teacher visiting Grandma. I wonder where people get their spending money."

"You should understand by now that the local economy depends entirely on remittances from abroad. Your grandparents live the way they do because of financial support from their children outside the area. Without those checks arriving by Western Union every month, the place would fall apart."

After they talked for a while, Peter said, "We were wondering when you'll be coming back. You need to start thinking of your future. If you plan to stay longer, you'd be better off going to Lagos, so your uncle can help you find a job."

Clint listened and said sharply, "I'll decide when I return from Calabar."

The connection suddenly cut off, and Clint realized he hadn't recharged his cell phone battery before recent power outages. His feeling of helplessness didn't abate with the short contact with his parents and being made aware of the fact that he had absolutely no control over his future if he decided to stay.

CHAPTER
TWENTY - THREE

One early morning in October, Clint was in a small canoe en route to Itu on the Cross River. There, he would transfer to a launch that regularly plied the route between Itu and Calabar. He looked forward to the visit, because his parents often spoke longingly of Calabar, where they spent their honeymoon.

He left the house at dawn with his hold-all, accompanied by one of Esther's boys, who carried his water supply and a canteen containing his lunch of jollof rice. The air was damp, and the leaves were heavy with dew. The damp air kept gnats and mosquitoes at bay.

The moon had long since set, and the sky was covered in various shades of gray clouds. In the eastern distance, the sky held the promise of the sun, which hadn't yet shown its face.

As he approached the water's edge, he saw the river teeming with early risers bathing before carrying their containers of water home. Several fishermen left or were preparing to leave to bring the day's catch. Clint's canoe man was getting impatient to start the journey and wanted to leave without Alfred, the gentleman Igwe designated to accompany Clint. Once Alfred arrived, they pushed out toward the creek that connected them to the Cross River.

Mangrove trees lined both banks. The dark-green water reflected the masses of leaves and tree debris that lay below. Occasionally, they encountered fishermen, who grunted greetings while focusing on pulling their nets from the river. The air was still except for the sound of the paddle, as it touched the water, and the occasional calls of animals and birds sheltering in the trees. There was a ripple of water, as a kingfisher spied his breakfast and swooped down to catch it.

With the sun's promised heat unfulfilled, Clint felt the dampness in his bones. Shivering, he drew his jacket tighter. Concentrating on keeping warm, and not being a morning person, anyway, he hunkered down on his knees, paying no attention to his companions, who, undeterred by the damp, chatted loudly.

The canoe was divided into three sections by planks affixed to its inner sides. The canoe man sat on the front plank, where he could steer. Alfred sat on the back plank, and Clint had the middle seat. The canoe carried bunches of plantain bound for the Itu market.

At a kilometer from their starting point, Clint saw a canoe filled with tall grass and broke his self-imposed silence. "Isn't that canoe filled with elephant grass? What will he do with it?"

"Those are achara stems, a type of grass that grows near the water's edge," Alfred explained. "He must've harvested them for today's market. We make delicious vegetable and fish soups with them. That must be at least 2,000 naira worth."

The canoe man pulled the pole to straighten the boat. "My wife asked me to get her some on my way back. In the past, they were abundant along this part of the creek."

"They've become scarce nowadays." Alfred turned to wave at canoes passing by. "You have to go far into the river to harvest them now."

Clint wondered whether he had, by chance, eaten achara soup without knowing it. He tried many kinds of soup at

Esther's, and sometimes at Igwe's, and he wasn't able to keep track of them all.

The only soup he cared for was bitter leaf and egusi soups, which he had before coming to Aro Chukwu.

As they approached the Cross River in their overloaded canoe, the water widened, and the canoe fought the strong current, swollen by the rains that swept mud and broken branches in its wake during the rainy season. The river's tributaries overflowed leaving the water a rusty color.

"The river must be carrying all the mud churned up during the rainy season," the canoe man said, looking upstream. "That explains the color. Later, it'll return to its normal bluish green, depending on the time of day."

The sun rose, and with it came midges, mosquitoes, and gnats. Attracted to the smell of human sweat, they bombarded the canoe. Even with his hat and sunglasses on, Clint wasn't spared. They swarmed him, and he had trouble remaining steady. His companions thought nothing of it, teasing him for sweating too much, as he smacked himself with the back of an exercise book he carried for jotting down notes about interesting fauna.

"How long will this attack last?" Clint asked.

Alfred looked smug. "It'll lessen over time as the heat rises, or you'll get used to it."

Traffic on the Cross River was heavy. They saw canoes of all types laden with bunches of palm fruit bound for the oil mill in Itu, while others carried plantain, bananas, yams, and assorted foodstuffs. Canoes coming in the opposite direction carried every imaginable type of manufactured goods, from zinc roofing sheets and assorted building materials to plastic containers. The river also carried a variety of debris, including discarded plastic, tires, and fallen branches. Clint and his companions tried to steer clear of the debris and the islands of water hyacinth and lilies.

Occasionally, they saw oilmen in motorboats scouting for possible new sites.

"I wish Aro Chukwu would get lucky, and we would discover oil,"

Alfred said. "That would really change our lives."

"I hope not," Clint said. "Oil is a curse."

"Curse or not, we want it, because it would bring development."

Clint, who knew of the problems in the Delta region, asked, "At what cost? It hasn't helped the Delta. It brought nothing but pollution."

"You should go to Eket and see how it changed from a village to a city. There's a lot of money there. Look at what's happening in Aro. We have no jobs."

Clint knew when to stop. How could he talk about the impact of oil exploration on the environment when the villagers were concerned only with obtaining money for their daily needs. He supposed people only cared for the environment after a certain stage in economic development. As far as Alfred, or any other man in Aro Chukwu, was concerned, pollution wasn't an immediate worry.

Clint changed the subject. "Has anyone proposed any industry for Aro Chukwu based on what's available?"

"How would I know?" Alfred asked, laughing. "I'm a nobody. I heard talk of a cement factory, but it's just talk. Nothing will happen. Sadly, it depends on the government in Umuahia." His voice was filled with hopelessness.

Clint had noted that feeling was very pervasive. Most people felt that not even a change in government would produce any change in their status.

He marveled at the bird life on the Cross River. He saw egrets, swallows, and kingfishers. In a tree on the nearest bank, he saw a really colorful bird that had to belong to the parrot family. Groups of monkeys and baboons hopped from tree to tree, and he wondered how long they would be allowed to enjoy the forest, given the pace of population growth and people's penchant for hunting most animals they saw for food.

When he saw birds he couldn't name, he wished for a book of tropical birds to guide him. Ubiquitous vultures circled overhead, telling him there was something dead on the islands or the banks. A group of dragonflies stopped near the canoe to drink. When Clint asked Alfred for the names of the birds and insects in Igbo, Alfred drew a blank.

"I don't know what they're called," he said. "They're just birds." "What about the dragonfly?"

"It's called that which drinks water with its bottom."

Clint laughed so hard he almost fell overboard. "What a colorful name. Much nicer than dragonfly."

On the far bank, he saw sunlight glinting on zinc and knew there were settlements in that area. As they passed some of the Ibibio villages Mary Slessor once visited, he wondered which of them Achi stopped at during his many shopping visits to Itu.

By noon, the sun's heat was relentless. He wished he brought an umbrella, as had the passengers in other canoes around them. His hat provided only a little shade.

To Clint's surprise, the canoe man made for the nearest bank that had a beach.

"I want to rest before continuing the trip," he explained. "This will give us an opportunity to eat and stretch our legs."

That was welcome news. Clint had already begun to tire of the monotonous journey.

They stopped at a nice beach with a reddish, sandy road leading up the hill into the village. Several canoes and men were on the beach, either mending nets or bargaining with customers over the price of fish.

Could this be one of the places Achi stopped on his way to Itu?

Clint wondered. Was this where he first saw the White woman who changed his life?

Since it was a market day, Clint decided to walk up the hill and look around. The amount of debris, including discarded plastic wrap and tires, shocked him, and he wondered why no one cared.

"This place isn't much different from the Aro villages in that regard," he muttered.

Walking toward the market, he soon came to a mission station and a primary school. Given the dominance of the Presbyterian sect in the area, he assumed it was one of the places Mary

Slessor visited. The lawn needed proper care, looking as if it had been hacked spasmodically with a machete.

Still, the mission post yard had beautiful frangipani, hibiscus flowers, and almond trees, whose pods were scattered over the ground. It seemed no one knew what they were. Clint admired the beautiful, dusty old church built in the style of the Obinkita church but without the stained-glass window.

Behind the church were the pastor's house and several other homes Clint assumed were for teachers. The village, he was told, wasn't far. From what he gathered, it was just a collection of thatched houses dropped there in no order.

Not wanting to hold up the canoe or attract the attention of little children, who invariably knew he was a stranger, he walked back to the beach, stopping at the market to buy a freshly grilled snapper to eat. His companions were glad to see him back so soon, and they quickly got into the canoe and headed toward Itu.

The late-afternoon sun was sinking, and Itu teemed with activity. The area from the beach and up the hill constituted one big market, with canoes being loaded and off-loaded and bargains being struck. Clint saw all kinds of boats and canoes.

On the far bank, a pontoon boat ferried people across between the two banks of the Cross River. Unlike during Achi's period, there were several power boats anchored at the wharf. The launch was expected in an hour, and travelers were already lining up for their return journey to Calabar.

Fascinated, Clint wanted to visit the Ikonetu mission post to look around. The place was even more interesting when he remembered that Achi spent several days there buying goods for resale at Aro Chukwu before venturing as far as Calabar.

"The wharf is new," Alfred said, "and the beach has recently been expanded. There's a road on the other side." He pointed. "See where the canoes and pontoons are? That roads leads to Aro Chukwu. Our traders took that road sometimes rather than a canoe from Amasu. Even now, you can get a taxi from Aro Chukwu to that spot."

Clint, wanting to linger in Itu, turned to Alfred. "Would you mind if we spent the night here instead of looking for transportation to Calabar?"

"Where?" Alfred was baffled.

"Surely you must have relatives here," Clint said nonchalantly. "Mazi Igwe told me so."

"Perhaps," Alfred said, sounding miffed, "but I have to find them first, since I only see them at home."

He reluctantly agreed to look around the market to see if he recognized anyone from his village.

"I would have liked to get to Calabar tonight," he said angrily. "My relatives will be meeting the launch." He scowled and wandered away, thoroughly upset. "This isn't what I expected. Instead of spending the night in the launch, now I have to sleep in someone's shack. I should have known this would happen."

Clint wandered from boat-to-boat, looking at the fishermen haggling with clients until he sat in a chair outside a stall where assorted plastic pans were sold. As he chatted with the stall man, a redheaded White man of medium height appeared and greeted the stall owner in a friendly way. While Clint watched, they conversed in Ibibio, making Clint wonder how long it took the White man to become fluent.

Baffled, Clint asked, "Are you from around here?"

"You could say so. I'm a VSO teacher in the secondary school up the hill." He seemed amused.

"What's VSO?"

"Volunteer Service Overseas. It's the British equivalent of the Peace Corps. By the way, I'm John from Scotland. And you?" He smiled broadly.

"I'm American by birth, but my parents are immigrants to the U.S. from Aro Chukwu. I'm currently visiting my grandparents there. You could say this is my gap period before graduate school." He laughed.

"The infamous Aro Chukwu? I always wanted to visit there. It's one of the places Mary Slessor visited. Are there any remnants of the Long Juju?"

Ignoring the jab, Clint asked, "Why'd you come here?"

"My grandparents were missionaries at Ikonetu up the hill and loved the place." John's voice grew animated. "My mother and one of her siblings were born here, and I grew up listening to stories about the Ibibios. After university, I thought it would be interesting to join the VSO and teach here for a while. I'm a biology teacher at the school."

"You speak the language very well. Did you have a teacher?"

John moved restlessly about like a caged animal. "I didn't really have to learn the language to function here. As you already know, Nigeria was a British colony, so many people speak English. I wanted to be able to move around and travel the Cross River. I felt knowing the language would be helpful. This is my second year here. You may think I speak it well, but I don't." He shook his head.

"Come on, John," the stall owner said, laughing. "You speak it well."

"Is there a hotel nearby? Alfred, my companion, and I may need one for the night. We didn't anticipate spending the night in Itu, but I didn't feel like continuing to Calabar after our long canoe journey from Aro Chukwu."

John thought for a moment. "I think there's a rest house somewhere, but I don't know. At the mission post, I understand they sometimes let rooms to visiting priests. Why don't you come with me, and we can see if they can accommodate you? At least you can be sure of mosquito netting over your bed."

Touched by the man's kindness, Clint looked for Alfred and saw him not far away, talking to some men. Since Alfred had been irritated by the change in plans, Clint was relieved when Alfred came over to talk.

"I found someone from my village, and he offered to put us up in his room not far from here." He glanced at John. "Perhaps you can go with Beke, and I'll stay to talk to my brother. We haven't seen each other since Ikeji."

That suited Clint. To avoid keeping John waiting, he and Alfred quickly arranged where to meet the following morning, and Clint accompanied John up the hill to the mission. John lived in a nearby teacher's house.

Once Clint was assured of a room, he went to John's house to talk for the evening.

"What are you plans after Itu?" John asked, sitting in his living room, drinking beer and eating corned beef sandwiches.

Clint thought for a moment. "Calabar, hopefully tomorrow. I was told there's a launch that runs from here and Calabar, but I haven't seen it, and it looks like it might have been discontinued. After that, I'll have to decide what's next."

"There's a small launch, but you may be able to get a ride in the morning from one of the oilmen prospecting for oil between here and Calabar. I don't want to give you false hope, though."

"It's worth checking out. Thanks." He remained silent for a moment, thinking how hard it must have been for John to leave behind the comforts of Scotland to live without any other White people around. "It must be lonely for you here."

"Not really. The kids are very nice, and I've made friends with the other teachers. On weekends, I usually go upriver with the fishermen stopping at villages along the way. I've been as far as Akpap. I'm trying to trace Mary Slessor's journey from Creek Town."

"I heard how she lived among the people of the Cross River even when the authorities forbade it. I heard she even shared quarters with natives, but I find the idea preposterous."

"I can understand how you feel, but the living conditions she left behind in Scotland at the time were only one step removed from what she found here. I think that's why she adapted so well."

As they talked, a car drove up, and a man in Western clothes came to say hello to John.

"I just got in from Eket and was on my way to visit my mother," the man said.

"Want to stay for a drink?" John asked. "No, thanks."

After the man left, John said, "He's an engineer with the oil company at Eket, but he was born and raised in Ikonetu. He usually stops to talk with me, but seeing you, he thought he would be intruding. His grandparents knew my grandfather, the missionary."

"What were your expectations when you arrived?" Clint studied John's face carefully.

John stood and began gathering dishes. "I can tell you that I had no expectations at all. I went through orientation, and we were told about the difficulties of living in Nigeria. There's the problem of how to get around without a car, the climate that's so different from Scotland, the food, the corruption, and many other problems."

He paused briefly to wash his hands. "Besides, I had my grandparents' experiences to think about. They absolutely loved the place and were sad when they had to retire to Scotland."

Coming back into the room after disposing of the plates, he said, "So I was prepared for it, but surprisingly, I haven't experienced any real problems, perhaps because I needed very little to feel comfortable.

"I try to eat what's available, and I have a Vespa, which enables me to get around. In Itu, I can buy anything I want. The shops, as you saw, are full of costly canned food, like corned beef, so occasionally I could eat that if I wanted. My only potential problems are malaria and dysentery, so I'm very careful about food. I take my malaria pills religiously.

"I have local friends like the stall man, and I go to Calabar during the vacation period to see other VSOs there, so we can travel to places like Obudu. I have one more year to go, but I'm thinking of extending it for another year." He sat down again and joined Clint. "And you?"

Clint was silent for a minute. "I haven't seen much of Nigeria except for Aro Chukwu. This is my first visit outside the area since I came. I'm going to Calabar, because my grandfather said it was the capital of the province for a long time, and many of its leaders trained at Hope Waddle. My parents had their honeymoon there. I just wanted to see it."

John became animated. "It's an interesting place. You should stick to Old Calabar and the Creek Town area. Visit the slave museum. I hope in the morning you can find a ride rather than take the launch. That can be very trying. There are so many people, you can hardly find a place to sit."

They talked until midnight, when Clint finally went to bed.

Clint heard school bells ringing and knew he had to get up. Soon, he bade John good-bye and walked to the waterfront to find transportation to Calabar. He was sorry to leave the mission post on the hill with its primary and secondary schools, teachers' houses, church, and beautifully tended yards.

At the waterfront, he joined Alfred, and they asked people about any Calabar-bound boat. Clint saw the engineer he met the previous night at the mission post. Luckily, he was going to Calabar for the weekend using a motorboat belonging to one of the oil companies prospecting for oil along the Cross River. The boat was manned and captained by another Nigerian officer, and there was room for Alfred and Clint.

When Clint offered to pay, the engineer waved him off. "Any friend of John's is my friend. His grandparents were very kind to my grandfather, and my father owed his education to them."

Later during the journey, he told Clint, "My grandfather worked for John's parents. They paid for my father's secondary education at Hope Waddell. John is like my brother."

The river was wider than previously, and it wasn't as easy to see the opposite coastlines as before. The friendly men gave Clint advice on where to stay and what to see in Calabar. He learned that the Calabar River was actually part of the Cross River as it emptied into the Bight of Biafra. They talked about the crocodiles and manatee common on the Cross River and told Clint that just recently a new species of crocodile had been found inhabiting the Calabar River. He learned that the new species' head was slightly larger than normal for a crocodile.

Clint looked for crocodiles and manatees, but the boat's speed meant he missed many of the river creatures they encountered.

When they reached Calabar, he was sorry to part with the engineer. They said good-bye and exchanged addresses. The engineer promised to look Clint up whenever he came to the U.S. but said in parting that his visits were mainly confined to Louisiana and Texas, and he rarely went to the East Coast.

CHAPTER TWENTY-FOUR

C lint spent his first night on old Calabar at the rest house John recommended. He remembered that his parents arrived in Calabar on the last day of the traditional Christmas celebration, and the streets were perhaps more crowded than when he arrived. Luckily, his parents obtained a hotel room, though at an exorbitant price. Since it was their honeymoon and first visit to Calabar, they were happy to pay it. His parents thought highly of Efik culture and food and were glad to be part of the celebration, even though they missed the days when the masquerades paraded the streets. He wished he could remember the name of their hotel and visit it so he could tell them he'd been there.

The rest house was a clean, cheap place that he felt sure would serve his own purpose, as he'd be there for three days at most.

Early the following morning, he went to the wharf to look around and visit some of the warehouses. As he walked around the wharf, looking at the activities in and around the big cargo ships moored there and at the canoes and small boats at the far end, he thought of Achi and wondered how he felt arriving from Aro Chukwu to buy yard goods. He probably took the launch to Calabar, since that would have been the quickest way, and must have arrived in early morning. He would probably have taken the overnight launch back to Itu. The quantity of the goods he bought must have been limited to the amount he could carry.

Strolling down the wharf and listening to the many voices of the crowd reminded Clint of the family myth that at some time, when Achi came to Calabar, he heard rumors that the sun would set, leaving the earth in darkness. He and all the traders assumed the event would last a long time, so Achi, who came to Calabar to buy clothes, immediately invested all his money in kerosene. With the impending perpetual night, he would make a sizeable profit, even though the price for a tin of kerosene had risen with the recent run on the liquid. The eclipse lasted only a few minutes, and the price of kerosene fell due to oversupply. Achi lost a lot of money and was never able to regain his capital and continue trading.

Staring at the wharf, Clint wondered how many tins of kerosene Achi bought. Did the other Aro Chukwu traders also bet on the prolonged eclipse? Those poor, illiterate, uninformed people, Clint thought, shaking his head.

As he walked the streets of Old Calabar, surrounded by a crowd of people pursuing their business, Clint mused, My parents don't know

where I am, and, apart from Alfred, I know no one here. He didn't even really know Alfred, because he was someone his grandfather assigned to him.

Alfred indicated that morning that the only reason he agreed to the Calabar trip was the opportunity to look for possible employment. While Clint was sightseeing, Alfred intended to meet a relative who was employed as a night guard by one of the companies in the wharf area.

Feeling alone in a sea of people, Clint was distraught. He feared it would be difficult to reach his family if he was hurt or in danger. He had his cell phone, but he had difficulty getting service ever since he arrived. He would continue to try to reach his mother. He began to think his decision to visit Calabar was impetuous.

Feeling extremely lonely, he couldn't understand why he was overwhelmed by such intense feelings. He tried to shake them off, thinking it was the heat and lack of good sleep from the previous night. He already decided not to go to Ikot Ishie to look for his father's relatives, because that would be imposing. That decision further irritated Alfred, but Clint knew Igwe would understand.

On a whim, he took a taxi to the slave museum on the waterfront. When he finally spoke to his parents on the phone that morning, Peace told him about their visit to the museum and how moved she felt by the exhibits detailing the horrible treatment of slaves on their way to the new world. Afterward, she said she refused to speak to her husband for the rest of the day.

"It was our first quarrel," she said.

Coming out of the museum, she turned to Peter and said, "I'm shocked that in the U.S., not enough is written about our collusion in this horrible trade. We sold our own people for trinkets!"

Peter, who felt he was better informed about the story of slavery in Nigeria, said, "Peace, listen. From what little I know of it, the people who sold them didn't know what their fates would be. You should remember they had their own slaves, so they didn't see anything wrong with the institution itself.

"My great-grandfather was brought to our area as a slave, and even in your own family, the man who ran constant errands for your father was the son of your grandfather's slave. In effect, he was your father's slave, even though he's no longer called that." Peace turned her back on him to show her anger.

Peter raised his voice and drove the final nail into the coffin. "You recently expressed the hope that his granddaughter would come to the U.S. as a nursemaid to our children when we have them."

Affronted, Peace said vehemently, "Nonsense! I don't regard her as a slave. She's practically my sister. We grew up together.

My father paid her school fees, and my wish for her to come to the U.S. is to give her a better life than her current one."

"Call it whatever you like, but my point is that our ancestors regarded slavery as the normal order of things. They had no compunction about selling those they captured in battle."

Clint recalled that conversation, as he looked at the exhibits. Like his mother, he found the images disturbing. Aside from him, there were few others in the building. Wandering the grounds, he noted the beautiful setting was incongruous. The beach next to the museum was deserted, but, as he walked farther, he saw fishermen's shacks in the distance. There were no swimmers or people playing in the water, either.

Walking to another museum nearby, he stopped to view the exhibits of the palm oil trade, old artifacts, and photos of old Calabar. At this museum, too, there were few visitors, although the food stalls near it were crowded.

When he returned to the rest house, he felt unwell. Despite the hot, humid night, he was chilled, but he thought nothing of it and went to bed.

He woke late the following morning and still felt low. He planned to take a taxi north of Calabar toward Ikom despite his mother's warning. The manager at the rest house mentioned a beautiful waterfall often visited by tourists.

His cell phone was working again, and a phone call from his mother changed his mind. Aghast at his intention to visit the waterfall, she reminded him of their accident on their honeymoon and insisted that under no circumstances should he take the road to Ikom.

"Are you crazy?" she asked. "I'm not saying you'll have an accident, but, if you do, where will you get help? There are no ambulances, and the hospitals aren't equipped to handle trauma cases. Please, I'm afraid for you. Humor me and don't go."

"But, Mom, it's been ages since you were here. The country has changed a lot since then. There's a teaching hospital in Calabar. I saw the sign for it when I saw the slave museum."

"Clint, humor me. You've seen better waterfalls before. You told me you saw a small one at Ibritam forest. You've been to Niagara Falls. The one in Ikom isn't like Victoria Falls. The place is nothing. I don't want you risking your life for it."

Her voice revealed how upset she was. She made Clint promise he wouldn't visit the waterfall.

Still not feeling well and dosing himself with Tylenol, Clint decided to go to Creek Town and visit the Mary Slessor church. He wandered around the area, speaking to a few of the extremely well- dressed parishioners leaving the building.

They told him the church had a partner church in Scotland and was frequently visited by Scottish parishioners. One of the teachers he met coming from the church mentioned that during the centennial of Mary Slessor's arrival in Calabar, a film was made about her life on the Cross River, and he should see it if he could.

The next day, he visited Hope Waddell, a very old school, according to the informative taxi driver. At the gate, with its redroofed building, several students stood around. Rather than answer his questions, they directed him to the principal's office.

Luckily for Clint, it wasn't a busy time, and the principal was willing to talk to a stranger from America.

"I'm glad you're visiting the school and hope that when you return, you'll have nice things to say about us. I can tell you only a little about the school, but I'll find a student to take you around."

"I'm most grateful," Clint said. "I just came to look around and never intended to disturb you. The students at the gate suggested I call at your office. My grandfather attended this school in the 1950s, so that was my primary motive for visiting."

The principal bade him sit in the opposite chair of his imposing desk, filled with files and books. An affable man, he gave Clint a short history of the school.

"This was a mission school until independence, when it became a state grammar school. It was founded in 1895 by

The Reverend Hope Masterson with Mary Slessor's urging. It began as a vocational school where students learned gardening, bakery, carpentry, engineering, and other subjects that were added as needed. It later became a grammar school.

"By 1984, the school buildings deteriorated because of neglect." He shook his head. "We owe a lot to our alumni, whose fundraising helped renovate and refurbish the buildings. Currently, we have over 2,000 pupils, some of whom are boarders."

Very impressed, Clint stood and thanked the man for his time. The principal walked him out of the administrative building and beckoned a student to show Clint the classes and student hostels.

After walking around the campus for half an hour, Clint became tired and returned to his lodging, anxious to rest and shake off his fever. He didn't want to alarm Alfred, who joined him at the rest house. Foregoing dinner, Clint said he was tired and needed rest.

—⁂—

The following day, Clint was sluggish and unusually quiet. "You don't seem your usual chatty self," Alfred said.

"I don't feel well," Clint replied, shivering. "I'm feverish."

"Then we'd better head home." Alarmed, Alfred didn't want to have a sick man on his hands.

"Perhaps so. Maybe we should look for a bus." He quickly began packing his small carryall.

They took a taxi to the motor park on the outskirts of town, where they found a bus going to Ikot Ekpene and were among the first to board. Alfred knew the bus wouldn't leave until it filled, so he secured a seat for Clint in the front, where he would be comfortable, until the full complement of passengers assembled.

Clint wasn't ready to sit down, so he got off the bus and looked for a place where he could rest and observe the happenings in the park. Fascinated by the touts luring passengers to the buses, he wondered if their fees depended on the number of people they brought. The young children carrying small packages of peanuts, akara balls, water, and all types of food caught his eye. He watched a little boy pickpocket a man in a flowing agbada costume. Clint could have tried to stop it, but he didn't want to become involved in the inevitable fight.

He was glad when Alfred said their bus was ready to go, and he should hurry to avoid being left behind. The bus was overcrowded.

Sitting beside the driver, Clint had some elbow room, while many passengers crowded into seats meant for one.

The road had been newly resurfaced. Despite the usual delays at the police checkpoints, they reached the Ikot Ekpene motor park in time to catch the last of the late-afternoon taxis to Aro Chuwku. They ate a hurried lunch at a new fast-food restaurant along the main street of Ikot Ekpene, and then they headed home as the only two passengers in the taxi. Although Aro Chukwu was only twentyfour miles from the Ikot Ekpene junction, the condition of the road meant the journey took three hours.

Through the drive, Clint felt sick and dizzy. The accommodating taxi driver stopped whenever necessary, because he felt sorry for Clint.

—⁊⁊⁊—

The taxi reached Esther's yard as the sun set. Clint staggered into the parlor and lay on the sofa, while Alfred went through the courtyard to find Esther and tell her Clint wasn't well and needed immediate attention.

Esther hurried into the parlor. "Clint? I didn't expect you back for another week. Alfred says you feel sick. Let me get you some food. That'll help."

Clint declined her offer.

Alfred gave her the details of their trip. He hadn't been with Clint for most of his wanderings, but Clint described his adventures in old Calabar and Creek Town. After a short summary, he excused himself, saying he was anxious to return to his family.

Esther made Clint take a hot bath, covered him with a blanket, and hoped that by morning in familiar surroundings, he would feel better. She blamed Igwe for putting Clint in danger. It was his fault for arranging the trip and filling Clint's head with the wonders of Calabar and its people. She hoped whatever Clint caught in Calabar wasn't serious.

Esther spent the night sitting in the parlor, praying and worrying about Clint. She felt Clint was the only good thing that resulted from the alliance with the Igwes. She never approved of the marriage, even though her husband did, given his friendship with Igwe. Peace met Peter in Washington where both were studying, and he bewitched her. How else could she explain the infatuation?

Esther's visits to their house in America didn't endear her to Peter, nor Peter to her, but she loved her grandchildren and would do anything for Clint. She told herself that first thing in the morning, she would go to Igwe's house and give him a piece of her mind for endangering Clint with stories about Calabar.

She didn't go to her room even for a short rest until the servants woke and began preparing for the morning.

CHAPTER
TWENTY-FIVE

Esther placed her hand on Clint's forehead. His temperature seemed dangerously high. "How do you feel?'

"Pretty worn out." Clint was shaking. "I threw up all night." He didn't open his eyes. After expending the effort to answer her, he lay still and quiet.

Without worrying about her disheveled appearance, Esther hurriedly took an okada, a motor bike taxi, to the new extension to confer with Igwe.

"If anything happens to Clint," she snapped, "you're responsible!

You just pray he gets well!"

Igwe was shocked by her appearance. "What are you saying? Did something happen?"

The arrangement was for Clint to stay with his relatives in Ikot Ishie and return in ten days. "I thought everything was all right, and Clint was still in Calabar. Has there been civil unrest in the city I haven't heard of?"

"He came home last night very sick."

Igwe shoved her aside and shouted for his driver to take all of them to the hospital.

On arrival at the only hospital in town, Igwe left Esther in the car and went inside to look for a friend who was a doctor, praying he was in the office at that time of the morning. Not having been inside the hospital since his retirement, he was shocked at how much it had deteriorated. Although aware of the dilapidated and unkempt surroundings, he wasn't prepared for what he found inside. The wards were as filthy as the grounds. Wastebaskets overflowed with rubbish, the mattresses were bare, and the patients on the beds wore only their individual wrappers. Some were being fed by relatives who came in early to give them breakfast. An orderly pushed a pail of dirty carbolic water and a mop, making Igwe wonder why the man went through the motions of cleaning, because all he did was push dirt from one end of the hall to the other.

Under no circumstances would he allow Clint to be moved into the hospital if his condition deteriorated. Depending on the doctor's prognosis, Igwe would arrange to have Clint sent to a private clinic in Umuahia, where he would receive better care.

He forced his thoughts away from the worst outcome. First, he needed to convince the doctor to accompany them to Esther's house for a diagnosis. He felt it was just as well he left Esther in the car, or she would have collapsed in shock at seeing the condition of the building. Then he would waste valuable time calming her down.

Igwe found Dr. Okoro, the lone doctor in the hospital, checking files of patient records. Surprised to see Igwe, he stopped his work.

"Mazi, what brings you here? Are you feeling poorly? You should have sent a messenger, and I would have come to your house."

Igwe looked at the tables piled high with files and fleetingly felt his visit was an imposition. "I'm well, but I have a big problem. My grandson, Clint, is ill." He looked up at the doctor. "Esther, my inlaw, said he came back last night from Calabar and has been sick the whole night. His temperature is very high. You know she was a nurse. She thinks he's got acute malaria, coupled with stomach flu, and she's very worried. He should be seen by a doctor before we make any plans to take him to Umuahia."

"Let me see," Dr. Okoro said calmly. "I don't have any operations scheduled today, so I can come with you right now to examine him. Let me get some drugs from the dispensary in case he's suffering from what you said."

Igwe was very grateful. The doctor accompanied them to Esther's house, where they found Clint feverish and sweating profusely, his discarded clothes strewn about the room. Even though the room felt like a hothouse, he complained of chills. His temperature was still very high. Esther and Igwe huddled outside, waiting for the doctor to finish his examination.

When Dr. Okoro emerged, he said, "Clint has a bad case of malaria and is hallucinating. The stomach flu has already run its course and can be contained with an antibiotic. I gave him the first dose. He'll need several quinine injections, the first of which I also gave, and I'll be back this evening to check his progress.

"Keep him as dry as possible to avoid pneumonia. If he can eat, give him light meals until further notice. I don't advise moving him to Umuahia unless the situation deteriorates further."

When Dr. Okoro left, Igwe suggested they move Clint to his house, where he could assign full-time help to watch him even overnight.

Esther rejected the idea. Shaking her head, she argued that she could manage his care and admitted she was rash when she accused Igwe of causing the illness.

Igwe wanted to inform Clint's parents of his condition.

Esther refused. "You'll worry them for nothing. Let's see how he reacts to the quinine injection and antibiotics before we start imagining the worst." She abruptly turned away and wiped her tearfilled eyes with the end of her wrapper.

Irritated, Igwe stared at her, wondering what changed between the time she rushed to his house to declare Clint was near death and the present moment.

As if sensing what he thought, she said in a calmer voice, "Mazi, you heard what the doctor said. If Clint doesn't respond to the treatment, I won't object to moving him and his parents being informed, but I'd hate to have them rush to Nigeria when there's no need."

As an afterthought, she added, "Let me get you some breakfast while we wait to see if Clint rouses sufficiently to ask for food."

Just as they sat down to eat, Pastor Ibekwe arrived, and Esther invited him in.

"I'm sorry to hear about the young man's illness," he said, his eyes sympathetic.

"How did you know?" Igwe asked.

"I sent him a message," Esther explained, "asking him to come to the house and pray for Clint's recovery."

"I went to the church before coming and offered prayers for his quick recovery," the pastor said. "We'll pray for him during the youth meeting this evening. Given the situation here, I know that you, Mama Esther, will be absent from the women's league meeting tomorrow. I'll alert them to pray for his recovery, too. Mazi, you should all believe he'll come out of this and be stronger. God won't allow harm to befall the innocent."

Igwe and Esther muttered, "Amen."

In his sleep, Clint felt himself walking up a steep mountain carrying a very heavy knapsack. He was there for a purpose. He sensed someone else walking on the opposite side of the mountain. The road he followed went straight to the top. Every step was difficult, and, after a quarter of the way, he stopped to rest.

Finding a bench on the side of the road, he was grateful to lie on it before continuing his journey, even though he still wore the heavy knapsack.

On his dying bed, Achi began his climb up the mountain, slowed by his heavy burden. A quarter of the way up, he gratefully saw a bench. He would rest awhile before continuing

Lying on the bench, he examined the obstacles he faced. The Christian God was a big taskmaster. He always put obstacles in one's way as a person struggled to reach the promised heaven, full of milk and honey, finally to sit at His right hand.

At first, accepting Christianity and its baptism worked to his advantage. After years of having no living child, he had three daughters—his oldest, who married into a good family, and two beautiful unmarried daughters. Just when he thought life was going well, God reminded him there were more obstacles to overcome.

He lost his wealth in a poor investment during the eclipse. Over the years, he adjusted to his poor status. With the help of the missionaries, his two remaining daughter received a primary education. Mary was the one he hoped would provide for him in his old age, and look at what happened. She died, because his wife tried to protect him from the shame of her pregnancy.

Every Sunday, he went to church and said, "Forgive us our trespasses, as we forgive those who trespass against us." He felt he was living a lie. He hadn't forgiven his wife for the death of their daughter, nor had he forgiven God for taking her away.

Lying on the bench one-quarter of the way up the mountain, Achi prayed he would be allowed to forgive and be rid of the burden he carried. If only he did that, he could continue his journey.

Clint thrashed in his bed, moaning and crying. The boy watching him ran out and called for Igwe and Esther, who rushed in.

"Clint, it's me," Igwe said. "I'm here. Wake up. Do you want something to eat?"

"Fetch a pail of hot water," Esther told the boy. "I want to bathe him and change his wet clothes."

Clint struggled to open his eyes, feeling extremely drowsy. He wanted to be left alone, but he understood his family's concern and their need for him to recuperate.

When the doctor arrived for his evening visit, he told Igwe and Esther that he thought the quinine injection was working. The blood sample he took that morning confirmed Clint had malaria.

"You said he went to Itu by canoe and on to Calabar. He must've been bitten by an anopheles mosquito there. It takes only one bite from a carrier to give someone malaria."

Shaking her head, Esther said, 'Doctor, you know that ever since he arrived, I've made sure this house is free of mosquitoes. We sprayed insecticides in his room every night, and we closed all the windows. I personally checked him every night to make sure the mosquito net was tucked into the bed, and I made sure he took his malaria drug every Sunday. I took every precaution to avoid this." Dr. Okoro, a handsome, thin, muscular man, rolled his eyes.

Before the doctor could speak, Igwe brusquely said, "No one's blaming you. If anyone is to be blamed, it's me for arranging the Calabar trip. Let's hope, with treatment, Clint is himself again."

"I gave him another quinine injection," the doctor said, picking up his bag before he left. "He should come out of it soon."

Igwe stayed for a few minutes after the doctor left. "If the situation changes during the night, send someone for me immediately. Otherwise, I'll see you in the morning."

He wasn't about to listen to Esther when it came to notifying Clint's parents. He usually called on Sunday evenings, when they could have a long chat about family shenanigans, but he wanted Peter to visit, so it seemed a good excuse.

Upon reaching his house, Igwe called Pater, even though it was midnight on a weekday.

"Papa?" Peter asked. "What's up? Why are you calling so late? Is everything OK?"

"Is Peace with you? Can you go to another room, so we can talk without disturbing her?"

Peter turned to Peace. "I'll go downstairs to deal with this. It'll be a long call, and I don't want to disturb you. You have to get up early tomorrow for work."

There was a period of silence, then Peter said, "OK, Papa. I'm downstairs. We can talk."

"I want you to know that the young man has contracted malaria.

He must've been bitten in Itu or Calabar. He's under good care. The doctor came this evening and said he's coming out of it, but he needs to rest. Esther doesn't want Peace to worry, but I felt I should let you know. You can decide if Peace should be told. If the situation changes, I'll call. I have your office number." "Can I speak to him?"

"He's at Esther's. I'm calling from home. As I said, there's no need to worry. He's on the mend. Apart from that, everything is OK here. Please don't call him yet. He needs to rest."

After the late-night call, Peter sat in the family room, staring at Clint's graduation photograph. He bent over and placed his head in his hands, silently praying nothing would happen to his son. His father wouldn't have called unless he was worried.

He had to travel to Nigeria. Ever since Clint left, and Sarah went to college in Washington, DC, he and Peace toyed with the idea of visiting Clint in Nigeria during Christmas, if Clint was there that long. Perhaps he could call and persuade Clint to come home for Christmas, but in case that didn't work, he would ask for vacation time and start looking for cheap tickets.

He wouldn't tell Peace until he was certain of his plans. By the time Peter returned to bed, Peace was asleep.

Still in a deep sleep, Clint rested enough on the bench to feel ready to continue his journey. Compelled to get up and walk toward the mountaintop, he groaned, tossing and turning. Somehow, he found himself halfway to the top. His steps were labored, and it was difficult to move each foot forward, so he slumped down on the mountainside.

There was no bench. He lay on the grass, fighting off gnats and midges. He scratched himself and moved in his sleep, once again requiring Esther to be summoned to restrain him.

Achi, burdened by his sorrows and inability to forgive, struggled to climb the mountain. Instead, he slumped down beside the road.

Just when he thought everything was getting better, the situation became worse. His last remaining unmarried daughter became wild and uncontrollable. She came home pregnant, and his wife was beside herself. She didn't dare try to abort the child for fear of losing another daughter.

"One thing stands between me and eternal life is my lack of forgiveness for those who I think wronged me or caused me shame," Achi said. "That's the burden I bear, as I try to climb this mountain."

"Forgive me!' Clint cried. "Forgive me!"

Esther shook him until he woke, then she asked, "Why are you crying? Where's the pain? What is there to forgive? Should I send for the doctor?"

"No, no." Clint was sweating profusely. He tried to get up to go to the bathroom, but Esther insisted he use the bedpan.

"I feel so thirsty."

"You should. You haven't had anything to drink all night." Esther bustled back and forth, calling maids for Fanta and water. She helped Clint put on dry clothes, changed his sheets, and once again, he lay down and dozed.

By the time the doctor arrived, Clint was asleep. The doctor awoke him to administer the injection.

"Make sure he drinks plenty of fluids," he told Esther and Igwe. "Don't force him to eat. He'll eat when he's better."

The news of Clint's illness reached most of the village, and a constant stream of people came to Esther's house to offer prayers for his recovery. When Igwe arrived, he took Esther aside and suggested they move Clint to his house, where he could rest undisturbed by the mob at Esther's home.

"Mazi Igwe, they mean well, and they're all praying for him." She gestured with both hands. "God will hear the prayers of so many. This grandson of mine has been with us only a little while, but everyone loves him. Do you know that even the Eze of Aro sent a message wishing him a quick recovery? He will get well!" She slapped her hand against a nearby stool for emphasis, then she opened her Bible to read about Jesus curing the sick and raising the dead.

For the whole day, unaware of the number of people praying for him, Clint lay asleep, tossing and turning in bed. Once more, he struggled up the mountain. He was there-quarters of the way up when disaster struck, and he couldn't move. He felt very tired, and his burden was heavier than ever. He needed to lie down and think.

Someone set a chair before him. He was glad for it and didn't question how it came to be there. He sat in it and gazed at the wildflowers. The mountain was barren of shrubs, but there were plenty of birds and butterflies. He watched the birds flit from grass to grass, picking up insects. The gentle breeze comforted him. He wished his could shrug off his knapsack, but he lacked the strength. Finally, he got up to proceed.

Three-quarters of the way up the mountain, Achi sat to rest and think. He felt God must hate him and was too unforgiving. His married daughter's husband lost his job and was accused of embezzling school funds.

"If he embezzled the funds," Achi asked himself, "what did he spend the money on?"

There was no evidence the money had been spent.

The in-law vehemently denied the charges, but the church school managers didn't believe him. Though an inquiry subsequently proved he was innocent, and the guilty party was the bookkeeper, the management decided the son-in-law's mismanagement caused the situation and ordered him to repay the embezzled amount as punishment. To repay that much meant he wouldn't have enough of his salary left to live on.

Achi blamed the Christian God for allowing an innocent man to be punished. Once again, he doubted his faith. How could he worship a God that allowed the innocent to be punished? No. He wouldn't forgive God. He would renounce Him and return to his life before the White people came.

Terribly agitated, Clint struggled to stand, but Esther held him, making him drink water. He tried to open his eyes but couldn't focus. Igwe, who was visiting, sent for the doctor, who came as quickly as he could.

He tried to allay their fears, saying Clint was improving. His temperature was down slightly, and his pain could be because of the aftereffects of malaria. He recommended they allow the drug to work its way through his system.

That night in his sleep, Clint felt his journey up the mountain was almost over. He just had to push through to the end. He got up, only to find the burden too heavy, so he sat down again.

Achi struggled to rise. Like Job, he still had to overcome his doubts. As he sat there, he saw his wife, extremely ill. He tried all the known herbs without success. In the end, she died, and he was left a widower.

The last blow was too much. He blamed himself for not telling her he forgave her, and he blamed God for taking Mboro from him. He was losing faith in the new religion.

On his deathbed, Achi remembered a sermon by his pastor about Job. Job lost his wealth and family and was taunted by Satan to denounce God, but Job's faith never wavered.

Remembering that sermon, Achi felt that perhaps everything that happened to him was God's way of testing his faith. He gave me all the things I have that made me happy, Achi thought, and it was His right to take those things away again.

I've been taught in the Bible that His Son died on the cross for our salvation. If I believe as I should that by His death my sins are forgiven, then I'll have eternal life.

He fell on his knees and recited Psalm 23, the first Bible passage he memorized during catechism. "The Lord is my shepherd..."

After he finished, he said, "I'll never doubt that Christ died for me, and through Him, my sins are forgiven."

Only then could he shed his burden. Walking up the mountain became easy.

In his sleep, Clint felt as if he were free of his burden, and the last mile passed easily. He breathed normally again. As he approached the mountaintop, he saw someone else up there. That was a surprise, because he saw no footprints on the path.

The other person walked toward him. When they met, Clint saw the man was his mirror image.

"You've been looking for me," the man said. "I'm glad you found me."

To Clint's surprise, he found himself saying, "Yes. I've searched far and wide for you."

"Now that you've found me, I have only one piece of advice. Go back to live your life. I came back as you, because I wanted to be able to learn the mysteries of the universe. I didn't have the opportunity to learn about the world outside my environment. I wanted to live a better life than the one I had during my lifetime.

"Go to school. Achieve something great. I find I can now accomplish many things through you. Go back to where you came from, learning everything you can, and live the life I longed for when I was alive. Don't look for me any further. I'm in you."

Before Clint could reply, the image changed, and he found himself sitting up and looking around the room. After he got up and saw it was morning, he went to the courtyard to ask for hot water to wash. He came back, dressed, and went to the parlor to wait for Esther to come from her room.

She was shocked when she found him sitting there, dressed. "Clint, you should lie down. You've been very ill. You must be weak." She hugged him in relief.

"You're right, Grandma, but I wanted to sit here awhile before going back to bed. I'm hungry, though, and I could do with some breakfast."

Later in the day, Igwe arrived to check on Clint. "You're sitting up!" He pulled out his cell phone. "Peter should be having breakfast about now before going to work. I'll call him."

Peter answered, and Igwe handed the phone to Clint, who said, "Hi, Dad. What's up?"

Peter's voice shook with emotion. "I should ask you that. I hear you gave your grandparents a scare. How do you feel?"

"A little weak, but otherwise as good as new. I wanted to tell you I'm coming back soon."

"How soon? Your mother and I were thinking of visiting shortly. We asked a travel agent to help us find cheap tickets. Depending on your plans, we can adjust ours."

"I wanted to come back within the fortnight, depending on when I can book a flight. I just made up my mind, and I have yet to discuss it with Grandpa. I don't see why you can't come, though. Don't come just on my behalf. I'll see in you a fortnight."

"Let me talk to Dad."

Clint handed Igwe the phone. Peter quickly explained the conversation with Clint, then he asked, "Dad, can you help, please? We've been very worried, and we planned to come there to bring Clint back. He insists we don't have to come, and it's just as well we haven't bought any tickets. We wanted to talk with you first. Do you think he can travel alone? He has an open-ended ticket, and you'll need to help him with booking his return. Peace's brother in Lagos can help, too. We'll contact him."

"He's right," Igwe said. "There's no need for you to come just for that. He's no longer in danger. In a few days, he'll be his usual self.

We like to see both of you, of course, but not this way.

"I need a change. I've been thinking of flying to Britain to visit your brothers. We've already discussed it, and perhaps I can combine that with a visit to see you. I'd enjoy that now that Clint and I are friends."

After their conversation, Igwe went to the courtyard to call Esther to the phone to talk to Peace. Soon, the news of Clint's recovery spread, and Esther's friends and acquaintances descended on the house to celebrate.

CHAPTER
TWENTY-SIX

B y the beginning of December, Clint fully recovered, looked forward to being reunited with his parents. His ticket was changed, and he would travel to Lagos to stay for a few days before going to the States. Igwe sent Clint's ticket to Lagos, and his uncle was able to validate it. Igwe would accompany Clint to Port Harcourt to catch his Lagos flight.

A few days before Clint's departure, Igwe invited a few family members and friends to a farewell party in Clint's honor. Included were Nick, Clint's constant companion, whose presence during Clint's illness endeared him to Esther. Nick's mother brought gifts of chicken, eggs, and oranges. Igwe also invited Ifeoma, who was just recently admitted to the Edinburgh University for an advanced degree in her specialty. Also present were the old men who contributed their time to explain the history of Aro Chukwu to Clint.

When Clint arrived at Igwe's house, he found his grandfather strolling in his garden. He stood beside the house, and Clint watched, as he leaned forward to retie the branches of a bean plant that separated from the main support post holding it in place.

Startled, Igwe welcomed Clint and invited him to join him in his stroll. They had time before Esther and the others would arrive.

The garden was in sharp contrast to the surrounding area, which was already showing the signs of the onset of the dry season.

"Hello, Grandfather. This place is like an oasis in the middle of the desert."

"You think so? Well! We try to give the plants their daily ration. Without care, we won't have fresh vegetables all year round. I'm lucky to have that bore hole for water."

As they strolled past the hibiscus, filled with flowers, and on to the bed of marigolds, Igwe admitted, "You gave us a fright. I'm glad you're feeling well. Speaking for myself, I don't want you to leave yet."

Clint deliberately arrived early to spend time with his grandfather before Esther came. There were things he wanted to know about the family, and he didn't want Esther hearing his questions. Igwe's wife was busy in the kitchen. It was the first time in a long time that Esther would come to the house as a guest, so Igwe wanted everything to be perfect. They had a lot to be thankful for.

"I don't want to return yet, either," Clint said wistfully. "You know, Grandpa, I was very angry with my parents when I arrived. I felt they had no right to raise me as an American without sharing any of their family history. I was particularly angry with my father for controlling my life.

"During a conversation with him the other day, he said if I wanted to stay in Nigeria, I should go to Lagos to find a job. He had already decided I should be in Lagos. He never asked what I wanted to do. He wanted me to go to law school, and, when I wanted time to think about it, he couldn't accept my decision.

"The only thing I want from my parents is to be allowed to make my own decisions and to have them support me in that. I also came here to find myself and think about what I want to be. I think I found what I came here for. I'm very grateful to all of you for putting up with me. I'm going back. When I get there, I'll reapply to law school and will most likely specialize in environmental or international law." Igwe embraced him. In a voice full of emotion, he said, "Your parents did what they think was right for you. They wanted the best for you. Your father's education was interrupted by the civil war. After the war, everything changed. We lost the war, and many were angry about it. To get back what we lost, we became selfish and inconsiderate of each other.

"Your father was a student activist in college. He fought against the university's misuse of funds meant for the students. He fought against the police for willfully stopping people to collect bribes. He fought against politicians brazenly using public funds as their own.

"We worried he would be jailed for his activities. He was an angry young man. We were happy when he was chosen by USAID to go to America for a conference, and I rejoiced when he decided to stay and complete his education. I can understand if he chose not to dwell on that period of his life."

Still holding Clint, he gazed into his eyes and laughed. "Looking at you, I can't help thinking of my grandfather. He was your height and carried himself the same way. He didn't have an easy life. We believe that death isn't the end of life, and each person who dies returns to us in the form of another person. We believe you are Achi come back."

He lowered his hands and continued his stroll. "He must have chosen to come back as my grandson, so he could live a better life than the one he had."

Clint, filled with gratitude, said, "Thank you, Grandfather. You've explained what I wanted to ask. Can you tell me where he was buried?"

"In the bedroom of his house, as is our custom."

They both looked up, as visitors began to arrive. Esther came straight from church. They met and had a wonderful family reunion.

Clint spent his last week in Aro Chukwu visiting his friends. Before he left for Lagos, he went to Amanagwu to the house Achi built. While there, he visited the room where Achi was buried, which became his uncle's bedroom.

www.ingramcontent.com/pod-product-compliance
Lightning Source LLC
Chambersburg PA
CBHW070912120626
46546CB00001B/234